Historic Preservation

A Bibliography on
Historical Organization Practices

Historic
Preservation

Edited by

Frederick L. Rath, Jr.
and
Merrilyn Rogers O'Connell

American Association for State and Local History
Nashville, Tennessee

Library of Congress Cataloging in Publication Data

Rath, Frederick L
 A bibliography on historical organization practices.

 Includes Index.
 CONTENTS: [1] Historic preservation.
 1. Historic buildings—United States—Conservation and restoration—Bibliography.
2. Historic sites—United States—Conservation and restoration—Bibliography.   3. Historic Buildings—Conservation and restoration—Bibliography.   4. Historical museums—Bibliography.   5. Museum techniques—Bibliography.   I. O'Connell, Merrilyn Rogers, joint author.
II. Title.
Z1251.A2R35   [E159]   016.973   75–26770
ISBN 0–910050–17–1 (v. 1)

Printed in the United States of America

Contents

Preface

One of the best indications of the growth of historical organizations and their work is the proliferation of publications in the field. Nearly a decade ago the New York State Historical Association published the first comprehensive bibliography for the profession, *NYSHA Selective Reference Guide to Historic Preservation*. It was a slender paperback volume of 133 pages and its compilation was done by the present editors on a part-time basis. Four years later, in 1970, a greatly expanded hard-cover edition called *Guide to Historic Preservation, Historical Agencies, and Museum Practices: A Selective Bibliography* was published. The contents included a new chapter on preservation, and there were expanded sections and many more new sources of materials.

By that time, it was evident that a part-time effort was not sufficient to keep abreast of the spate of books, pamphlets, and articles being published. In 1971, the National Museum Act (administered by the Smithsonian Institution) granted funds to support the continuation and expansion of the Bibliographic Project. Merrilyn Rogers O'Connell of the original team became active director of the project and was joined by a full-time editorial associate and part-time assistant. The New York State Historical Association provided office space in its library.

The staff has worked actively to compile a major bibliographic archive and prepare material for publication of the third revised edition of the *Guide*. References were subjected to more comprehensive processing and classifying with multiple usage and long-range continuity in mind. A key-sort punch card retrieval system was adopted for immediate flexibility and future conversion to computerization. The intent of the project has been to establish a permanent continuing record of all significant references in the field.

Again, the explosion of printed materials for the profession proved to be unpredictable. Major developments on federal and state levels, the increased number of training programs, and the continued popular interest in American history and culture resulted in the publication of more monographs, pamphlets, and periodicals than ever.

When the project was half-finished it became apparent that the production of a single-volume edition in three years was not feasible; the number of entries for historic preservation and conservation already equaled the number of entries in the entire second edition. The compiler-editors decided to view the bibliography as a set of separate but related volumes on specific topics. Completion of the present volume on historic preservation within the originally projected time schedule was given top priority and efforts were begun to secure funding for the additional time that would be required for compilation on other subjects.

Soon after the change in compilation plans it also became necessary to make new arrangements for publication. The New York State Historical Association, which from the beginning had sponsored the project and served as publisher, found itself unable to continue in that role. The American Association for State and Local History, acting quickly to ensure continuation of the work, agreed to become its sponsor, made immediate plans for publication of this volume, and obtained additional grant support from the National Museum Act.

The bibliography continues to be selective rather than definitive. It seeks to include all the most significant references. Some older materials, particularly periodical litera-ture, and some superseded materials have been dropped. The compilers have also exercised an arbitrary discretion in not listing articles in obscure or unobtainable editions or periodicals. Although some early seminal or definitive references are still included, the concentration is on books, pamphlets, and articles published since 1945. In a number of specialized areas, references have been gleaned from allied fields wherever it might be helpful.

As in the second edition, all entries for books and pamphlets follow the Library of Congress main headings and have additional data based on the Library of Congress catalog card information. Thus, all include the following: number of pages or number of volumes; illustrations (if any), including drawings, plans, photographs, or other graphic material; bibliography or bibliographical footnotes (if any); and the designation "paper" or "mimeo" wherever the entry is not a hard-cover publication.

The primary purpose of the bibliography is to be a working tool, providing the first steps on research trails. To add to its practicality, the compilers have included descrip-tive notes where the title of the book or article did not give a clear idea of subject matter. In the same vein, a periodicals or notes section has been added at the end of chapters and subchapters where deemed needed. The appendix lists all periodicals from which articles have been cited, with addresses and subscription information. The index, derived from the punch card system, is deliberately comprehensive, so that the most obscure references, coauthors, editors, or even allusions can be tracked down easily.

Compilation for the volume on historic preservation was stopped on December 31, 1973, although there are notes on several major references scheduled for publication in 1974.

There are two other departures from what may be considered standard biblio-graphic practice which give further dimension to the usefulness of the work. A Basic Reference Shelf was introduced in the first edition and repeated in the second edition. In the third edition, each topical volume has its own Basic Reference Shelf which has been expanded and more thoroughly annotated.

To add to the overall perspective of the volume, a discursive section follows on major related organizations both national and foreign and international. Their programs are summarized so that readers will know where to go for services and further infor-mation.

To produce a work of this kind, the help of many organizations and individuals is necessary. The Smithsonian Institution, as administrator of National Museum Act funds, made the expanded Bibliographic Project possible. We are especially grateful to the Advisory Council and to Paul N. Perrot and Frederick Schmid. The New York State Historical Association provided not only rooms for the small staff but also the full services of its fine library. We wish to recognize the constant encouragement of Dr. Louis C. Jones, now Director Emeritus of the Association. Special assistance in organizing the expanded project was gratefully received from George R. Clay of Arlington, Vermont, who helped us to adapt his Indecks system to our particular needs, and Mike Gladstone of the Publishing Center for Cultural Resources, New York City, who shared his knowledge of printing processes to our advantage.

During the course of the Bibliographic Project, a number of persons served on the staff in full or part-time positions: Rosemary Sullivan Reese; Anne Bland; Marjorie Searl; Deborah Autorino; and Philip D. Spiess II, now on the staff of the National Trust. Without their help, this volume would not have been possible.

In compiling this volume, *Historic Preservation*, several individuals served as able, cheerful, and unpaid reviewers of the materials in their specialties: Frank B. Gilbert, formerly of the New York City Landmarks Commission; Paul R. Huey, New York State Office of Parks and Recreation, Division for Historic Preservation; John I. Mesick, Albany, New York; Edward M. Risse, Columbia, Maryland; and John G. Waite, New York State Office of Parks and Recreation, Division for Historic Preservation. Special acknowledgment is given to the following contributors for their continuing assistance in locating and verifying unusual references and sources: Judith Holliday, Librarian, Cornell University Fine Arts Library; and Brigid Rapp, Librarian at the National Trust for Historic Preservation.

There were other organizations and individuals who also advised and assisted with this volume and deserve our thanks and the list must start with the National Trust for Historic Preservation whose field this is. Its growing library and archives, the expertise of its fine staff, and the increasing number of papers and articles produced by the organization or with its assistance—all made our work easier. Other organizations always willing to assist include the American Institute of Architects, the American Society of Planning Officials, the Ancient Monuments Society (Britain), the Association for Preservation Technology, the National Trust for Places of Historic Interest or Natural Beauty (Britain), the National Park Service, and the Society for the Protection of Ancient Buildings (Britain). And to this list we must also add these individuals, who helped whenever we called on them: Stephen W. Jacobs and Barclay G. Jones, Cornell University; Edmund E. Lynch, New York State Office of Parks and Recreation, Division for Historic Preservation; A. Russell Mortensen, National Park Service; Mrs. Dorothy Mortensen, Advisory Council on Historic Preservation; and George E. Pettengill, American Institute of Architects.

It almost goes without saying that we were delighted to have had the assistance of Dr. William T. Alderson, Director of the American Association for State and Local History, throughout the project. When we needed a new publisher we had an understanding friend who appreciated the expanded scope of the bibliography and presented the proposal to his officers and Council for approval. We are happy that they are willing to embrace a project that has meant so much to us.

And so, as we have said in earlier editions, happy hunting!

Frederick L. Rath, Jr.
Deputy Commissioner for Historic
Preservation, New York State
Office of Parks and Recreation

Merrilyn Rogers O'Connell
Director, Bibliographic Project

A Bibliography on Historical
Organization Practices

Historic Preservation

Basic Reference Shelf

The Basic Reference Shelf includes volumes, booklets, and reprinted articles that should be part of the working library of every organization and individual involved in historic preservation. Each entry includes a more extensive annotation than in previous editions to provide users with a better idea of its content. Most references contain important bibliographies or are bibliographies in a specialized area, which will provide leads to other sources. Most of the items are listed in the National Trust Preservation Bookstore catalog.

In addition to *The National Register*, published copies of your own state and local surveys and inventories should be included on the reference shelf.

Also recommended is membership in one or more major preservation organizations in order to keep up with the developments in a rapidly growing field and to receive their important publications. Addresses and program summaries are given at the end of the references.

Alderson, William T., Jr. "Securing Grant Support: Effective Planning and Preparation," *History News*, 27:12 (December 1972), Technical Leaflet no. 62 (new series). ♦ Suggests guidelines found successful by agencies that have received grants, and points out pitfalls.

Bullock, Orin M., Jr. *The Restoration Manual: An Illustrated Guide to the Preservation and Restoration of Old Buildings.* Norwalk, Conn.: Silvermine Publishing Co., 1966. 181 pp., photos, prints, drawings, glossary, bibliog. ♦ Chapters include: architecture and engineering, historical research, archeological research, architectural research, restoration and specifications, building maintenance, building interpretation. The appendix, "Restoration and Preservation of Historic Buildings," is reprinted from *Building Research*, 1:5 (September-October 1964), entire issue.

Condit, Carl W. *American Building: Materials and Techniques from the First Colonial Settlement to the Present.* Chicago History of American Civilization Series no. 25. Chicago: University of Chicago Press, 1969. 329 pp., photos, prints, drawings, diagrams, bibliog.,

paper and hardcover. ♦ The focus is on the materials and techniques of construction, rather than the cosmetics, of American buildings. The four parts deal with colonial building development, the agricultural republic, rise of the industrial republic, and industrial and urban expansion in the twentieth century.

Fitch, James Marston. *American Building, 1: The Historical Forces That Shape It.* 2nd ed., rev. and enl. Boston: Houghton Mifflin Co., c1947, 1966. 350 pp., photos, prints, drawings, diagrams, bibliog. notes, paper and hardcover. ♦ A comprehensive view of architecture in the United States, taking into account the materials, the needs, the technical equipment, esthetic theory and creative genius that shaped saltbox and skyscraper.

Historic American Buildings Survey. *Recording Historic Buildings: The Historic American Buildings Survey.* Compiled by Harley J. McKee. Washington, D.C.: U.S. National Park Service, 1970. 165 pp., photos, drawings, diagrams, tables, bibliog. ♦ The basic text on techniques for recording buildings by drawing, photography, and documentation.

Hosmer, Charles B., Jr. *Presence of the Past: A History of the Preservation Movement in the United States Before Williamsburg.* New York: G. P. Putnam's Sons, 1965. 386 pp., photos, notes, bibliog. ♦ The first record of the history of the preservation movement in broad terms and early efforts in the United States. It sets forth the strengths and weaknesses, successes and failures of various approaches. The extensive bibliography lists letters and interviews, manuscript material, government documents, magazines, proceedings, reports, leaflets, and books. Volume 2, covering the history to 1949, is in preparation.

Hulan, Richard, and Stephen S. Laurence. *A Guide to the Reading and Study of Historic Site Archaeology.* Museum Brief no. 5. Columbia, Mo.: Published for the Conference on Historic Site Archaeology by the Museum of Anthropology, University of Missouri, 1970. 127 pp., paper. ♦ Bibliography, with editorial comment in the introduction to each chapter, of the best and most authoritative books and articles on historical archaeology available to the general reader, the student, and the professional.

Insall, Donald W. *The Care of Old Buildings Today: A Practical Guide.* London: The Architectural Press, 1972. 197 pp., photos, diagrams, bibliog. ♦ Published in conjunction with the Society for the Protection of Ancient Buildings, the book shows owners and architects how to dispel the threats of decay, neglect, and the developer's bulldozer. The first section deals with the administrative problems, legal background, and sources of financial help in Great Britain, and the second section covers specific restoration techniques.

Menges, Gary L. *Historic Preservation: A Bibliography.* Exchange Bibliography no. 79. Monticello, Ill.: Council of Planning Librarians, 1969. 61 pp., paper. ♦ Preservation of buildings, sites, and towns with emphasis on the United States. Chapters include case studies by state, architectural surveys, legal aspects, restoration and maintenance, environmental aesthetics.

Miner, Ralph W., Jr. *Conservation of Historic and Cultural Resources.* Chicago, Ill.: American Society of Planning Officials, 1969. 56 pp., photos, bibliog., paper. ♦ Report defines historic and cultural conservation; traces the changing emphases of the preservation movement; and outlines an approach to a comprehensive program through surveys, legal techniques, public and private options.

Morrison, Jacob H. *Historic Preservation Law.* 2nd ed. Washington, D.C.: National Trust for Historic Preservation, 1965. 198 pp., photos, prints, bibliog., table of cases. ♦ Legal references for individuals, organizations, and public officials concerned with maintaining landmarks, and a compilation of municipal and state statutes, ordinances, court decisions, and enactments. The hardcover edition is out of print; a reprinted paperback edition will be available in 1974 from the National Trust for Historic Preservation.

Morrison, Jacob H. *Supplement to Historic Preservation Law.* New Orleans, La.: Author, 1972. 98 pp., paper. ♦ Updates the 2nd ed., covering the progress of preservation law, preservation at the federal, state, and local levels, historic district acts, special legislative acts concerning eminent domain and tax abatement, and decisions of the courts.

Murtagh, William J. "Financing Landmark Preservation." Reprinted from "New Twists in Financing Historic Preservation," American Institute of Architects *Journal,* 45:3 (March 1966), pp. 70-74. ♦ Reviews briefly examples of acquiring historic properties by purchase, gift, bequest, federal aid, adaptive use, foundation support, mortgage, and revolving funds.

The National Register of Historic Places, 1972. 2nd ed. Washington, D.C.: National Park Service, 1973. 603 pp., illus. ♦ The official schedule of the nation's cultural property, national, state and local, worth saving. The current edition lists over 3,500 buildings, structures, objects, sites, and districts.

National Trust for Historic Preservation. *How to Evaluate Historic Sites and Buildings.* A report by the Committee on Standards and Surveys. Rev. ed. Washington, D.C.: The Trust, 1971. 2 pp., leaflet. ♦ The basic statement on criteria in the field.

National Trust for Historic Preservation, and Colonial Williamsburg. *Historic Preservation Tomorrow: Revised Principles and Guidelines for Historic Preservation in the United States, Second Workshop, Williamsburg, Virginia.* Williamsburg, Va.: The Authors, 1967. 57 pp., photos, prints, drawings, bibliog., paper. ♦ Revision of the principles and guidelines, drafted in 1964, which were rendered obsolete with the passage and implementation of historic preservation legislation by the 89th Congress in 1966. The report includes objectives and scope of the preservation movement; survey, evaluation, and registration; planning for preservation; education and training for restoration work; and points to consider in surveying.

New York (State). Office of Parks and Recreation, Division for Historic Preservation. *Historic Resources Survey Manual.* 2nd ed. Albany, N.Y.: The Division, 1974. 76 pp., photos, drawings, maps, bibliog., paper. ◆ Model manual designed to be used by volunteer groups or individuals. Methods of organizing local survey teams and the components of surveys are described.

Noel Hume, Ivor. *Historical Archaeology.* New York: Alfred A. Knopf, 1969. 335 pp., photos, diagrams, charts, bibliog. ◆ A comprehensive guide for amateurs and professionals to the techniques and methods of excavating historical sites. The book treats preparation for digging, how to proceed, different types of sites, recording and presenting the story, treatment, study and storage.

Pyke, John S., Jr. *Landmark Preservation.* 2nd ed. New York: Citizens Union Research Foundation, 1972. 32 pp., photos, drawings, diagrams, appendix, bibliog., paper. ◆ Includes the challenge and economics of landmark preservation, types of preservation programs, the work of the New York City Landmarks Commission, and elements of an effective program. The appendix lists where to go for assistance.

United States Conference of Mayors, Special Committee on Historic Preservation. *With Heritage So Rich: A Report.* Albert Rains, Chairman; Laurance G. Henderson, Director. 1st ed. New York: Random House, Inc., 1966. 230 pp., plates, photos, bibliog. ◆ Report of a special study of the state of preservation in the United States that provided impetus for passage of the National Historic Preservation Act of 1966. Chapters, written by authorities in special fields of preservation, include an historical overview, origins of preservation in the United States, buildings that have been lost, the Historic American Buildings Survey, preservation in Europe, and photographic essays.

U.S. Advisory Council on Historic Preservation. *Guidelines for State Historic Preservation*

Legislation. Historic Preservation Workshop, National Symposium on State Environmental Legislation, March 15-18, 1972. Washington, D.C.: The Council, 1972. 61 pp., bibliog., paper. ◆ Prepared to promote a higher and more uniform standard of performance within the nationwide historic preservation movement, the guidelines should be evaluated in the context of the needs of each state. Sections include the state historic preservation agency, conservation of archeological resources, protection and recovery of underwater historic properties, state advisory council on historic preservation, state historical trust, enabling legislation for local preservation activities, preservation procedures to guide state agencies. An appendix reviews tax incentives.

U. S. Office of Archeology and Historic Preservation. *Historic Preservation Grants-in-Aid: Policies and Procedures.* Washington, D.C.: National Park Service, National Register of Historic Places, 1973. 101 pp., diagrams, charts, forms, index, paper. ◆ Outlines the format, scope, and content of the state historic preservation plan, the annual program grant, and administration of grants. The appendices include sample forms and charts.

U. S. Office of Archeology and Historic Preservation. *How to Complete National Register Forms.* Washington, D.C.: National Park Service, National Register of Historic Places, September 1972. 64 pp., appendices, paper. ◆ Explanations of the purpose and criteria of the National Register, nomination procedures, and processing nominations are given. Instructions for completing the forms are covered in detail, and the appendices include sample forms, copies of the laws relating to the National Register, and the State Preservation Officers list.

Ziegler, Arthur P., Jr. *Historic Preservation in Inner City Areas: A Manual of Practice.* Pittsburgh, Pa.: Allegheny Press, 1971. 77 pp., photos, drawings, paper. ◆ A practical manual of principles, directions, and experience of the Pittsburgh History and Landmarks Foundation, focusing on restoration in historic districts without dislocating the residents. The manual also emphasizes the importance of community participation.

AMERICAN ASSOCIATION FOR STATE AND LOCAL HISTORY
1400 Eighth Avenue South
Nashville, Tennessee 37203
Membership, professional services, publications, training programs.

NATIONAL TRUST FOR HISTORIC PRESERVATION
740-748 Jackson Place, N.W.
Washington, D.C. 20006
Membership, professional services, publications, training programs, properties, National Trust Preservation Bookstore.

ASSOCIATION FOR PRESERVATION TECHNOLOGY
Meredith H. Sykes, Secretary-Treasurer
Box 2682
Ottawa, Ontario, Canada
Membership, bulletin and newsletter, meetings.

SOCIETY FOR INDUSTRIAL ARCHEOLOGY
Vance Packard, Treasurer
William Penn Memorial Museum
Pennsylvania Historical and Museum Commission
P.O. Box 1026
Harrisburg, Pennsylvania 17108
Membership, newsletter, occasional publications, meetings.

SOCIETY OF ARCHITECTURAL HISTORIANS
Room 716
1700 Walnut Street
Philadelphia, Pennsylvania 19103
Membership, newsletter, journal, tours.

1

Historic Preservation in Perspective

In 1845 Walt Whitman referred to the "pull-down-and-build-over-again spirit" of America, a cumbersome phrase from the lips of a fine poet who must have been overcome by the evidences of willful destruction in his day. Things have not changed much since. The battle to save the most significant sites, buildings, and objects in American history and culture continues to be waged.

Fortunately, there are increasing numbers of those who rage against the death toll. Among them, surely, a principal voice is that of Ada Louise Huxtable of the Editorial Board of the *New York Times*, who noted at the end of 1973 that "the two chief ingredients of urban renewal are destruction and irony." The irony lies in the fact that the federal government has tried to take a much more constructive, a much more positive, role in historic preservation in recent years. But sometimes the wheels grind slowly.

Historians deal constantly in perspective, for they know something about the repetitive patterns of ignorance and error. Students of the historic preservation movement are frequently appalled that so many individuals and communities, suddenly conscious of their heritage, are doomed to make mistakes first made scores of years ago simply because they lack perspective and information. This chapter is designed to help correct that by presenting the materials that serve as background, both long-range and short; by giving hard information about the organizations that are leading the fight nationally and internationally; and even by citing the materials that tell us the extent of our losses.

In addition, the chapter deals with that most important of subjects, principles and objectives. To meet the challenge of those who believe that progress consists of tearing down the familiar to replace it with the monstrous there must be standards, there must be criteria. And finally, there must be those who are trained as professionals to assist the millions of people who are learning to care about their environment, natural and manmade, so there are leads to the graduate programs set up for those who would make a career in historic preservation. (Other programs, graduate and undergraduate, dealing with other aspects of the overall field will be cited in later volumes.)

Most frequently, historic preservation causes are dealt with on an emergency basis. Lest the cause be lost because of lack of substance in the foundation, time still should be made to give solidity to the frame.

5

National Preservation Organizations

American Association for State and Local History (AASLH), 1400 Eighth Avenue South, Nashville, Tennessee 37203.

The American Association for State and Local History, founded in 1940, is a nonprofit educational organization dedicated to advancing knowledge, understanding, and appreciation of localized history in the United States and Canada. It serves amateur and professional historians, individuals and organizations, and includes in its broad spectrum such groups as historical museums and libraries, junior history clubs, historic sites, manuscript collections, and large as well as small historical societies.

To encourage the development of popular knowledge about American history, the Association launched the magazine *American Heritage* in 1949. Within five years it became a bimonthly, hardcover magazine published professionally by American Heritage Publishing Company and cosponsored by the Association. Royalties help provide some of the financial resources needed to carry out the Association's broad educational program. In recent years, the National Endowment for the Humanities, the National Endowment for the Arts, the Council on Library Resources, and the National Museum Act have provided funds to the Association to support special training programs, seminars for historical agency personnel, consultant services, and publications.

Membership in the Association is open to professionals, institutions, libraries, and individuals.

PROFESSIONAL SERVICES: Clearinghouse for inquiries from individuals and organizations; cassette lectures produced from seminar lectures; research surveys about the profession; job placement service; Federal Programs Committee; consultant service to historical societies and museums; annual awards of merit and commendation for outstanding contributions to the field by individuals and organizations; cooperative programs with state and regional conferences of historical organizations; annual meeting; joint meetings with related historical organizations.

PUBLICATIONS: *History News*, monthly magazine of up-to-date news of members, events, new ideas, reviews of books, and a Technical Leaflet series of how-to-do-it articles; *Directory of Historical Societies and Agencies in the United States and Canada*, biennial; books and booklets; job placement newsletter, quarterly; *Newsletter*, occasional, special issues on matters of urgent importance; catalog of Association books, technical leaflets, cassette lectures.

TRAINING PROGRAMS: Cosponsor of annual Williamsburg Seminar for Historical Administrators; seminars on publications, administration of historical agencies and museums, historical museum techniques, management and interpretation of history museums; training seminars and regional workshops for beginning professionals and small agency directors.

National Trust for Historic Preservation (NTHP), 740–748 Jackson Place, N.W., Washington, D.C. 20006.

The National Trust for Historic Preservation was chartered by Congress in 1949 "to further the national policy of preserving for public use America's heritage of historic districts, sites, buildings, structures, and objects; to facilitate public participation in the historic preservation movement and to serve that movement through educational and advisory programs; and to accept and administer for public benefit and use significant historic properties."

Membership in the National Trust is open to individuals, organizations, and businesses interested in historic preservation. Programs are supported by membership dues, endowment funds, contributions, and matching grants from the U.S. Department of the Interior, National Park Service, under provisions of the National Historic Preservation Act of 1966.

Programs are carried out under seven departments: Education, Field Services, Historic Properties, Plans and Development, Public Affairs, Publications, and Office of the President. Advisory services are provided to preservation groups, community leaders, and city planning officials, and special liaison is maintained with federal programs. The National Trust is also in contact with numerous related groups, both national and international, concerned with architecture, urban history, landscape architecture, and other special interests. Information on preservation legislation, architectural surveys, and preservation projects is distributed throughout the country.

Regional offices are also maintained: Midwestern Regional Field Office, 1800 South Prairie Avenue, Chicago, Illinois 60616; Western Regional Field Office, 802 Montgomery Street, San Francisco, California 94133; New England Regional Field Office, 141 Cambridge Street, Boston, Massachusetts 02114.

PROFESSIONAL SERVICES: Clearinghouse of current information on preservation theories, techniques, standards, legislation; advisory services and visits by professional staff and consultants; lectures and visual aid materials; preservation archives and library; annual meeting and preservation conference; regional preservation workshops and conferences; consultant service grants and National Historic Preservation Fund (brochure available); tours in the U.S. and abroad.

PUBLICATIONS: *Preservation News*, monthly newspaper of preservation activities; *Historic Preservation*, illustrated quarterly journal; *Member Organizations and Their Properties*, annual directory; *Annual Report*; technical reports; conference proceedings; leaflet series; Trust property brochures; *Work*, bimonthly bulletin listing employment opportunities in historic preservation. A Preservation Bookstore is located at the National Trust headquarters and a catalogue is available.

TRAINING PROGRAMS: Cosponsor of annual Williamsburg Seminar for Historical Administrators: annual Woodlawn Conference for Historical Museum Associates; field seminars; youth work-study programs.

PROPERTIES OPEN TO THE PUBLIC: Belle Grove (Va.), Chesterwood (Mass.), Cliveden (Pa.), Decatur House (D.C.), Lyndhurst (N.Y.), Oatlands (Va.), Pope-Leighey House (Va.), Shadows-on-the-Teche (La.), Woodlawn Plantation (Va.), Woodrow Wilson House (D.C.).

PROPERTIES LEASED FOR ADAPTIVE USE: Casa Amesti (Calif.), Cooper-Molera Adobe (Calif.).

U.S. National Park Service (NPS), Department of the Interior, Washington, D.C. 20240. The National Park Service was created as a bureau of the Department of the Interior by Congress in 1916 and was charged with the administration of the small number of existing national parks and monuments, including some archeological and historical areas. The Historic Sites Act of 1935 established "a national policy to preserve for public use, historic sites, buildings and objects of national significance for the inspiration and benefit of the people of the United States." With new powers and responsibilities, the National Park Service embarked on a national preservation program.

Added to this legislative lineage is the National Historic Preservation Act of 1966 which significantly broadened the scope of national preservation policy. Under this new authority, the National Register of Historic Places was greatly expanded, a national Advisory Council on Historic Preservation was appointed, and a system of matching grants-in-aid to the states and the National Trust for Historic Preservation was established. An Office of Archeology and Historic Preservation was organized in 1967 to manage the increased responsibilities.

NATIONAL PARK SYSTEM: The Park System is composed of natural, historical, and cultural areas, totaling 298 as of January 1, 1973. Field direction is provided through eight regional offices: New England Region, Boston; Northeast Region, Philadelphia; Southeast Region, Atlanta; Midwest Region, Omaha; Southwest Region, Santa Fe; Western Region, San Francisco; Pacific Northwest Region, Seattle; parks and memorials in Washington, D.C. are administered by the Office of National Capital Parks. Functions of planning, design and construction of physical facilities in the parks are carried out by the Denver Service Center. Production of publications, museum exhibits, and audiovisual programs is carried out by the Harpers Ferry Center. Cooperative research programs are conducted in conjunction with several universities throughout the country.

PUBLICATIONS: The National Park Service publication program is as varied as the parks it serves, from archeological studies and architectural records to maps and posters. There is an informational folder published for most of the parks. One hundred parks have interpretive handbooks and folders, all reasonably priced and sold in the visitor centers. The program further serves the public with fishing, boating, and camping information booklets; and, with the Administrative Policy series, it opens to the public rules, regulations, and standards by which the parks are managed and maintained.

TRAINING CENTERS: The Albright Training Center, Grand Canyon National Park, Arizona, is maintained for orientation and skills training for all new employees; the Mather Training Center, Harpers Ferry, West Virginia, is maintained for teaching interpretive methods. There are also a number of short courses at both centers for new and experienced rangers and interpreters. The Park Service maintains career and seasonal employment services for the park system.

PARK PRACTICE PROGRAM: Begun in 1957, the Park Practice Program is a mutual program of service to park and recreation people, co-sponsored by the National Conference on State Parks, National Recreation and Park Association, and the National Park Service.

The program is a series of publications for individuals and organizations concerned with parks, recreation, and conservation. It seeks to communicate interesting and high quality practical information on planning, designing, operating and administering recreation facilities. The publications are available through full membership or individual subscriptions. The Park Practice Program is located at the National Recreation and Park Association, 1601 N. Kent Street, Arlington, Virginia 22209.

Grist—bimonthly, tested time-, effort-, and money-saving technical ideas and devices for more effective park operation; Guideline—bimonthly, members exchange methods of management, administration, and interpretation of park and recreation facilities; Trends—quarterly, features new and important issues relating to parks, recreation, and conservation; Design—semiannually, innovative structural designs and layout plans for park and recreation sites to better serve visitor needs; Plowback—discontinued.

EASTERN NATIONAL PARK AND MONUMENT ASSOCIATION: The Association is a private, nonprofit organization formed in 1948 to promote the historical, scientific, educational, and interpretive activities of the National Park Service, principally in the eastern half of the United States, through grants-in-aid for research, publication of historical literature, development of park libraries, acquisition of museum objects, subsidies for experimental interpretive techniques, and acquisition of lands needed to prevent intrusions on present areas. It is located at 311 Walnut Street, Philadelphia, Pennyslvania 19106. Its publications include: Newsletter, twice a year to members; Agency News, sent to agents five to seven times a year covering new sales facilities, sales techniques, changes in policies and personnel; Annual Report; publications for sale at National Park Service sites.

SOUTHWESTERN MONUMENTS ASSOCIATION: The Association is a nonprofit publishing and distributing organization supporting historical, scientific, and educational activities of the National Park Service. It was formed in 1946 to provide accurate information concerning the Southwest to the traveling public; to stimulate and encourage scientific research in the historical and natural sciences within the National Park System areas in the Southwest; to publish informational and technical papers dealing with various historical and natural sciences; to develop and maintain in the National Park Service areas reference libraries available to the public; and to assemble and safeguard in the National Park Service areas of the Southwest study collections and exhibits germane to these areas. The Association publishes a catalog, Books on the National Park System in the West and Related Subjects, listing items distributed through its sales centers.

ADMINISTRATION: Because of the expansion of nonpark programs such as the National Register, grants, surveys, and interagency services, the National Park Service reorganized its divisions in the historic preservation field into two major offices in 1973. The Office of Archeology and Historic Preservation handles all nonpark programs; and Park Historic Preservation is responsible for programs within the parks. The Advisory Council on Historic Preservation is a separate office, under the Director of the National Park Service.

Park Historic Preservation, under the reorganization of NPS historic preservation programs in 1973, combines the divisions for history, archeology, and architecture. The Division of History is responsible for the research and recommendations on all historical matters for the National Park Service. It does the basic research for the whole program of preservation and interpretation in all of the national park sites, and carries on annual research programs and individual studies. The Division of Archeology conducts archeological investigations in areas of the National Park System where prehistoric and historic people have lived. Its Archeological Research series is a program for the publication of information derived from archeological projects, and made available in the form of published reports for use in libraries and research institutions. The archeology program, begun in 1906 and expanded by the preservation legislation of 1935 and 1966, is served by the Southwest Archeological Center, Globe, Arizona, and the Southeast Archeological Center, Macon, Georgia. The Division of Architecture is responsible for the restoration of historic structures under the control of the National Park Service. It conducts all the research, planning, and execution of the restorations, and also conducts a training program to perpetuate the traditional building crafts necessary for truly accurate restorations.

The Office of Archeology and Historic Preservation was first organized in 1967 from existing professional staffs within the National Park Service. Its purpose was to carry out more fully the preservation policies of the federal acts of 1906, 1935, and 1966. In 1973 all nonpark programs in historic preservation were reorganized under the Office and included four main divisions: Division of the National Register, Division of Grants, Division of Historic and Architectural Surveys, Division of Interagency Services.

Division of the National Register: The National Register of Historic Sites and Places was officially established, in name and scope, by the National Historic Preservation Act of 1966, although the Historic Sites Act of 1935 provided for a survey of significant historic sites and buildings. Under the Secretary of the Interior, and administered by the National Park Service, the National Register is the official list of the nation's cultural property that is worth saving, and is a protective inventory of irreplaceable resources relative to the progress of American history and the enhancement of the physical environment. All historical areas in the National Park System, together with those properties eligible for designation as National Historic Landmarks, are of national significance and thus qualify automatically for inclusion in the National Register. With the expansion of the Register authorized by the 1966 Act, properties of national, state, and local significance may be nominated by the states and upon approval by the National Park Service are formally placed on the Register. Criteria for inclusion in the Register are described in a leaflet, *The National Register of Historic Places*. In general, these criteria emphasize the quality of significance in American history, architecture, archeology, and culture that is present in districts, sites, buildings, structures, and objects.

State Historic Preservation Officers (formerly State Liaison Officers) are appointed by the governor of their state to supervise the program within the state, and officially make their state's nominations to the National Register. States are expected to prepare and have printed a State Historic Preservation Plan, to consist of three volumes or parts: (1) The Historic Background, giving an historical summary of the state, a history of preservation in the state, the state's philosophy of preservation, preservation planning's relationship to other state planning, preservation problems within the state, and an explanation of the state's procedures for nominating properties to the Register; (2) The Inventory, discussing the inventory's purpose, scope, and organization, and listing the inventory under both theme and county; and (3) The Annual Preservation Program, which gives an annual status report on the state's program, including a review of grants, the annual updating of Volumes I and II, and both long-range and immediate plans. The three-volume state plan is considered a public document, and the states are urged to publish and distribute full or abridged versions of their plan to acquaint and interest the public in the state's historic preservation effort. A state's eligibility to receive federal grants for preservation depends on National Park Service approval of each volume, and each volume must be reviewed by the state's governor before submission. It is not required to revise Volumes I and II, any new additions appearing in Volume III.

The State Historic Preservation Officer Policy Group (formerly the Advisory Committee to the National Register) is a committee of seven members selected from the various State Historic Preservation Officers. It is responsible for assisting the Keeper of the National Register in establishing procedural and administrative policy in carrying out the state grants-in-aid programs. The group meets several times yearly in Washington, D.C.

The National Register will be published on a biennial basis; the second edition became available in 1973. An annual revision of the National Register is published by the Government Printing Office and contains the monthly supplements to the Register which are printed in the Federal Register as additions are formally made to the complete list. In 1969 the National Park Service also published the Advisory List to the National Register of Historic Places, which included historic places not then listed in the National Register itself but which were to be considered as potential entries for the National Register. The list was culled from the National Survey of Historic Sites and Buildings and the Historic American Buildings Survey. Its purpose was to recommend to the various states historic sites which they might desire to nominate to the National Register.

Division of Grants: The National Historic Preservation Act of 1966 authorized federal grants-in-aid to the states for preservation purposes. These grants may be used in the preparation of the State Historic Preservation Plan or in the acquisition of individual properties which must be first listed on the National Register. These properties must also need financial assistance. The state may also distribute grant monies for individual projects to other eligible recipients. To qualify for aid, properties must be listed in the National Register, be consistent with a statewide historic preservation plan approved by the Secretary of the Interior, and need financial assistance or be owned by the National Trust for Historic Preservation. The State Historic Preservation Officer directs his state's grant-in-aid program, its historic surveys, and its preservation planning.

Division of Historic and Architectural Surveys: The Division is responsible for carrying out the Historic American Buildings Survey, the National Historic Landmarks

Program and its supportive programs, and the Historic American Engineering Record.

Historic American Buildings Survey: The Survey was established to record, as completely as possible, American building art, including all construction types, all use types, and all periods and regions throughout the country and the territories. Architectural merit and historical association constitute the basic criteria. The National Park Service began the Survey in 1933 with architects, draftsmen, and photographers employed under several federal relief programs. In 1934 the National Park Service entered into an agreement with the American Institute of Architects and the Library of Congress to conduct the Survey on a permanent basis. The National Park Service administers the planning and operation of the Survey with funds appropriated by Congress and supplemented by gifts from individuals, foundations, and associations; sets up qualitative standards; organizes projects; directs the preparation of records and places them with the Library of Congress. The Library preserves the records, makes them available for study, and supplies reproductions through its Photoduplication Service. The American Institute of Architects provides professional counsel through its national membership. The Survey became a long-range program under the Historic Sites Act of 1935.

With the passage of the Historic Preservation Act of 1966, the responsibilities of the National Park Service in this field were greatly increased to include enlarging the National Register and providing grants-in-aid to the states for historic site surveys and preservation. Today, the National Park Service conducts a broad national program of intensive architectural surveys on a shared-fund basis in cooperation with state and local governments, preservation groups, and historical societies. The program includes annual measured drawing projects done by student architects and university faculty supervisors; inventory recording projects conducted to evaluate large areas; architectural photogrammetry of skyscrapers and buildings of complex design; projects in industrial archeology undertaken in cooperation with the Smithsonian Institution; historic district studies; landscape architecture recordings; and civil engineering projects in cooperation with the American Society of Civil Engineers.

Several detailed catalogs listing HABS records are available, including the old national series and a new series of revised and expanded state and regional publications. Reprints may be ordered from the National Technical Information Service, 5283 Port Royal Road, Springfield, Virginia 22151. The new series of revised catalogs of the records by individual state and urban areas are done generally in cooperation with state organizations.

National Historic Landmarks Program: As defined by the National Park Service, a National Historic Landmark is "a district, site, building, structure, or object nationally significant in American history, architecture, archeology, or culture." It may be publicly or privately owned, but is judged by the Secretary of the Interior to possess significance for all Americans. The Historic Sites Act of 1935 provided for the National Survey of Historic Sites and Buildings and set up, within the National Park Service, the Advisory Board on National Parks, Historic Sites, Buildings and Monuments to advise the Secretary of the Interior on eligible sites and structures for the Survey program. The expanded program, under its present name of the National Historic Landmarks Program, was begun in 1960, and furthers the policies of the historic preservation acts of 1906, 1935, and 1966, in designating properties worthy of preservation. Supportive programs include the National Survey of Historic Sites and Buildings, the Natural Landmarks Program, and the National Environmental Education Landmarks Program.

National Survey of Historic Sites and Buildings: This Survey is the vehicle for studying and identifying prospective National Historic Landmarks. In order to cover fully every aspect of American life and thought from prehistoric days to the present, American history has been divided into major themes, subthemes, and facets, dealing with chronological periods, political and military events, economic and industrial affairs, artistic and intellectual currents, and settlement and social patterns, as outlined in *The National Park System Plan: Part I—History*. Sites associated with these themes are surveyed and evaluated, and the findings are then presented in a formal study. State and local agencies, historians, architects, archeologists, and colleges and universities participate in this process, cooperating with the National Park Service's professional staff. The study reports are turned over to the Advisory Board on National Parks, Historic Sites, Buildings and Monuments which then submits its recommendations to the Secretary of the Interior, who determines final eligibility. The full findings of the National Survey of Historic Sites and Buildings are being published in a series of approximately twenty-five volumes, five of which have been published to date.

Once a site's eligibility as a National Historic Landmark has been announced, the owner may apply for Landmark designation. A certificate and a bronze plaque, which attest to the significance of the site, are given and an appropriate ceremony may be held if the owner so desires. Continuing integrity of the site is essential if it is to remain a National Landmark. Any change can constitute cause for withdrawal of the designation. The National Park Service has guidelines for both commercial and private uses of a Landmark, and for architectural modifications of the interior and exterior fabric of the site. These guidelines, as well as the criteria for originally determining the status, are described in a leaflet, *The National Historic Landmarks Program*.

Supportive programs, the National Environmental Education Landmarks Program and the Natural Landmarks Program, are described in their respective leaflets, available from the National Park Service.

Historic American Engineering Record: Closely related to the Historic American Buildings Survey, the Record was begun in 1969. The National Park Service conducts a national program of intensive surveys of engineering works on a shared-fund basis with professional engineering societies, state and local governments, historical societies, and preservation groups. The purpose of HAER is to record a complete summary of engineering technology for surveying significant examples of engineering solutions which demonstrate the work of the various branches of the engineering profession: civil, mechanical, architectural, electrical, hydraulic. The program began with the Historic American Buildings Survey in 1933, which included a variety of works such as bridges, dams, projects in industrial archeology, and mill complexes. In 1964 the American Society of Civil Engineers set up a Committee on the History and Heritage of American Civil Engineering. It has designated engineering landmarks, worked on a series of books on engineering history, and published a biographical dictionary of civil engineers.

When the HAER was established in 1969, an agreement similar to that of the HABS was entered into, with the National Park Service administering the program and conducting the research, the American Society of Civil Engineers providing professional counsel and financial assistance, and the Library of Congress keeping the records and making them available for study and copying through its Photoduplication Service. In 1971 the American Society of Mechanical Engineers formed a History and Heritage Committee, which also assists the HAER.

Two types of surveys are conducted: a regional survey identifying landmarks on a geographic basis which may begin as an inventory; and an industrial survey which identifies landmarks on the basis of the type of industry and may focus on a particular firm or cover a given industry entirely within a particular area. Survey records include architectural and engineering drawings, photographic and photogrammetric records, and historical research and technical documentation. Some documentary reports on the surveys have been published; state catalogs of the material will ultimately be produced by the National Park Service.

Division of Interagency Services: The Division coordinates efforts for the preservation of prehistoric and historic ruins, earthworks, and building excavations through stabilization programs; makes advisory studies relative to the disposal of federal property for museum purposes under the Surplus Property Acts of 1944, 1961, and 1972; and offers recommendations based on its studies. It also assists in carrying out the provisions of Executive Order 11593.

Under its Archeological Salvage Program, sponsored by the National Park Service since World War II, the Division is responsible for the recovery of archeological remains in reservoir areas and other locations where construction activity threatens archeological and historic sites. The program to salvage materials and information has been developed in cooperation with local institutions and other government agencies. The Division also coordinates research and allocates funds to qualified agencies and institutions which conduct the actual salvage work.

ADVISORY COUNCIL ON HISTORIC PRESERVATION: The Advisory Council is an independent federal agency, formally established in 1967 under the provisions of the National Historic Preservation Act of 1966. The Council is comprised of the secretaries of the Interior, Housing and Urban Development, Commerce, the Treasury, Agriculture, and Transportation, and the Attorney General, the Administrator of the General Services Administration, the Chairman of the National Trust for Historic Preservation , the Secretary of the Smithsonian Institution, and ten citizens appointed by the President.

The Council advises the President and Congress on matters relating to historic preservation; coordinates the preservation efforts of federal, state, and local agencies, and private individuals and institutions; and studies the adequacy of legislative and administrative statutes relative to preservation in the states and local areas and the effects of tax policies at all levels on historic preservation. The Director of the National Park Service or his designee is the executive director of the Council.

Financial and administrative services are provided by the Department of the Interior, as arranged between the Chairman of the Council, who is designated by the President, and the Secretary of the Interior. The basic administration of the Advisory Council falls under the National Park Service. The Council meets four times a year.

Responsibilities of the Advisory Council are provided by the Act of 1966 and its amendment of 1970. The Council advises on the dissemination of information pertaining to historic preservation; encourages training and education in the field of historic preservation, in cooperation with the National Trust for Historic Preservation and other agencies; recommends to the Secretary of State the members of the official United

States delegation to the International Centre for the Study of the Preservation and the Restoration of Cultural Property (the Rome Centre); and serves as coordinator of the United States membership. The Council is becoming increasingly involved in the matters of surplus property transfer, adaptive usage, and environmental impact, particularly visual pollution. The Council works closely with the National Register to insure quality and consistent preservation throughout the country at all levels.

The review powers of the Advisory Council are established in Section 106 of the National Historic Preservation Act of 1966. The Council comments upon federal, federally assisted, or federally licensed undertakings that will affect properties listed in the National Register of Historic Places. The Council defines "undertaking" as any federal action, activity, or program, such as the issuance of a license or permit, the granting of funds, or the development or funding of master or regional plans. The Council reviews and processes a large number of plans and proposals of varying complexity, presently exceeding 300 cases a year. The Council comments to federal agencies in two ways: either by a negotiated "Memorandum of Agreement," approved by the Chairman, or by written recommendations to the head of the department after consideration by the full Council. Printed annually in the *Federal Register*, the "Procedures for Compliance" establish and explain the commenting process. Although Section 106 does not give the Council the power to veto federal undertakings that affect historic properties, it requires that agencies consider historical values in project planning. When conflicts cannot be avoided, the Advisory Council provides a forum for assessing the national interest and recommending courses of action.

Under Section 2(b) of Executive Order 11593, review powers extend essentially the same protection to non-Register properties owned by the federal government as Section 106 affords to those in the National Register. Section 1(3) of Executive Order 11593 requires federal agencies to establish procedures, in consultation with the Advisory Council, to ensure that federal plans and projects contribute to the preservation and enhancement of nonfederally owned historic properties.

In implementation of Section 102 of the National Environmental Policy Act, the Council staff reviews numerous environmental impact statements each year to determine whether cultural values have been considered in reaching decisions on "major actions" affecting the human environment.

The Council publishes a descriptive brochure; *Guidelines for State Historic Preservation Legislation* (1972); *Digest of Cases, 1967–1973* (1973); an annual report; brochures on the National Register and the International Centre and its training courses; *Issue Paper on Revenue Sharing (August 1, 1973; The Environmental Protection Tax Act of 1973: An Analysis for the Advisory Council on Historic Preservation, September 24, 1973.*

Foreign and International Preservation Organizations

Canada

Heritage Canada, Box 1358, Station B, Ottawa, K1P 5R4, Canada.

Heritage Canada is a nonprofit corporation formed in 1973 to promote, preserve and develop articles, buildings, and landscapes for the enjoyment of present and future generations. It also holds in trust for the nation buildings and landscapes that are its heritage. It works closely with provincial representatives, other voluntary organizations and individuals concerned with heritage preservation, and enlists the support of individuals and groups in the protection of old buildings and natural areas.

Heritage Canada has an executive director and small staff of experts on property management, restoration architecture and engineering, membership services, and public relations. Policies are directed by a thirty-member Board of Governors, and its work complements the National and Historic Parks Branch, Parks Canada, of the Department of Indian and Northern Affairs. Initially, the Branch provides research and technical assistance.

Membership is open to anyone interested in the preservation of individual buildings, groups of buildings, and areas of historical and natural value that are of national significance. Members are entitled to voting privileges, periodicals and reports, and use of a library.

PROFESSIONAL SERVICES: Communications center for voluntary associations and individuals; information and program material for local associations; advice and possible financial help to local associations; public education programs; cooperation with the Canada Council, the provinces, universities and technical colleges to provide training courses for restoration architects and skilled craftsmen; resource and clearinghouse for exchange of technical information at the national and international level; charter tours; Awards for Heritage Conservation.

PUBLICATIONS: Periodic report; magazine by mid-1974.

PROPERTY: Property may be acquired by donation, bequest, purchase, lease, or exchange and may include real and personal property. Real property of special significance, "Heritage Property," is held in trust and not sold or mortgaged, but may be leased or transferred to federal, provincial, or municipal departments or agencies or private agencies for appropriate use. Worthwhile buildings renovated for adaptive use are placed under restrictive covenants for protection. Acquired property, of commercial value only may be operated for its revenue, sold, leased, or mortgaged. Personal property may be declared "Heritage Property" and retained as an integral part of a building or landscape, or such collections may be turned over to appropriate federal agencies.

National Historic Parks and Sites Branch, Parks Canada, Department of Indian and Northern Affairs, Ottawa K1A OH4, Canada.

The passage of the Dominion Forest Reserves and Parks Act in 1911 was a significant milestone in the federal government's commemorative program. Prior to this date the government's involvement was through financial contributions to commemorative activities. This act created within the Department of the Interior a Dominion Parks Board to administer national and historic parks. In 1917 Fort Anne at Annapolis Royal, Nova Scotia, was transferred from the Department of the Militia and declared Canada's first National Park of historic significance. Upon the recommendation of the Commissioner of the Dominion Parks Board, a seven-member Historic Sites and Monuments Board of Canada was formed to advise the Minister on the matter of sites of national historical interest. The second National Historic Park was established in 1927, and by 1950 there were nine such parks, receiving over 150,000 visitors annually.

Part II of the National Parks Act of 1930 provided that the Governor in Council may set apart any land, the title to which is vested in Her Majesty as a National Historic Park, to commemorate an historic event of national importance, or to preserve any historic landmark, or any object of historic, prehistoric, or scientific interest of national importance, and may from time to time make any changes in the area to set apart that which he may consider expedient. Until 1953 the Historic Sites and Monuments Board of Canada operated under Order in Council authority and no provision was made for Parliament's formal review of the Board's decisions.

The Historic Sites and Monuments Act of 1953 provided the statutory base for the operation of the Board for the first time. The significant change brought about by the Act was the definition of the role of the Board as adviser to the Minister, whose statutory responsibility it became to develop and implement a national program of commemorating historical sites. Further legislation was enacted in 1955 and 1959 to amend and broaden the scope of the original act.

The Canadian Historic Sites Division, later renamed the National Historic Sites Service, was created within the National and Historic Parks Branch of the Department of Northern Affairs and National Resources in 1955 to develop, interpret, operate and maintain historic parks and sites and to act as secretariat for the Board. In April 1973 the National Historic Sites Service became the National Historic Parks and Sites Branch.

ADMINISTRATION: The Branch is divided into five regions, each with a central headquarters: Western Region, Calgary, Alberta; Prairie Region, Winnipeg, Manitoba; Ontario Region, Cornwall, Ontario; Quebec Region, Quebec; Atlantic Region, Halifax, Nova Scotia. Canada's National Historic Parks and Sites Branch is responsible for more than eighty major parks and sites, of which some forty-seven are operational and the remainder under development. These parks and sites preserve some of the most outstanding historical features in Canada for the benefit, education, and enjoyment of the Canadian people. The Branch administers the parks and sites and serves as secretariat to the Historic Sites and Monuments Board of Canada, an independent body which makes recommendations to the Minister regarding matters of national historic and architectural significance. It also administers a national historical marker program, under which some 650 commemorative plaques have so far been erected across Canada.

CANADIAN INVENTORY OF HISTORIC BUILDING: Computerized survey designed to identify and record surviving structures from the pre-1880 period in Eastern Canada and the pre-1914 period in the western and northern parts of the country. Phase I, a survey of building exteriors, has recorded some 100,000 structures to date. Phase II, just begun, will involve the recording of interior details from some 6,000 to 10,000 structures selected from the mutual survey.

RESEARCH AND PUBLICATIONS: Archeological and historical research studies in support of the identification and development of national historic parks and sites; *Manuscript Report* series, unpublished research papers with copies deposited with the Public Archives of Canada and the provincial archives for public use; *Canadian Historic Sites* series, occasional papers in archeology and history available for sale through Information Canada, Ottawa; park folders and information leaflets; *National Historic Sites Policy* (1968); *The Canadian Inventory of Historic Building* (1972).

Great Britain

Ancient Monuments Society, 33 Ladbroke Square, London W11 3NB, England.

The Society was founded in 1924 for the study and conservation of ancient monuments, historic buildings, and fine old craftsmanship. It contests plans to demolish buildings of architectural or historic interest and conducts public enquiries where necessary. It also campaigns to increase the number of conservation areas, to extend the boundaries of those already in existence, and to prevent a creeping erosion of the character by new building that is inappropriate or out of scale.

Through its membership program, liaison is maintained with local communities and other amenity societies. Much work is done by members, particularly those who are professionally qualified to report on plans to demolish listed buildings and to represent the Society at public enquiries.

PUBLICATIONS: *Transactions*; and reprinted articles on specialized topics.

Civic Trust, 17 Carlton House Terrace, London SW1 Y 5AW, England.

Founded in 1957, the Civic Trust is an independent body supported by voluntary contributions. Its objectives are to encourage high quality in architecture and planning; to preserve buildings of distinction and historic interest; to eliminate and prevent ugliness, whether from bad design or neglect; to stimulate interest in the good appearance of town and country; and to inspire generally a sense of civic pride.

It has initiated hundreds of ideas and has provided leadership to stimulate similar projects. It has moved over 650 semimature trees into London as part of a wider campaign to plant more trees. It stimulates voluntary action to remove eyesores which mar town and countryside. The Trust gives support and advice to over 1,000 local civic and amenity societies throughout Britain. The relationship between the Civic Trust and a local amenity society registered with it is a mutually reinforcing one. Both organizations retain complete independence but the society receives certain services from the Trust and the Trust is kept informed of grass-roots activities.

There are four Associate Trusts: Scottish Civic Trust, 24 George Square, Glasgow C2; Civic Trust for Wales, 6 Park Place, Cardiff CF 1 3 DP; Civic Trust for the North West 56 Oxford Street, Manchester M 1 6 EU; Civic Trust for the North East, 34/35 Saddler Street, Durham.

PROGRAMS: Presents annual awards, to encourage high standards in architecture which pays due respect to the surroundings; assists and advises on planning projects and proposals; promotes the adoption of legislation on amenity problems such as the drafting of the Civic Amenities Act (1967); provides traveling exhibitions, conferences, expert studies, and films to focus attention on town planning and architecture.

PUBLICATIONS: *Civic Trust Newsletter*, bimonthly to registered societies, up-to-date information about action by government, local authorities, and voluntary organizations;

Publications and Visual Aids, catalog of publications, films, slides, photographs, exhibitions; *Guide to Slide and Photograph Collection*.

The National Trust for Places of Historic Interest or Natural Beauty, 42 Queen Anne's Gate, London WS1 H 9AS, England.

The National Trust was founded in 1895 by three imaginative people who foresaw that industrialism would be an increasing threat to the countryside and ancient buildings of England, Wales, and Northern Ireland. It was formed as a public company not trading for profit, and with power to acquire and preserve for the nation places of historic interest or natural beauty. In 1907 the Trust was incorporated by an Act of Parliament which gave it its mandate "to promote the permanent preservation for the benefit of the nation of land and buildings of beauty or historic interest." It granted the Trust its unique power to declare property inalienable.

In 1937 Parliament further enabled the Trust to hold country houses and their contents, as well as land and ancient buildings. Under the Country House Scheme, a country house, with or without its contents, may be presented to the Trust with an adequate endowment fund to maintain it in perpetuity. In return the donor and his descendants may continue living in the house rent-free, subject to public access and to certain controls which ensure that the original character and fabric of the property are preserved. A 1946 act permitted the Trust the right to appeal to a joint committee of both Houses of Parliament if a public authority proposed to take its land by use of compulsory powers. Another program provides for the acquisition of portions of the coastline unspoiled by development.

The Trust is administered by an executive staff of about seventy in the head office in London or at sixteen regional offices covering the whole of England, Wales, and Northern Ireland. Policy is determined by the governing body, the Council, half of which is appointed by national institutions and half elected by the Trust members. There is an Executive Committee, volunteer committees, and eighty-five local bodies connected with single properties.

The Trust has 349,000 members; owns some 380,000 acres of land, including 300 miles of coastline, and has protective covenants over an additional 61,000 acres; and manages more than 200 houses and gardens open to the public at a charge.

PUBLICATIONS: *The Continuing Purpose*, by Robin Fedden, an account of the Trust's history, aims and work (o.p.); *The National Trust Guide*, official guide to the houses and gardens; *The National Trust and the Preservation of Historic Buildings*, how the Country House Scheme works; program leaflets; property guidebooks and leaflets; *Prehistoric Properties of the National Trust*.

The National Trust for Scotland, 5 Charlotte Square, Edinburgh EH2 2DU, Scotland.

The National Trust for Scotland was founded in 1931 to promote the preservation of places of historic interest or natural beauty. In its care are over eighty properties including castles, gardens, cottages, tracts of mountainous country, and picturesque burghs. The Trust is a charity supported by legacies, donations, and annual subscriptions of its members who now total 64,000.

By Act of Parliament, the Trust has the power to make conservation agreements which now provide protection for 51,634 acres and seventy-three miles of coastline. A Gardens Committee was formed in 1950 to build up a fund for the maintenance of notable gardens among the properties in the Trust's care and to enable the Trust to accept other gardens for preservation. In 1960 the Trust pioneered in the restoration of "little houses," and its Little House Improvement Scheme has been chosen one of four British projects to be featured during European Architectural Heritage Year 1975. Some 125 dwellings, ten museums, shops and other places of business have been completed through the use of a revolving fund.

ACTIVITIES AND SERVICES: Tours and expeditions, April–November, to Trust and related sites; winter lecture series; special occasions; cruises; slide and lecture kits, and films. Cooperative programs are carried out with the Forestry Commission, Nature Conservancy, Crofters Commission, Scottish Tourist Board, Countryside Commission for Scotland, Scottish Civic Trust, Highlands and Islands Development Board, and the Association for the Preservation of Rural Scotland.

PUBLICATIONS: *Year Book; Conserve and Provide*, a history of the Trust by R.J. Prentice; *The National Trust for Scotland*, Volume V of a five-volume work on the two Trusts by Peter Ryan; *Freedom of Scotland: The National Trust for Scotland*; *Scotland's Gardens Scheme Handbook;* guidebooks, maps and folders for properties; *Newsletter; News Sheets.*

The Society for the Protection of Ancient Buildings, 55 Great Ormond Street, London WC1 N 3JA, England.

The Society, founded in 1877, advises on all problems affecting old buildings, giving technical advice on their treatment and repair. Buildings, ecclesiastical and secular, large and small, including mills, dovecotes, and bridges, come within the scope of the Society. It investigates cases of buildings suffering from neglect or threatened by damaging treatment or with destruction. It prepares surveys and reports on the historic areas of cities, towns, and villages, and is willing to advise planning authorities and others on the designation of conservation areas. It also keeps records of past repair work and cases. An index of houses threatened with demolition is maintained and possible purchasers are provided with information.

Membership is available for those who are interested in the care and preservation of old buildings and who adhere to the principles laid down in the founder's manifesto.

ACTIVITIES: Public lectures on specific subjects dealing with old buildings, and speakers on all aspects of the Society's work; exhibitions; conferences on problems in the field of historic preservation.

TRAINING PROGRAMS: Annual courses on the repair of ancient buildings for architects, surveyors, and builders; special scholarships which enable architectural students to study old buildings and their repair.

PUBLICATIONS: General and technical information on the history and care of old buildings, their features and fittings; news sheet, circulated to members about four times a year; catalog of publications, available on request.

International

Council of Europe, Council for Cultural Cooperation, c/o Director of Education and of Cultural and Scientific Affairs, Council of Europe, Strasbourg, France.

The Council of Europe was established by ten nations on May 5, 1949, and since then its membership has increased to eighteen. Its aim is "to achieve a greater unity between its members for the purpose of safeguarding and realizing the ideals and principles which are their common heritage and facilitating their economic and social progress." This aim is pursued by discussion of questions of common concern and by agreements and common action in economic, social, cultural, scientific, legal and administrative matters.

The Council for Cultural Cooperation was set up by the Committee of Ministers of the Council of Europe on January 1, 1962, to draw up proposals for the cultural policy of the Council of Europe; to coordinate and give effect to the overall cultural program of the organization; and to allocate the resources of the Cultural Fund. It is assisted by three permanent committees of senior officials: for higher education and research, for general and technical education, and for out-of-school education. All the member governments of the Council of Europe, together with Spain and the Holy See, which have acceded to the European Cultural Convention, are represented on these bodies.

EUROPEAN ARCHITECTURAL HERITAGE YEAR, 1975: The Council of Europe has designated 1975 as European Architectural Heritage Year. Five years ago the Council sponsored the successful European Conservation Year 1970. Just as that campaign focused attention on the need to conserve the environment, the broad aim of the present one is to halt the steady loss of irreplaceable buildings and the erosion of character in historic European towns.

The detailed objectives of the Heritage Year are to awaken the interest of the European peoples in their common architectural heritage; to protect and enhance buildings and areas of architectural or historic interest; to conserve the character of old towns and villages; and to assure for ancient buildings a living role in contemporary society. National committees, backed up by government money and patronage, have now been established in most European countries.

International Council of Monuments and Sites (ICOMOS), ICOMOS/International, Hotel St. Aignan, 75 rue du Temple, Paris, 3ème, France.

The International Council of Monuments and Sites, organized in 1965, is an international organization designed to link public authorities, departments, institutions, and individuals interested in the preservation and study of monuments and sites. Its activities include encouraging the preparation and adoption of international recommendations for the study, preservation, and restoration of monuments, sites, and artistic objects; cooperating in the development of documentation centers, inventories, directories, maps, and photographic archives; and disseminating information of all techniques for the preservation, restoration, and development of monuments and sites.

ICOMOS is supported by a membership program and by national committees of well-known preservationists which have been formed in forty-six countries to date. National Committees take steps to implement the general and national programs of

ICOMOS. The U.S. National Committee is headed by Robert R. Garvey, ICOMOS Vice President, 1522 K Street, N.W., Suite 430, Washington, D.C. 20005.

Temporary or permanent study groups and international committees, composed of a limited number of experts, carry out specialized studies on professional problems. Such committees are the International Committee for Architectural Photogrammetry organized jointly with the International Society for Photogrammetry, and the International Committee for Documentation.

PROGRAMS: Triennial General Assembly; symposiums, study meetings for the examination of urgent and important problems connected with architectural heritage; collaboration with UNESCO, the International Centre for the Study of the Preservation and the Restoration of Cultural Property (Rome Centre), International Council of Museums, International Union of Architects, and other related regional or international organizations.

UNESCO/ICOMOS INTERNATIONAL DOCUMENTATION CENTRE FOR THE PROTECTION OF THE ARCHITECTURAL HERITAGE: A proposal was first explored in 1966. The U.S. National Committee commissioned an analysis of function and scope of such a center and in 1970 ICOMOS adopted the report. A detailed proposal is now being implemented under the joint auspices of UNESCO and ICOMOS. The center functions as an international information agency for problems of historic preservation. Through the facilities of a reference library and a professional staff, institutions and individuals will be put in touch with international experts who can answer their queries. Staff will maintain contact with other documentation and information services around the world. The Centre is located at the Paris headquarters of ICOMOS.

PUBLICATIONS: *Monumentum*, a semiannual scholarly journal devoted to articles and scientific texts dealing with either doctrine or legislation, or with the restoration, revivification, or enchancement of monuments, sites, or groups of ancient buildings; *ICOMOS Bulletin*, devoted to news of the organization and the National Committees, and a portion devoted to the conservation problems of an individual country; Symposium Reports, published in a series of specialized brochures.

History of the Preservation Movement

Albright, Horace M. *Origins of National Park Service Administration of Historic Sites.* Philadelphia: Eastern National Park and Monument Association, 1971. 24 pp., photos, paper.

Albright, Horace M., and Frank J. Taylor. *Oh, Ranger!* National Park Service Centennial Edition. Riverside, Conn.: Chatham Press (distr. by Viking Press, N.Y.), 1972. 239 pp., illus., paper.

American Society of Planning Officials. "Planning for Preservation of Historical Areas," *Planning 1954*, pp. 75-86. ◆ Remarks by J.

Ben Rouzie, Arch R. Winter, Albert Simons, and Robert M. Lillibridge on programs in New Orleans, Louisiana; Mobile, Alabama; Charleston, South Carolina; Chicago, Illinois.

Ashbee, Charles Robert. "The Growing Regard for Amenities and the Preservation of History." In *Where the Great City Stands; A Study in the New Civics* (London: Essex House Press, 1917), pp. 22-25.

Ashbee, Charles Robert. *A Report by Mr. C. R. Ashbee to the Council of the National Trust for Places of Historic Interest and Natural Beauty, on His Visit to the United States on the Council's Behalf, October, MDCCCC to February, MDCCCCI.* London: Essex House Press, 1901. 24 pp.

Bailey, Worth. "Safeguarding a Heritage: An Account of the Historic American Buildings Survey," *Historic Preservation*, 15:4 (1963), pp. 143-148. ♦ See also: Washington, D.C.: National Park Service, January 1963. 6 pp., photos, paper.

Bannister, Turpin C., ed. "Preservation of Historic Monuments," *Journal of the Society of Architectural Historians*, 1:3-4 (July-October 1941), special issue. 60 pp., bibliog., mimeo.

Barrington, Lewis. *Historic Restorations of the Daughters of the American Revolution.* New York: R. R. Smith, 1941. 320 pp., photos, index.

Bingaman, John W. *Guardians of Yosemite: Story of the First Rangers.* n.p.: 1961. 123 pp., illus.

Buck, Paul H. *The Evolution of the National Park System of the United States.* Washington, D.C.: U.S. Government Printing Office, 1946. 74 pp., bibliog. ♦ M.A. thesis, Ohio State University, 1922; reprinted by the National Park Service for official use only.

Butterfield, Roger P. "Henry Ford, the Wayside Inn, and the Problem of 'History is Bunk,'" *Massachusetts Historical Society Proceedings*, 77 (1965), pp. 53-66.

Chittenden, Hiram Martin. *The Yellowstone National Park; Historical and Descriptive . . . .* New and enl. ed., entirely revised. Cincinnati, O.: Stewart & Kidd Co., 1915. 397 pp., illus., maps, bibliog. ♦ First published in 1895; revised editions by others up to 1940.

Chorley, Kenneth. "Primer for Preservation: What's Wrong with Historic Preservation," *History News*, 19:6 (April 1964), Technical Leaflet no. 19 (old series). ♦ See also: *Primer for Preservation: A Handbook for Historic-House Keeping* (Cooperstown, N.Y.: New York State Historical Association, 1956), pp. 2-22; *New York History*, 37:2 (1956), pp. 141-150.

Clary, David A. *"The Place Where Hell Bubbled Up": A History of the First National Park.* Washington, D.C.: National Park Service, 1972. 68 pp., photos, drawings, map. ♦ A centennial history of Yellowstone, and its development from an Army-protected to a national park.

Crampton, Louis C. *Early History of Yellowstone National Park and Its Relation to National Park Policies.* Washington, D.C.: U. S. Government Printing Office, 1932. 148 pp., bibliog., legislative chronology, (o.p.).

♦ Focus on the establishment of the national park idea in 1872 with the creation of Yellowstone National Park.

Dale, Anthony. "Listing and Preserving Historic Buildings, Part I: The European Picture," *Architectural Review*, 138 (August 1965), pp. 97-104.

Dale, Anthony. "Listing and Preserving Historic Buildings, Part II: U.S.A., Canada, South Africa, Australia and New Zealand," *Architectural Review*, 149 (October 1966), pp. 277-279.

Everhart, William C. *The National Park Service.* Praeger Library of U. S. Government Departments and Agencies, no. 31. New York: Praeger, 1972. 276 pp., illus., bibliog.

Ferriday, Peter. "The Church Restorers," *Architectural Review*, 136 (August 1964), pp. 86-95.

Finley, David E. *History of the National Trust for Historic Preservation, 1947-1963.* Washington, D.C.: National Trust for Historic Preservation, 1965. 115 pp., photos, charts, appendix, index.

Goodwin, Rutherfoord. *A Brief and True Report Concerning Williamsburg in Virginia; Being an Account of the Most Important Occurrences in that Place from Its First Beginning to the Present Time.* 3rd ed., rev. and enl. Richmond, Va.: Printed for Colonial Williamsburg, Inc. by A. Dietz and Son, 1940. 406 pp., illus., maps, plans, appendix.

Hampton, H. Duane. *How the U.S. Cavalry Saved Our National Parks.* Bloomington, Ind.: Indiana University Press, 1971. 246 pp., photos, map, bibliog., index.

Hartzog, George B., Jr. "Mission 66 and Parkscape," *Historic Preservation*, 18:4 (July-August 1966), pp. 140-143.

Hays, Samuel P. *Conservation and the Gospel of Efficiency: The Progressive Conservation Movement, 1890-1920.* Harvard Historical Monograph Series no. 40. Cambridge, Mass.: Harvard University Press, 1959. 297 pp., bibliog. note, bibliog. footnotes.

Historic American Buildings Survey. "Documenting a Legacy: 40 Years of the Historic American Buildings Survey." Reprinted from the Library of Congress *Quarterly Journal*, October 1973. 28 pp., photos, drawings, paper.

Hosmer, Charles B., Jr. *Presence of the Past: A History of the Preservation Movement in the*

United States Before Williamsburg. New York: G. P. Putnam's Sons, 1965. 386 pp., photos, notes, bibliog., index. ◆ The first record of the history of the preservation movement in broad terms and early efforts in the United States. It sets forth the strengths and weaknesses, successes and failures, of various approaches. The extensive bibliography lists letters and interviews, manuscript material, government documents, magazines, proceedings, reports, leaflets, and books. Volume 2, covering the preservation movement to 1949, is in preparation.

Huth, Hans. "Preservationism: A Selected Bibliography," *Journal of the Society of Architectural Historians,* 1:3-4 (July-October 1941), pp. 33-45.

Jacobs, Stephen W. *Architectural Preservation: American Development and Antecedents Abroad.* A dissertation submitted to the Department of Art and Archaeology. Princeton, N.J.: Princeton University, April 1966. 451 pp., bibliog., paper.

Jacobs, Stephen W. "Architectural Preservation in the United States: The Government's Role," *Curator,* IX:4 (December 1966), pp. 307-330.

Jones, Louis C. "Primer for Preservation: A Look at Historic Preservation," *History News,* 19:6 (April 1964), Technical Leaflet no. 19 (old series). ◆ See also: *Primer for Preservation: A Handbook for Historic-House Keeping* (Cooperstown, N.Y.: New York State Historical Association, 1956), p. 23; *Antiques,* 70:1 (July 1956), p. 38.

Kocher, A. Lawrence, and Howard Dearstyne. *Colonial Williamsburg: Its Buildings and Gardens, A Study of Virginia's Restored Capital.* Rev. ed. New York: Holt, Rinehart & Winston, 1961. 104 pp., illus. bibliog.

Lee, Ronald F. *The Antiquities Act of 1906.* Evolution of Federal Participation in Historic Preservation series no. 1. Washington, D.C.: National Park Service, Office of History & Historic Architecture, Eastern Service Center, 1970. 120 pp., photo, tables, appendices, bibliog. notes, paper. ◆ Also available from: National Technical Information Service, 5285 Port Royal Road, Springfield, Virginia 22151.

Lee, Ronald F. *Family Tree of the National Park System: A Chart with Accompanying Text Designed to Illustrate the Growth of the National Park System, 1872-1972.* Philadelphia: Eastern National Park and Monument Association, 1972. 99 pp., color chart, chronological tables, index.

Lemann, Bernard. "Keeping Time in Perspective." Reprinted from American Institute of Architects *Journal,* November 1968. 7 pp., photos. ◆ Excerpts from "Historic Areas and Structures" and "The Vieux Carré - A General Statement," on useful integration of historic landmarks and their restoration. Available from the National Trust for Historic Preservation.

Lillibridge, Robert M. "Historic American Communities: Their Role and Potential," *Journal of the American Institute of Planners,* Part I: 19:3 (Summer 1953), pp. 131-138; Part II: 19:4 (Fall 1953), pp. 219-226.

Lord, Clifford L., ed. *Keepers of the Past.* Chapel Hill, N.C.: University of North Carolina Press, 1965. 241 pp. ◆ Chapters deal with Ann Pamela Cunningham and Mount Vernon; Adina De Zavala and the Alamo; William Sumner Appleton and the Society for the Preservation of New England Antiquities; Stephen H. P. Pell and Fort Ticonderoga; John D. Rockefeller and the Sleepy Hollow Restorations and Williamsburg.

Morrison, Jacob H. "Variation on an Old Theme," *Historic Preservation,* 14:2 (1962), pp. 74-77. ◆ Focus is primarily on the legal battles involving the Vieux Carré, New Orleans.

Nash, Roderick, "The American Invention of National Parks," *The American Quarterly,* 22:3 (Fall 1970), pp. 726-735.

National Trust for Historic Preservation, and The Colonial Williamsburg Foundation. *Historic Preservation Today: Essays Presented to the Seminar on Preservation and Restoration, Williamsburg, Virginia, September 8-11, 1963.* Charlottesville, Va.: University Press of Virginia, 1966. 265 pp., tables, bibliog. footnotes, appendix, index, paper. ◆ Papers and comments on a group of international experts on all phases of government and private preservation.

Pan American Symposium on the Preservation and Restoration of Historic Monuments, St. Augustine, 1965. *Old Cities of the New World; Proceedings. . . .* Sponsored by the Organization of American States, National Trust for Historic Preservation, and St. Augustine Historical Restoration and Preservation Commission. San Agustin Antiguo: 1967. 1 vol. (various pagings), illus., map. ◆ Also published in Spanish.

24

Peterson, Charles E. "Historic Preservation U.S.A.: Some Significant Dates." Reprinted from *Antiques,* 89:2 (February 1966), pp. 229-232. 4 pp., photos, prints, chronology, paper.

Pettengill, George E. "AIA in the Preservation Movement," American Institute of Architects *Journal,* 19:6 (June 1953), pp. 271-274.

Robbins, Roy M. *Our Landed Heritage: The Public Domain, 1776-1936.* Reprinted from the Princeton University Press edition. Lincoln, Neb.: University of Nebraska Press, 1962. 450 pp., illus., maps, bibliog., paper.

Shankland, Robert. *Steve Mather of the National Parks.* New York: Alfred A. Knopf (Borzoi Books), 1951. 326 pp., photos, map, appendices, bibliog., index.

Swain, Donald C. *Wilderness Defender: Horace M. Albright and Conservation.* Chicago: University of Chicago Press, 1970. 347 pp., photos, bibliog., index.

Tilden, Freeman. *The National Parks.* 2nd rev. ed. New York: Alfred A. Knopf, 1970. 584 pp., illus., map.

Tilden, Freeman. *The State Parks: Their Meaning in American Life.* Foreword by Conrad L. Wirth. New York: Alfred A. Knopf, 1970. 494 pp., photos, plates, maps, appendices, index.

United States Conference of Mayors, Special Committee on Historic Preservation. *With Heritage So Rich: A Report.* Albert Rains, Chairman; Laurance G. Henderson, Director. 1st ed. New York: Random House, Inc., 1966. 230 pp., plates, photos, bibliog. ◆ A report of a special study of the state of preservation in the United States that provided impetus for passage of the National Historic Preservation Act of 1966. Chapters, written by authorities in special fields of preservation, include an historical overview, origins of preservation in the United States, buildings that have been lost, the Historic American Buildings Survey, preservation in Europe, and photographic essays.

U.S. National Park Service. *Historic Preservation: Policies of the National Park Service.* 1968 reprint from *Administration Policies for Historical Areas of the National Park System.* Washington, D.C.: U.S. Government Printing Office, 1969. 22 pp., paper. ◆ Contents include history of government involvement, preservation policy, administrative policy, research policy. Appendices cover administra-

tive criteria for historical areas and historic landmarks.

U.S. National Park Service. *That the Past Shall Live: The History Program of the National Park Service.* Text by Shirley Hurst, Washington staff, in collaboration with John A. Hussey, Region Historian, Region Four Office. Washington?: 1959? 39 pp., illus.

Wolfe, Albert B. "Conservation of Historical Buildings and Areas—Legal Techniques." Reprinted from the *Proceedings* of the American Bar Association, Section of Real Property, Probate & Trust Law, August 1963. 11 pp. ◆ Contents include preservation in general and early projects of the Society for the Preservation of New England Antiquities; constitutionality based on police power; inventories and surveys used; preservation legislation; districts and boundaries. Available from the National Trust for Historic Preservation. See also: *Planning 1964* (Chicago: American Society of Planning Officials, 1964), pp. 208-214.

Historic Preservation Today

American Institute of Architects. "The Architect as a Preservationist," *Architect's Handbook of Professional Practice.* Chap. 21. Washington, D.C.: The American Institute of Architects, 1971. 8 pp., index, leaflet.

Balk, Alfred. "Our Embattled Landmarks," *Saturday Review,* 49:26 (June 25, 1966), p. 18. ◆ An editorial on landmarks in imminent danger, e.g., St. Louis, Chicago, New Orleans.

Benedict, Sarah. "Group Action in Preservation," *Antiques,* 95:3 (March 1969), pp. 388-389. ◆ Historic sites federation in Tennessee.

Biddle, James. "Historic Preservation is Getting Growing Attention from Federal, State, Local, and Private Agencies." Reprinted from the *Journal of Housing,* 28:5 (May 1971). 8 pp., photos, leaflet.

Blair, Lachlan F. "Planning for Historic Preservation," *History News,* 17:1 (November 1961), pp. 14-15.

Briggs, Martin Shaw. *Goths and Vandals: A Study of the Destruction, Neglect, and Preservation of Historic Buildings in England.* 1952. Reprint. New York: Somerset Publishers, 1972. 251 pp., illus.

Brown, William E. *Islands of Hope: Parks and Recreation in Environmental Crisis.* Washington, D.C.: National Recreation and Park Association, 1971. 194 pp., bibliog. ◆ Contents include chapters on environmental reform, environmental management, environmental interpretation, environmental education, and the environment of change.

Bryant, James A.; Mrs. George E. Downing; and H. G. Jones. "The Role of State Programs," *Historic Preservation,* 23:1 (January-March 1971), pp. 37-49. ◆ Urban effects of statewide preservation projects in Michigan; description of surveys sponsored by Rhode Island Historical Preservation Commission; North Carolina grants-in-aid to local projects in urban areas.

Chesley, Gene A. "Encore for 19th Century American Theaters," *Historic Preservation,* 25:4 (October-December 1973), pp. 20-24.

Civic Trust. "Conservation Areas; Preserving the Architectural and Historic Scene." A Civic Trust survey with contributions by Maurice Barley and others. Reprinted from *Architects' Journal,* January 1967. 87 pp., illus., plans. ◆ A survey of the problems and opportunities for area and group preservation offered by the Civic Amenities Act of 1967. Reprint available from Harrison Publishers, London.

Civic Trust. *Conservation in Action: A Progress Report on What Is Being Done in Britain's Conservation Areas, Based on the Civic Trust Conference Held at the Royal Festival Hall.* London: The Trust, 1972. 104 pp., photos, map, diagrams, paper. ◆ Contents cover conservation principles; policy and participation; planning issues; restoration-maintenance-enhancement; paying for it; call to action.

Clay, Grady. "Townscape and Landscape: The Coming Battleground," *Historic Preservation,* 24:1 (January-March 1972), pp. 34-43. ◆ Major forces at work where preservationists must compete such as building construction, move to the suburbs, quick assemblage of huge building formations.

Cliver, E. Blaine. "Reconstruction: Valid or Invalid?" *Historic Preservation,* 24:4 (October-December 1972), pp. 22-24.

Colony, John J., III. "Preservation in Small Towns: Why Save Harrisville?" *Historic Preservation,* 24:2 (April-June 1972), pp. 22-25.

Conference on the Conservation, Restoration and Revival of Areas and Groups of Buildings of Historic Interest, 1st, Caceres, Spain, 1967. *First Conference on the Conservation, Restoration and Revival of Areas and Groups of Buildings of Historic Interest, Cacares, Spain, 15-19 III 1967.* Paris: ICOMOS, 1968. 92 pp.

Conference on the Conservation, Restoration and Revival of Areas and Groups of Buildings of Historic Interest, 2nd, Tunis, 1968. *Second Conference on the Conservation, Restoration and Revival of Areas and Groups of Buildings of Historic Interest, Tunis, 9-16 IV 1968.* Paris: ICOMOS, 1969. 194 pp., photos, maps.

Conference on the ICOMOS Documentation Centre, Brussels, 1966. *Conference on the ICOMOS Documentation Centre, Brussels, 13-15 XII 1966.* Paris: ICOMOS, 1969. 97 pp.

"Conservation," *Architectural Review,* 148:886 (December 1970), special issue. 61 pp., photos, maps, prints, drawings, plans. ◆ Articles include: "European Conservation Year"; "Continuing Disasters"; "Dropping the Pilot?—York, Bath, Chester, Chichester"; "Achievements and Prospects;" "Four Case Studies—Edinburgh, Paris, Sfax, Rome"; "Conservation Conspectus—Social Aspects, Housing Rehabilitation, Traffic Engineering and Management, Cost Benefit Analysis, Participation"; "The Art of Infill"; "Rehabilitation."

The Conservation Foundation. *National Parks for the Future: An Appraisal of the National Parks as They Begin Their Second Century in a Changing America.* Washington, D.C.: The Foundation, 1972. 254 pp., bibliog. on National Parks.

Crosby, Theo. *The Necessary Monument: Its Future in the Civilized City.* Greenwich, Conn.: New York Graphic Society, Ltd., 1970. 128 pp., appendices, bibliog., prints, diagrams, photos. ◆ Includes a discussion of the architectural monument in the modern city in terms of the monument reborn (Paris Opera), the monument in balance (Tower Bridge), and the monument destroyed (Pennsylvania Station).

Daifuku, Hiroshi. "The Significance of Cultural Property." In *The Conservation of Cultural Property with Special Reference to Tropical Conditions* (Paris: UNESCO, 1968), pp. 19-26.

Dale, Anthony. "Listing and Preserving Historic Buildings: Part I: The European Picture,"

Architectural Review, 138 (August 1965), pp. 97-104.

Dale, Anthony. "Listing and Preserving Historic Buildings: Part II: U.S.A., Canada, South Africa, Australia and New Zealand," *Architectural Review,* 149 (October 1966), pp. 277-279.

deAndrade, Rodrigo M.F. "The Conservation of Urban Sites." In *The Conservation of Cultural Property with Special Reference to Tropical Conditions* (Paris: UNESCO, 1968), Chapter 11, pp. 153-168.

Delaney, Barbara Snow. "Preservation: Canada 1967," *Antiques,* 92:1 (July 1967), pp. 100-105.

Delaney, Barbara Snow. "Preservation 1966," *Antiques,* 90:4 (October 1966), pp. 526-533. ◆ Charleston, South Carolina; Annapolis, Maryland; Newport, Rhode Island.

Delaney, Barbara S.; Robert L. Raley; and Molly A. Ten Broeck. "Preservation 1968," *Antiques,* 93:4 (April 1968), pp. 511-517. ◆ Benefit Square, Providence; Old Brandywine Village, Inc., and Tredyffrin Township, Pennsylvania.

Dober, Richard P. "The Three Thousand Decisions," *Historic Preservation,* 14:4 (1962), pp. 126-133. ◆ Preservation of campus architecture.

Dunn, Alan. *Architecture Observed.* 1st ed. New York: Architectural Record Books, 1971. 144 pp., cartoon drawings. ◆ A collection of the author's cartoons which have appeared regularly in *Architectural Record* over the past thirty-five years. They point out impudent burlesques on the absurdities of modern architecture.

Feiss, Carl. "Preservation of Historic Areas in the United States," *Historic Preservation,* 16:4 (1964), pp. 132-149.

Florida Historic Preservation Planning: A Symposium; Proceedings. Edited by Samuel Proctor. Tallahassee, Fla.: Division of Archives, History and Records Management of Florida, 1971. 33 pp., photos, prints, paper. ◆ Publication of the proceedings of the symposium held at the College of Architecture and Fine Arts at the University of Florida, January 14-15, 1971.

Great Britain. Ministry of Housing and Local Government. *Historic Towns: Preservation and Change.* London: Her Majesty's Stationery Office, 1967. 49 pp., illus.

Greater London Council. Historic Buildings Board. *The Work of the Historic Buildings Board of the Greater London Council.* 3rd ed. Publication 7168. London: Greater London Council, 1971. 61 pp., photos, drawings, cartoons, prints, maps, list of organizations, tables, index, paper. ◆ Discusses the work of the Board, its projects, grants, plaque placing and listing programs, restoration work, properties, and the 36-volume *Survey of London.* Cover title: *Do You Care About Historic Buildings?*

Hall, Peter Nelson. "Minirara, Minneapolis' Internationally Historic Falls," *Historic Preservation,* 23:3 (July-September 1971), pp. 36-44.

Hartzog, George B., Jr. "Mission 66 and Parkscape," *Historic Preservation,* 18:4 (July-August 1966), pp. 140-143.

Haskell, Douglas; Lachlan F. Blair; and John R. Searles, Jr. "Is There Preservation Planning for the City of Tomorrow?" *Historic Preservation,* 13:4 (1961), pp. 168-179.

Historic American Buildings Survey. *Preservation Through Documentation.* Washington, D.C.: U.S. Government Printing Office, 1968. 16 pp., photos, drawings, diagrams, maps, paper.

Historic Preservation, 14:2 (1962), pp. 44-78. ◆ Special issue on preservation of courthouses and city halls, and includes examples; "Criteria for Historic District Selection"; "How to Save a Courthouse"; and "A Law for the Preservation of a Historic District."

Historic Towns and Cities Conference, York, England, 1968. *Conservation and Development in Historic Towns and Cities.* Edited by Pamela Ward. New Castle-Upon-Tyne, England: Oriel Press, 1968. 275 pp., illus., plans, maps. ◆ Chapters include economics, traffic, management, research, design, policy. Chapter on "Historic Buildings Law" is a recent listing of relevant legislation in Great Britain.

Horler, Miklos. "Preservation in Europe, 1969: The Historic Quarter of Buda," *Antiques,* 96:6 (December 1969), pp. 918-920.

Insall, Donald W. *Historic Buildings: Their Care and Repair and the Availability and Training of Planners, Architects, Contractors and Craftsmen.* An International Enquiry prepared for the Council of Europe. London: Council of Europe, 1972. 109 pp. ◆ Includes an introduction; form of enquiry; list of member countries giving replies; selected list of authorities recommending architects who specialize in restoration work; selected list of organizations recommending contractors skilled in the repair of historic buildings; selected list of organizations recommending craftsmen, specialists and suppliers. A copy of the unpublished report is on deposit in the National Trust for Historic Preservation library.

International Council of Monuments and Sites. *Application of Photogrammetry to Historic Monuments, Saint-Mandé, 4-6 July 1968.* Vol I. Paris: The Council, 1968. 181 pp., charts, bibliog.

International Federation for Housing and Planning, Standing Committee on "Historic Urban Areas." *Historic Urban Areas: Venice Meeting Acts.* Publication No. 1. Torino, Italy: Urbanistica, 1965? 115 pp., illus., maps, plans.

Jacobs, Stephen W. "Architectural Preservation in Europe: French and English Contributions," *Curator,* 9:3 (November 1966), pp. 196-215.

Kidney, Walter. "New Life for a Dead Letter Office," *Progressive Architecture,* 53 (November 1972), pp. 100-105. ♦ Report of Pittsburgh's old North Side Post Office restored to new use as the Pittsburgh History and Landmark Museum.

Knight, Carleton, III. "Seattle, A City Where Preservation is a Priority," *Preservation News,* 13:11 (November 1973), p. 8.

Landahl, William L. *Perpetuation of Historical Heritage for Park and Recreation Departments.* Management Aids Bulletin no. 55. Wheeling, W. Va.: American Institute of Park Executives, Inc., 1965. 40 pp., appendix, bibliog.,paper.

Latus, Mark. "Preservation and the Energy Crisis," *Historic Preservation,* 25:2 (April-June 1973), pp. 10-13.

Libal, Dobroslav, and Eduard Stach. "Preservation in Europe, 1969: Prague," *Antiques,* 95:6 (June 1969), pp. 842-846.

Lynch, Kevin. *What Time Is This Place?* Cambridge, Mass.; M.I.T. Press, 1972. 277 pp., illus., bibliog., index, appendix. ♦ Focus on progress, time perception, cities transforming, presence of the past, change.

Lynn, James T. "Preservation and Revenue Sharing," *Preservation News,* 13:9 (September 1973), p. 8.

McCahill, Peter J. "Saving a Neighborhood Through Historic Preservation," *Journal of Housing,* 24:3 (April 1967), pp. 168-172. ♦ Discusses the Ansonborough area rehabilitation program of Historic Charleston.

Mackey, M. Cecil. "Transportation and the Preservation Ethic," *Historic Preservation,* 21:1 (January-March 1969), pp. 5-7.

Melvin, Peter. "Conservation and the Built Environment," *Progressive Architecture,* 53 (November 1972), pp. 86-91. ♦ Review of the conservation acts of the United Kingdom; public participation; economic viability; individual list of buildings; new structures and the great need for public awareness of environmental quality.

Menges, Gary L. *Historic Preservation: A Bibliography.* Exchange Bibliography no. 79. Monticello, Ill.: Council of Planning Librarians, 1969. 61 pp., mimeo. ♦ Preservation of buildings, sites, and towns with emphasis on the United States. Chapters include case studies by state; architectural surveys; legal aspects; restoration and maintenance; environmental aesthetics.

Miller, James Nathan. "Preservation for Profit: Restorations Come Alive," *National Civic Review,* 60:10 (November 1971), pp. 542-547. ♦ Condensed version in *Reader's Digest,* October 1973, pp. 30-36, entitled "Bonanza in Old Buildings."

Miner, Ralph W., Jr. *Conservation of Historic and Cultural Resources.* Chicago: American Society of Planning Officials, 1969. 56 pp., photos, bibliog., paper. ♦ Defines historic and cultural conservation; traces the changing emphases of the preservation movement; and outlines an approach to a comprehensive program through surveys, legal techniques, public and private options.

Minost, Maurice. "Preservation in Europe, 1969: Paris, the Quartier du Marais," *Antiques,* 96:3 (September 1969), pp. 406-408.

Montague, Robert L., and Tony P. Wrenn. *Planning for Preservation.* Chicago: American Society of Planning Officials, 1964. 42 pp., tables, bibliog. notes, appendix, paper. ♦ Reviews legal trends; problems and current capabilities in preservation law; survey of economic effects of preservation on property values, taxation and tourism; and the development of municipal historic district ordinances.

"Monuments in Peril: A World Campaign to Protect Our Cultural Heritage," *UNESCO Courier*, 18:1 (January 1965), special issue.

Morton, Terry Brust. "The Washington Megalopolis: Some Current Village Preservation Problems," *Historic Preservation*, 15:3 (1963), pp. 108-115. ◆ Discusses areas protected by historic legislation in Leesburg, Annapolis, Alexandria, and Georgetown, and urges architectural integrity in restorations and new structures.

Muskie, Edmund S. "Viewpoint," *History News*, 26:1 (January 1971), pp. 9-10. ◆ Stresses the importance of historians' efforts to preserve their local heritage.

National and Historic Parks Branch. *National Historic Sites Policy*. Ottawa: Department of Indian Affairs and Northern Development, 1968. 32 pp., English and French text, paper.

National Trust for Historic Preservation. *A Guide to State Programs*. 1972 ed. Washington, D.C.: The Trust, 1972. 200 pp., paper. ◆ Rev. ed. in preparation.

National Trust for Historic Preservation. *Historic Preservation and the Business Community*. Abstracts of the speeches presented at the 23rd Annual Meeting and Preservation Conference, October 2-5, 1969, Denver, Colorado. Washington, D.C.: The Trust, n.d. 36 pp., photos, drawings, map. ◆ See also: *Historic Preservation*, 21:4 (October-December 1969), pp. 2-36.

National Trust for Historic Preservation. *Preservation in the West: The 1971-72 Report of the Western Regional Field Office of the National Trust for Historic Preservation.* By John L. Frisbee, Ill. Washington, D.C.: The Trust, 1973. 49 pp., illus., appendix. ◆ Contents: the historic preservation movement in the western states; public programs; private programs; major preservation problems; National Trust involvement in the West; new directions for National Trust involvement; recommendations for state involvement.

National Trust for Historic Preservation. *Summary Report: San Diego Regional Preservation Workshop, 1971*. Washington, D.C.: The Trust, 1971. 62 pp. ◆ Summary of preservation activity in the states, in Washington, D.C., and in the private sector.

National Trust for Historic Preservation, **and The Colonial Williamsburg Foundation.** *Historic Preservation Today: Essays Presented to the Seminar on Preservation and Restoration, Williamsburg, Virginia, September 8-11, 1963.* Charlottesville, Va.: University Press of Virginia, 1966. 265 pp., tables, bibliog. footnotes, appendix, index, paper. ◆ Papers and comments of a group of international experts on all phases of governmental and private preservation.

New York (City). Council on the Environment. *Responding to the Urban Challenge: The National Park Service in New York City*. New York: The Council, 1972. 362 pp., diagrams, maps, paper.

New York (State). Commission on Cultural Resources. *State Financial Assistance to Cultural Resources: Report*. New York: 1971. 163 pp., illus.

Péladeau, Marius B. "Maine: Preservation Yankee Style," *Historic Preservation*, 25:4 (October-December 1973), pp. 4-11.

"Preservation: The Heritage of Progress," *Historic Preservation*, 13:3 (1961), entire issue. ◆ Exhibit of photographs assembled by the National Trust for Historic Preservation to exemplify the main currents of the preservation movement in this country and in other nations.

"Preservation and the Bureau of Outdoor Recreation," *Historic Preservation*, 16:6 (November-December 1964), pp. 209-214.

"Preservation for the People," *Historic Preservation*, 24:2 (April-June 1972), pp. 30-43. ◆ Four articles describing unique preservation problems confronting some of America's minorities.

"Preservation in Context," *Progressive Architecture*, 53 (November 1972), pp. 64-69. ◆ Discussion of preservation at a symposium cosponsored with Italian Art and Landscape Foundation, going beyond buildings to the broader implications of ecological and social problems and using Italy as a case in point.

Pyke, John S., Jr. *Landmark Preservation*. 2nd ed. New York: Citizens Union Research Foundation, 1972. 32 pp., photos, drawings, diagrams, appendix, bibliog., paper. ◆ Includes the challenge and economics of landmark preservation, types of preservation programs, the work of the New York City Landmarks Commission, and elements of an effective program. The appendix lists where to go for assistance.

Rath, Frederick L., Jr. "Primer for Preservation: The Challenge and a Plan," *History News,* 19:3 (January 1964), Technical Leaflet no. 16 (old series). 4 pp. ♦ See also: *Primer for Preservation: A Handbook for Historic-House Keeping* (Cooperstown, N.Y.: New York State Historical Association, 1956), pp. 4-6. *Antiques,* 70:1 (July 1956), pp. 41-43.

Rath, Frederick L., Jr., and Merrilyn Rogers O'Connell, comps. *Guide to Historic Preservation, Historical Agencies, and Museum Practices: A Selective Bibliography.* Cooperstown, N.Y.: New York State Historical Association, 1970. 369 pp., index. ♦ Guide to books, articles, and organizations and sources of information dealing with the field of historic preservation. Major sections cover preservation, administration, care of collections, research, and interpretation.

"Restoration and Preservation," *Architectural Review,* 148:885 (November 1970), entire issue. ♦ Review of preservation projects in England and East Germany, training for restoration, and surveys.

Rohrbach, Peter Thomas. "The Poignant Dilemma of Spontaneous Restoration," *Historic Preservation,* 22:4 (October-December 1970), pp. 4-10. ♦ Discussion of the East Capitol Hill restoration, Washington, D.C.

Ross, Marion D. "Preservation in Small Towns: Jacksonville," *Historic Preservation,* 24:2 (April-June 1972), pp. 28-29. ♦ Also photo story by Jack E. Boucher, "Jacksonville in HABS Color," pp. 26-27.

Satterthwaite, Ann. "A New Meaning for Landscape," *Historic Preservation,* 25:3 (July-September 1973), pp. 4-9.

"Saving Places for People: Large Scale Preservation," *Progressive Architecture,* 53 (November 1972), pp. 70-85. ♦ Four cities—Louisville, Lockport, Lowell, Seattle—approach the task of preserving neighborhoods with different methods and different results. Also available as a reprint in *Your Community Workbook,* published by the Public Awareness Program, New York State Council on Architecture, 810 Seventh Avenue, New York, New York 10019.

Scott, Mellier Goodin. *The States and the Arts: The California Arts Commission and the Emerging Federal-State Partnership.* Berkeley, Calif.: Institute of Governmental Studies, University of California, 1971. 129 pp., bibliog., paper.

Slayton, William L., et al. "Toward a Broader National Preservation Program," *Historic Preservation,* 18:6 (November-December 1966), entire issue. ♦ Includes reports on National Park Service, Department of Housing and Urban Development, General Services Administration, Department of Commerce Bureau of Public Roads, Philadelphia City Planning Commission, Pennsylvania Historical and Museum Commission.

Smith, Sherwin D. "The Great Landmarks Fight—Private Loss vs. Public Gain." *New York Times Magazine,* March 26, 1966, pp. 108 ff.

Snow, Barbara. "Philadelphia Story Continued," *Antiques,* 89:4 (April 1966), pp. 546-547. ♦ Effect of proposed Delaware Expressway on historic Southwark district of Philadelphia.

Snow, Barbara. "Preservation, 1962: Old and New Frontiers," *Antiques,* 81:4 (April 1962), pp. 416-419. ♦ Projects in Galena, Illinois, and Jacksonville, Oregon.

Snow, Barbara. "Preservation Notes: The Philadelphia Story—Part II," *Antiques, 83:3 (March 1963), p. 344.*

Stevens, S. K., et al. "The Federal Responsibility in Historic Preservation," *Historic Preservation,* 20:1 (January-March 1968), pp. 8-36. ♦ Articles on Department of the Interior, Department of Transportation, Department of Housing and Urban Development.

Sturdy, David. *How to Pull a Town Down: A Handbook for Local Councils.* London: Society for the Protection of Ancient Buildings, 1972. 16 pp., photos, paper. ♦ A satire on the rapid pace of demolishing historic buildings in England published to raise funds for the Society. Text of handbook reprinted in *Historic Preservation,* 25:2 (April-June 1973), pp. 14-17.

Swaine, Anthony. "Preservation in Europe, 1969: The Port and Town of Faversham, England," *Antiques,* 96:1 (July 1969), pp. 88-90.

Symposium on Monuments and Society, Leningrad, U.S.S.R., 2-8 IX 1969. Vol. III. Paris: ICOMOS, 1971. 155 pp., photos.

Taupin, Jean Louis. "Avignon: The Surroundings of the Palace of the Popes," *Antiques,* 96:3 (September 1969), pp. 409-411.

Tordeur, Jean. "Preservation in Europe, 1969: The Grand Béguinage at Louvain, Belgium; The Quartier des Arts in Brussels," *Antiques,* 96:4 (October 1969), pp. 592-597.

United Nations Educational, Scientific and Cultural Organization. *International Campaign for Monuments.* Paris: UNESCO, 1964. 23 pp., illus. ◆ Campaign to deepen awareness and to facilitate the preservation of the cultural heritage of mankind while at the same time enhancing this heritage by making monuments an integral part of everyday life.

United Nations Educational, Scientific and Cultural Organization. *Preserving and Restoring Monuments and Historic Buildings.* Museums and Monuments Series no. XIV. Paris: UNESCO, 1972. 267 pp., photos, diagrams, charts, bibliog., paper.

United Nations Educational, Scientific and Cultural Organization. *Protection of Mankind's Cultural Heritage: Sites and Monuments.* Paris: UNESCO, 1970. 73 pp., illus.

U. S. Advisory Council on Historic Preservation. *Issue Paper on Revenue Sharing, August 1, 1973.* 2nd paper. Washington, D.C.: The Council, 1973. 25 pp., paper.

U.S. Advisory Council on Historic Preservation. *A Report to the President and the Congress of the United States for the Years 1971-1972.* Washington, D.C.: U.S. Government Printing Office, 1973. 31 pp., photos, appendices. ◆ Appendices include: project review, section 106; comments on federal undertakings; special studies; international responsibilities; new legislation; membership in the International Centre.

U.S. Advisory Council on Historic Preservation. *A Report to the President and to the Congress, June, 1971.* Washington, D.C.: U.S. Government Printing Office, 1971. 32 pp., photos, drawings, paper.

U. S. Council on Environmental Quality. "Improving Land Use; Preserving Our Natural Heritage." In *Environmental Quality: The Third Annual Report of the Council on Environmental Quality* (Washington, D.C.: U. S. Government Printing Office, 1972), pp. 133-142. ◆ Includes national land use policy; tax incentives for better land use; key federal land use decisions; national parks centennial.

U. S. Council on Environmental Quality. "Land Use." In *Environmental Quality: The First Annual Report of the Council on Environmental Quality* (Washington, D.C.: U.S. Government Printing Office, 1970), pp. 165-197. ◆ Includes status of the land; influence of government; land use controls, police power, eminent domain, planning, role of private agreements, permits, tax policy; needed reforms; land use impact of federal activities.

U. S. Council on Environmental Quality. "National Parks." In *Environmental Quality: The Third Annual Report of the Council on Environmental Quality* (Washington, D.C.: U.S. Government Printing Office, 1972), pp. 311-335. ◆ Includes a century of parks; national parks' role in recreation; environmental quality in national parks; proposals for change; national parks worldwide; footnotes.

U. S. Council on Environmental Quality. "NEPA — Reform in Government Decision-making." In *Environmental Quality: The Third Annual Report of the Council on Environmental Quality* (Washington, D.C.: U.S. Government Printing Office, 1972), pp. 221-267. ◆ Includes origins of the National Environmental Policy Act; impact statement process; the courts and NEPA; footnotes. Appendix B—The National Environmental Policy Act of 1969, Public Law 91-190, January 1, 1970 (42 U.S.C. 4321-4347), pp. 352-257.

U. S. Council on Environmental Quality. "The Past Year, Federal and International Activity: Land Use." In *Environmental Quality: The Second Annual Report of the Council on Environmental Quality* (Washington, D.C.: U.S. Government Printing Office, 1971), pp. 19-24. ◆ Includes national land use policy; parks and wilderness areas; siting power plants and protecting mining lands; land controversies; protecting historic buildings.

U.S. Council on Environmental Quality. "The Urban Environment—Toward Livable Cities." In *Environmental Quality: The Fourth Annual Report of the Council on Environmental Quality* (Washington, D.C.: U. S. Government Printing Office, 1973), pp. 1-41. ◆ Includes review of downtown setting and design; four neighborhoods—city as a place to live, historic neighborhood, preservation of neighborhood with and without dislocation; footnotes.

U. S. Environmental Protection Agency. *Manual: Review of Federal Actions Impacting the Environment.* Washington, D.C.: The

Agency, 1972. 41 pp., forms, appendices, paper.

U. S. Environmental Protection Agency, Office of Public Affairs. In Productive Harmony: Environmental Impact Statements Broaden the Nation's Perspectives. By Carolyn Harris. Washington, D.C.: The Agency, 1972. 12 pp., leaflet. ◆ Description of the National Environmental Policy Act; definition of an impact statement; purpose and content of a statement; preparation of a statement; role of the Council on Environmental Quality and EPA; trends.

U. S. National Parks Centennial Commission. Preserving a Heritage. Final Report to the President and Congress of the National Parks Centennial Commission, Washington, D.C.: The Commission, 1973. 196 pp., photos, tables, bibliog., appendix.

U. S. Office of Archeology and Historic Preservation. Historic Preservation Grants-in-Aid (as of October 31, 1972). Washington, D.C.: National Park Service, 1972. 42 pp. ◆ Provides a complete list of all existing grants awarded since the passage of the Historic Preservation Act of 1966; summary of the historical significance of a project site and the assistance work; and the site ownership and dollar amount of assistance.

U. S. Office of Archeology and Historic Preservation. Summary Report of the 1967-68 Regional Conferences on the New Preservation Under the National Historic Preservation Act of 1966, Public Law 89-665. Washington, D.C.: 1968. 101 pp., illus.

Van Ravenswaay, Charles. "Planning for Preservation." In Historic Preservation Tomorrow (Williamsburg, Va.: National Trust for Historic Preservation and Colonial Williamsburg, 1967), pp. 15-29.

Washington Preservation Conference: Proceedings. Sponsored by Society of Architectural Historians, Latrobe Chapter, and National Trust for Historic Preservation, April 14-15, 1972. Washington, D.C.: National Trust for Historic Preservation, 1972. 210 pp., cartoons, landmarks list, list of preservation organizations and programs, bibliog., paper. ◆ Conference topics include transfer of development rights, role of the government, urban renewal economics, private enterprise, environmental aspects.

Weinberg, Robert C. "Preservation, at Long Last," American Institute of Architects Journal, 47:5 (May 1967), pp. 114-115. ◆ Brief history of the New York Landmarks Preservation Commission, its trials and errors.

White, Dana F. "Back Bay Boston: A Museum Experiment with Urban History," Museum News, 48:7 (March 1970), pp. 20-25. ◆ The focus of the Back Bay Exhibition upon a single precinct or district of the city may serve as a model for the organization of future museum exhibitions on the dynamics and problems of other American cities.

White House Conference on Natural Beauty, Washington, 1965. Report to the President: Statement by the Chairman and Summations by the 15 Panel Chairmen; and, The President's Response: Remarks of the President. Washington, D.C.: U. S. Government Printing Office, 1965. 47 pp.

Wolfe, Albert B. "Conservation of Historical Buildings and Areas—Legal Techniques." Reprinted from the Proceedings of the American Bar Association, Section of Real Property, Probate & Trust Law, August, 1963. 11 pp. ◆ Contents include preservation in general and early projects of the Society for the Preservation of New England Antiquities; constitutionality based on police power; inventories and surveys used; preservation legislation; districts and boundaries. See also: Planning 1964 (Chicago: American Society of Planning Officials, 1964), pp. 208-214.

Wrenn, Tony P. "Conservation, Preservation, and the National Registry," Historic Preservation, 18:4 (July-August 1966), pp. 164-169.

Young, Wayland Hilton, Baron Kennet. Preservation. London: Maurice Temple Smith, Ltd., 1972. 224 pp., photos, maps, appendix, index. ◆ Gives background on preservation movement in Britain, together with review of recent changes; advice to amenity societies; and extensive description of case histories of preservation projects.

Ziegler, Arthur P., Jr. Historic Preservation in Inner City Areas: A Manual of Practice. Pittsburgh, Pa.: Allegheny Press, 1971. 77 pp., photos, drawings, addresses of useful agencies, paper. ◆ A practical manual of principles, directions, and experience of the Pittsburgh History and Landmarks Foundation, focusing on restoration in historic districts without dislocating the residents. The manual also emphasizes the importance of community participation.

Zykan, Josef. "Preservation in Europe, 1969: Urban Sites in Austria," *Antiques,* 96:2 (August 1969), pp. 214-217.

Preservation Principles and Objectives

Browne, Kenneth. "Aspects of Conservation 1: Defining the Conservation Area," *Architectural Review,* 144 (October 1968), pp. 269-272.

Feiss, Carl. "Criteria for Historic District Selection," *Historic Preservation,* 14:2 (1962), pp. 67-73.

Feiss, Carl, and Terry Morton. "True or False—Living Architecture, Old and New," *Historic Preservation,* 20:2 (April-June 1968), pp. 50-58.

International Federation for Housing and Planning Council. "Resolution on the Preservation and Use of Buildings of Architectural and Historical Importance," *Ekistics,* March 1962, pp. 182-183.

Kerr, Robert J., II. "Historic Preservation—A Pragmatic Approach," American Institute of Architects *Journal,* 41:4 (April 1964), pp. 36-38. ◆ Importance of integrity of design in historic preservation.

Little, Bertram K. "Selection of New England Houses for Preservation," *Museum News,* 26:10 (November 15, 1948), pp. 6-7. ◆ Criteria for the selection of historic buildings for restoration and operation by the Society for the Preservation of New England Antiquities.

National Trust for Historic Preservation. *How to Evaluate Historic Sites and Buildings.* A report by the Committee on Standards and Surveys. Rev. ed. Washington, D.C.: The Trust, 1971. 2 pp., leaflet. ◆ The basic statement on criteria in the field.

National Trust for Historic Preservation. *A Report on Principles and Guidelines for Historic Preservation in the United States.* Washington, D.C.: The Trust, October 31, 1964. 23 pp., leaflet. ◆ Includes restoration principles, education, surveys, criteria, training, responsibility, legislation, administration. See also: National Trust for Historic Preservation. *Historic Preservation Today . . .* (Charlottesville, Va.: University Press of Virginia, 1966), appendix, pp. 243-256.

National Trust for Historic Preservation, and Colonial Williamsburg. *Historic Preservation Tomorrow: Revised Principles and Guidelines for Historic Preservation in the United States, Second Workshop, Williamsburg, Virginia.* Williamsburg, Va.: The Authors, 1967. 57 pp., photos, prints, drawings, bibliog., paper. ◆ A revision of the principles and guidelines, drafted in 1964, which were rendered obsolete with the passage and implementation of historic preservation legislation by the 89th Congress in 1966. The report includes objectives and scope of the preservation movement; survey, evaluation and registration; planning for preservation; education and training for restoration work; and points to consider in surveying.

Ostrowski, W. "Preservation and Use of Urban Monuments and Historic Urban Areas: General Report/Recommendations," International Federation for Housing and Planning *Bulletin,* 5-6 (1961), pp. 132-156.

South Carolina, Department of Parks, Recreation and Tourism. *Policy for South Carolina State Historic Parks and Sites.* Columbia, S.C.: The Department, 1973. 18 pp., paper.

Streatfield, David. "Standards for Historic Garden Preservation and Restoration." Reprinted from *Landscape Architecture,* 59:3 (April 1969), pp. 198-204. 8 pp. photos.

United Nations Educational, Scientific and Cultural Organization. *Convention Concerning the Protection of the World Cultural and Natural Heritage.* Recommendation adopted by the General Conference at its seventeenth session, Paris, 16 November 1972. Paris: 1972. 60 pp., paper.

United Nations Educational, Scientific and Cultural Organization. *Recommendation Concerning the Preservation of Cultural Property Endangered by Public or Private Works.* Recommendation adopted by the General Conference at its fifteenth session, Paris, 19 November 1968. Paris: 1968. 25 pp., paper.

United Nations Educational, Scientific and Cultural Organization. *Recommendation*

Concerning the Protection, at National Level, of the Cultural and Natural Heritage. Recommendation adopted by the General Conference at its seventeenth session, Paris, 16 November 1972. Paris: 1972. 29 pp., paper.

United Nations Educational, Scientific and Cultural Organization. *Recommendation Concerning the Safeguarding of the Beauty and Character of Landscapes and Sites.* Recommendation adopted by the General Conference at its twelfth session, Paris, 11 December 1962. Paris: 1962. 17 pp., paper.

United States Conference of Mayors, Special Committee on Historic Preservation. "Findings and Recommendations." In *With Heritage So Rich* (New York: Random House, Inc., 1966), pp. 203-211.

U. S. National Park Service. *Criteria for Selection of National Parklands and National Landmarks.* Rev. ed. Washington, D.C.: U. S. National Park Service, 1971. 30 pp., illus., paper.

U. S. National Park Service. *Historic Preservation: Policies of the National Park Service.* 1968 reprint from *Administration Policies for Historical Areas of the National Park System.* Washington, D.C.: U. S. Government Printing Office, 1969. 22 pp., paper.

"The Venice Charter," *Historic Preservation,* 17:1 (January-February 1965), pp. 20-23. ◆ International Charter for Preservation and Restoration of Monuments, prepared by the International Congress of Architects and Technicians of Historic Monuments.

Weinberg, Robert C. "Pitfalls and Plausibilities of Landmark Preservation," American Institute of Architects *Journal,* 44:1 (July 1965), pp. 50-57. ◆ Notes on what considerations should go into the decision to preserve a building, and comments on aesthetical and historical concerns and importance of total environmental preservation.

NOTES

United Nations Educational, Scientific and Cultural Organization, Recommendations. A recommendation is an international instrument and, as such, has no expiry date. It is a legal instrument in which Member States are invited to adopt whatever legislation or take other steps required to apply international principles and norms within their respective territories.

United Nations Educational, Scientific and Cultural Organization, World Heritage Convention. The Convention defines cultural heritage as architectural work, archeological remains, inscriptions, cave dwellings, groups of buildings and other features valuable in history, art, or science. Natural heritage includes physical and biological formations, habitats of threatened plant and animal species, and natural sites outstanding for their scientific values, conservation potential, or natural beauty. The World Heritage List includes sites, cultural and natural, nominated by their respective countries, considered of universal value. The World Heritage in Danger List includes sites seriously threatened and in need of immediate assistance. Aid is in the form of personnel services, materials, or money. Technical information and assistance depend on governmental and nongovernmental organizations, i.e., International Centre, ICOMOS, International Union for Conservation of Nature and Natural Resources. The World Heritage Fund is made up of voluntary or mandatory contributions by Member States. The United States was the first to ratify the Convention, November 13, 1973.

Preservation Training Programs

Dalibard, Jacques. "Training Architects for Conservation: The Prospects in Canada," *Bulletin of APT,* III:1 (1971), pp. 64-66.

Fitch, James Marston. "Professional Training for the Preservationist." Reprinted from the AIA *Journal,* 51:4 (April 1969), pp. 57-61. 5 pp., photos, drawings.

Insall, Donald W. *Historic Buildings: Their Care and Repair and the Availability and Training of Planners, Architects, Contractors and Craftsmen.* An International Enquiry prepared for the Council of Europe. London: Council of Europe, 1972. 109 pp. ◆ Includes form of enquiry and addendum; list of countries giving replies; selected list of authorities recommending architects who specialize in restoration work; selected list of organizations recommending contractors skilled in repair of historic buildings; selected list of organizations recommending craftsmen, specialists, and suppliers. A copy of the unpublished report is on deposit in the National Trust for Historic Preservation library.

National Trust for Historic Preservation. *Conference on Training for the Building Crafts, November 19-20, 1971, Washington, D.C.: A Summary Report.* Washington, D.C.: The Trust, 1972. 68 pp., paper.

National Trust for Historic Preservation. *Historic Preservation: Careers for Archaeologists, Curators, Historians, Landscape Architects, Lawyers, Planners.* Washington, D.C.: The Trust, n.d. 8 pp., mimeo. ♦ Includes listings of undergraduate programs, graduate programs, foreign courses, and short courses. Brochure is continually updated, and is available from the office of Community Education Coordinator.

Whitehill, Walter Muir. "Education and Training for Restoration Work." In *Historic Preservation Tomorrow: . . .* (Williamsburg, Va.: National Trust for Historic Preservation and Colonial Williamsburg, 1967), pp. 31-36.

NOTES

Columbia University, School of Architecture, New York, New York 10027. Program: M.S. in Historic Preservation for architects and landscape architects, two years, specialized faculty and visiting experts, includes seminars, field trips, and internships. Prerequisite, undergraduate degree in architecture, landscape architecture, art history, or cultural history.

Cornell University, College of Architecture, Sibley Dome, Ithaca, New York 14850. Program: two years or four years, interdisciplinary program, M.A. or Ph.D. in History of Architecture and Urban Development with preservation planning as a minor subject.

Institute of Advanced Architectural Studies, University of York, Kings Manor, York, England. Program: one-year diploma course in conservation studies including conservation of buildings, architectural history, construction, history of landscape design, and townscape and conservation areas.

International Centre for the Study of the Preservation and the Restoration of Cultural Property (Rome Centre), 13 Via di San

Michele, 00153, Rome, Italy. Program: wide range of six-month training courses in the conservation of sites, buildings, and objects of cultural and historical importance. Three regular courses, as well as individualized personally designed programs, are offered to architects, urban planners, archeologists, art historians, engineers, conservators, and scientists from the world over. In the United States, contact United States International Committee, Advisory Council for Historic Preservation, 1522 K Street, Suite 430, Washington, D.C. 20005, for a brochure.

Longwood Program in Ornamental Horticulture, College of Agricultural Sciences, University of Delaware, Newark, Delaware, 19711. Program: two years, M.A. in Ornamental Horticulture, with emphasis on historic gardens.

University of Florida, Department of Architecture, Gainesville, Florida 32601. Program: two years, M.A. in Architecture with specialization in architectural history, including courses in historic preservation, or with specialization in historic preservation. Prerequisite, B.A. in architecture.

University of Georgia, School of Environmental Design, Athens, Georgia 30601. Program: two years, M. Landscape Architecture with concentration in historic preservation. Courses include design, architecture, landscape architecture history, and management.

University of Michigan, Program in American Culture, Ann Arbor, Michigan 48103. Program: M.A. or Ph.D. in American Culture with possible specialization in architectural history or urban studies.

University of Virginia, School of Architecture, Fayerweather Hall, Charlottesville, Virginia 22901. Program: two years, M.A. in architectural history, including courses in historic preservation. Also, B. of Architecture students may major in architectural history.

What Has Been Lost

Briggs, Martin Shaw. *Goths and Vandals: A Study of the Destruction, Neglect, and Preservation of Historic Buildings in England.* 1952. Reprint. New York: Somerset Publishers, 1972. 251 pp., illus.

Great Britain. Royal Commission on the Ancient and Historical Monuments and Construction of England. *Monuments Threatened or Destroyed: A Select List: 1956-1962.* London: Her Majesty's Stationery Office, 1963. 84 pp., photos, maps, plans, glossary, index, paper.

Greiff, Constance M., ed. *Lost America: From the Atlantic to the Mississippi.* Princeton, N.J.: The Pyne Press, 1971. 244 pp., photos, prints, index.

Greiff, Constance M., ed. *Lost America: From the Mississippi to the Pacific.* 1st ed. Princeton, N.J.: The Pyne Press, 1972. 243 pp., photos, index.

Hobhouse, Hermione. *Lost London.* Boston: Houghton Mifflin Co., 1972. 250 pp., photos, prints, drawings, maps, index.

Howells, John M. *Lost Examples of Colonial Architecture: Buildings That Have Disappeared or Been So Altered As to Be Denatured.* New York: Dover Publications, 1963. 248 pp., photos, prints, index, paper.

Saalman, Howard. *Haussman: Paris Transformed.* New York: George Braziller, Inc., 1971. 128 pp., illus., bibliog., paper.

Silver, Nathan. *Lost New York.* New York: Schocken Books, c1967, 1972. 242 pp., photos, prints, drawings, index, paper.

2

Preservation Law

In the last twenty-five years, slowly and steadily there has grown up a frequently bewildering body of law that circumscribes, delineates, and sometimes directs the course that an historic preservation project can take. There is no good answer to the problem of finding a way through this difficult legal maze. If a lawyer who has taken a special interest in some aspects of the field can be found, snare him if possible. If not, search for one who has an honest bent in the direction of and concern for his environment and then learn to ask the right questions.

This chapter gives an overview of the areas into which preservation law has extended and the legal basis for historic preservation at all levels. A number of sources interpret and explain federal preservation legislation; others discuss specific laws and cases.

Federal, state, and local laws and regulations must be reviewed and understood — and used intelligently. Especially since 1966, the federal government has become increasingly concerned with environmental questions and has made protection possible in some cases where federal funding is involved. What is still needed are more directions and guidelines and greater implementation of state and local preservation laws.

There are a number of legal techniques that can be used in local historic preservation projects, ranging from basic zoning and building code requirements to the most recent device, transfer of development rights.

A thorough review of the chapter and consultation with a sympathetic lawyer might help you determine what laws and ordinances are needed in your state and community in order to heighten the chance for more effective control in the future.

Preservation Law: An Overview

American Law Institute. *A Model Land Development Code.* Nos. 1–. Philadelphia, Pa.: The Institute, 1968-. ◆ Tentative Draft No. 1, 1968, 271 pp.; Tentative Draft No. 2, 1970, 124 pp.; Tentative Draft No. 3, 1971, 123 pp.; Tentative Draft No. 4, 1972, 55 pp.; Tentative Draft No. 5, 1973, 57 pp.

Berlin, Roisman & Kessler. *Law and Taxation: A Guide for Conservation and Other Nonprofit Organizations.* Washington, D.C.: The

Conservation Foundation, 1970. 47 pp., paper.

Betebrenner, Lyle. "Esthetics." In *City Planning and Zoning in American Legal Periodicals* (Eugene, Ore.: Council of Planning Librarians, Exchange Bibliography no. 28, 1965), pp. 47-50.

Biddle, James. "Federal Legislation and Historic Preservation," *Museum News,* 46:8 (April 1968), pp. 22-24.

Brecher, Joseph J., and Manuel E. Nestle. *Environmental Law Handbook.* Berkeley,

Calif.: California Continuing Education of the Bar, 1970. 343 pp., illus., forms, bibliog. ♦ Contains "The National Environmental Policy Act," pp. 309-311.

Cambridgeshire and Isle of Ely, England. County Planning Department. *A Guide to Historic Buildings Law.* 2nd ed. rev. Cambridge, Eng.: Cambridgeshire and Isle of Ely County Council, 1970. 54 pp. ♦ Includes planning acts and associated legislation, ancient monuments acts and those associated with repair grants, housing acts, National Trust acts, other legislation, and an explanation of the Historic Buildings Bureau.

Civic Trust. *The Civic Amenities Act, 1967.* London: The Trust, 1967. 8 pp., paper. ♦ Provides for preservation of areas and buildings, planting more trees, disposal of junk cars and other bulky rubbish, and imposes new duties on local authorities and new responsibilities on individuals.

"Congressional Struggles with Coastal-Zone and Land-Use Policy," *C F Letter,* August 1972, entire issue. 12 pp.

Dale, Anthony. "Listing and Preserving Historic Buildings: Part I: The European Picture," *Architectural Review,* 138 (August 1965), pp. 97-104.

Dale, Anthony. "Listing and Preserving Historic Buildings: Part II: U.S.A., Canada, South Africa, Australia and New Zealand," *Architectural Review,* 149 (October 1966), pp. 277-279.

Delafons, John. *Land-Use Controls in the United States.* 2nd ed. Cambridge, Mass.: M.I.T. Press, 1969. 203 pp.

Dosselman, Fred; David Callie; and John Banta. *The Taking Issue: An Analysis of the Constitutional Limits of Land Use Control.* Washington, D.C.: U. S. Government Printing Office, 1973. 329 pp., paper. ♦ Published for the Council on Environmental Quality and includes particular court cases on the history of land use control and the right of the government to take over property and inflict property restrictions on owners.

Duke University. School of Law. "Historic Preservation," *Law and Contemporary Problems,* 36:3 (Summer 1971), special issue. 135 pp., bibliog., paper. ♦ See also companion volume by the National Trust for Historic Preservation, *Legal Techniques in Historic Preservation.*

Garvey, Robert R., and Terry B. Morton. *The United States Government in Historic Preservation* 1968. Reprint. Washington, D.C.: National Trust for Historic Preservation, 1973. 37 pp., photos. ♦ A brief section noting major developments in the federal government's role in historic preservation since 1968 has been added in the reprint.

Gray, Oscar S. *Cases and Materials on Environmental Law.* Washington, D.C.: Bureau of National Affairs, 1970. 1252 pp. ♦ Designed as a legal source book with a section covering historic preservation law. Cases include Vieux Carré property decisions. The volume is updated by supplemental pocket parts.

Great Britain. Laws, Statutes, etc. *Civic Amenities Act of 1967, Chapter 69.* London: Her Majesty's Stationery Office, 1967. 24 pp.

Green Springs Association. *Comments and Information on Environmental Impact of Proposed Reception and Diagnostic Center in Green Springs.* Green Springs, Va.: The Association, 1971. unpaged, photos, maps, bibliog. ♦ Statements by experts on the environmental impact on the historic community, and mentions alternate sites and considerations. Compiled for inclusion in Law Enforcement Impact Report. See also: U.S. Department of Justice, *Green Springs Environmental Impact Statement.*

Menges, Gary L. "Environmental Aesthetics." In *Historic Preservation: A Bibliography* (Monticello, Ill.: Council of Planning Librarians, Exchange Bibliography no. 79, 1969), 54-57.

Menges, Gary L. "Legal Aspects." In *Historic Preservation: A Bibliography* (Monticello, Ill.: Council of Planning Librarians, Exchange Bibliography no. 79, 1969), pp. 45-51. ♦ Includes architectural controls and aesthetics, historic preservation law in the U.S., historic preservation law in Great Britain, environmental aesthetics.

Miner, Ralph W., Jr. "Tools for Program Implementation: Public Options." In *Conservation of Historic and Cultural Resources* (Chicago: American Society of Planning Officials, 1969), pp. 23-32. ♦ Includes zoning, historic districts, scenic easements, urban renewal, federal assistance, tax incentives, public acquisition.

Montague, Robert L., III. "Planning for Preservation in Virginia." Reprinted from *Virginia Law Review,* 51:6 (1965), pp. 1214-1227.

Morrison, Jacob H. *Historic Preservation Law.* 2nd ed. Washington, D.C.: National Trust for Historic Preservation, 1965. 198 pp., photos, prints, bibliog., table of cases. ◆ Legal references for individuals, organizations, and public officials concerned with maintaining landmarks; also contains a compilation of municipal and state statutes, ordinances, court decisions, and enactments. The hardcover edition is out of print; a reprinted paperback edition will be available in 1974 from the National Trust for Historic Preservation.

Morrison, Jacob H. *Supplement to Historic Preservation Law.* New Orleans, La.: Author, 1972. 98 pp., paper. ◆ Updates the second edition, covering the progress of preservation law, preservation at the federal, state and local levels, historic district acts, special legislative acts concerning eminent domain and tax abatement, and decisions of the courts.

Morrison, Jacob H. "Variations on an Old Theme," *Historic Preservation,* 14:2 (1962), pp. 74-77. ◆ Preservation legal battles, primarily the Vieux Carré.

Mortensen, Dorothy. "Dateline: Washington," *History News,* 21:12 (December 1966-). ◆ Monthly column, begun by Ronald F. Lee, relating to federal legislation and preservation programs.

National Trust for Historic Preservation. *The Law in Preservation Issues.* Abstracts of five-minute reports, Third Annual Breakfast Meeting for Architects, Lawyers, Planners, etc., Charleston, S.C., November 7, 1970. Washington, D.C.: The Trust, n.d. 9 pp., photos, drawings, paper.

National Trust for Historic Preservation. *Legal Techniques in Historic Preservation.* Selected Papers from the Conference on Legal Techniques in Preservation sponsored by the National Trust for Historic Preservation, May 1971. Washington, D.C.: The Trust, 1972. 40 pp., bibliog. footnotes, paper. ◆ See also companion volume by Duke University School of Law, "Historic Preservation," *Law and Contemporary Problems, ...*

"The Preservation Congress," *Historic Preservation,* 18:6 (November-December 1966), pp. 271-274. ◆ See also: Washington, D.C.: National Trust for Historic Preservation, 1966. 5 pp., leaflet.

Singer, David B. *Can We Legislate Beauty?* Riverside, Calif.: J. F. Davidson Associates, 1972. 9 pp., bibliog.

U. S. Advisory Council on Historic Preservation. *Digest of Cases, 1967-1973.* Washington, D. C.: The Council, April 1973. 34 pp., paper. ◆ Summary of the twenty-six cases which have been brought before the Council for full hearing and review under the provisions of Section 106 of the Historic Preservation Act of 1966.

U. S. Advisory Council on Historic Preservation. "Procedures for the Protection of Historic and Cultural Properties," *Federal Register,* 39:18 (Friday, January 25, 1974), Part II.

U.S. Council on Environmental Quality. "Environmental Impact Statements: A New Ingredient in Federal Decisionmaking." In *Environmental Quality: The Second Annual Report of the Council on Environmental Quality* (Washington, D. C.: U.S. Government Printing Office, 1971), pp. 25-27. ◆ See also: Appendix G—"Statements on Proposed Federal Actions Affecting the Environment: Guidelines," pp. 309-326.

U. S. Department of Justice. *Green Springs Environmental Impact Statement.* (Draft). Washington, D.C.: U. S. Government Printing Office, n.d. 90 pp., photos, drawings, diagrams, maps, tables. ◆ See also: "Environmental Impact Statement," three volumes of supporting material on alternatives, results of the proposal and exhibits in support and opposition, prepared for the U.S. Department of Justice, Law Enforcement Assistance Administration by the Environmental Impact Statement Section, National Clearinghouse for Criminal Justice, Planning and Architecture. Volume I also prepared by Impact Report Committee, Department of Welfare and Institutions, Virginia, for the Division of Corrections, Department of Welfare and Institutions, Virginia. Copies on file in the library of the National Trust for Historic Preservation. See also: Green Springs Association, *Comments and Information . . . .*

U. S. National Park Service. *Historic Preservation Handbook: Part II, Section 106, A Guide to the History, Meaning, Procedures and Implications of Section 106 of the Preservation Act of 1966.* Washington, D. C.: National Park Service, National Register of Historic Places, 1971. 29 pp., mimeo. ◆ Draft copy on file in the library of the National Trust for Historic Preservation.

U.S. Office of Archeology and Historic Preservation. *Summary Report of the*

1967-68 Regional Conferences on the New Preservation Under the National Historic Preservation Act of 1966, Public Law 89-665. Washington, D.C.: 1968. 101 pp., illus.

U. S. Public Land Law Review Commission. *One Third of the Nation's Land: A Report to the President and to the Congress.* Washington, D.C.: U.S. Government Printing Office, 1970. 342 pp., illus., maps, bibliog. references.

Utley, Robert M. "Federal Historic Preservation Programs," *History News,* 22:10 (October 1967), pp. 214-216. ◆ Explains four laws passed by the 89th Congress involving federal government in historic preservation.

Wentworth, Mrs. Eric. "An Amendment to the Rescue," *Historic Preservation,* 17:5 (September-October 1965), pp. 176-177. ◆ Kennedy-Tower amendment to the Federal Housing Act of 1965 allowing federal funds to be used for moving, new foundation and new site preparation for historic buildings in urban renewal developments. Also cites the case of the Plymouth Heritage Trust, Plymouth, Massachusetts.

Wolfe, Albert B. "Conservation of Historical Buildings and Areas—Legal Techniques." Reprinted from the *Proceedings* of the American Bar Association, Section of Real Property, Probate & Trust Law, August 1963. 11 pp. ◆ Contents include preservation in general and early projects of the Society for the Preservation of New England Antiquities; constitutionality based on police power; inventories and surveys used; preservation legislation; districts and boundaries. Available from the National Trust for Historic Preservation. See also: *Planning 1964* (Chicago: American Society of Planning Officials, 1964), pp. 208-214.

Wrenn, Tony P. *Preservation Legislation.* Washington, D.C.: National Trust for Historic Preservation, n.d. 8 pp., leaflet.

NOTES

The American Law Institute, 4025 Chestnut Street, Philadelphia, Pennsylvania 19104. The American Law Institute is a private organization devoted to reforming the law, and is playing a central role in the quiet revolution to reshape archaic land-use laws in the U.S. In 1963, ALI began work on a Model Land Development Code. The project will not be completed until 1974, but the ALI has made each tentative part of the Code public upon its drafting. The Council on Environmental Quality re-lied on the tentative Code in drafting 1971 amendments to the initial national land-use policy legislation. ALI concepts are also used by state legislatures drafting laws to take control of land use out of the hands of local authorities. A major contribution has been to define limits for the state role and develop such concepts as "districts (or areas) of critical state concern," and "development of state or regional benefit."

National Trust for Historic Preservation, Legal Services. The Legal Services of the Department of Field Services outlines current major legal cases involving historic preservation and publishes them in *Preservation News.* The outlines are also maintained in the Trust files.

Preservation Law: Federal

Executive Order 11593. *Protection and Enhancement of the Cultural Environment.* 36 F.R. 8921, May 13, 1971. Washington, D.C.: U.S. Government Printing Office, 1971. 3 pp. ◆ With reference to the National Environmental Protection Act, the order instructs all federal agencies to provide leadership in historic preservation and to guarantee the preservation of federally owned cultural resources and institute procedures to assure that federal plans and programs contribute to the preservation and enhancement of nonfederally owned sites, structures, and objects of historic, architectural, or archeological significance. Also printed in: *Environmental Quality: The Second Annual Report of the Council on Environmental Quality* (Washington, D.C.: U.S. Government Printing Office, 1971), Appendix H, pp. 327-329.

U.S. Congress. House. Committee on Banking and Currency. *Summary of Housing and Urban Development Act of 1966* (H.R. 15890) *As Ordered Reported on June 28.* Eighty-ninth Congress, second session. Washington, D.C.: U.S. Government Printing Office, 1966. 19 pp.

U.S. Congress. House. Committee on Interior and Insular Affairs. *Establishing a Program for the Preservation of Additional Historic Properties Throughout the Nation; Report to Accompany S. 3035, August 30, 1966.* Eighty-ninth Congress, second session, House. Report no. 1916. Washington, D.C.: U.S. Government Printing Office, 1966. 18 pp.

U. S. Congress. House. Committee on Interior and Insular Affairs. Subcommittee on National Parks and Recreation. *Federal City Bicentennial Development Corporation.* Hearings, Ninety-first Congress, second session, on H. R. 18677 and H.R. 19097. . . September 17 and 18, 1970. Washington, D.C.: U. S. Government Printing Office, 1971. 157 pp.

U.S. Congress. House. Committee on Interior and Insular Affairs. Subcommittee on National Parks and Recreation. *National Historic Preservation Act Amendments.* Hearing, Ninety-first Congress, second session, on H.R. 14896, January 29, 1970. Washington, D.C.: U. S. Government Printing Office, 1970. 85 pp.

U.S. Congress. House. Committee on Interior and Insular Affairs. Subcommittee on National Parks and Recreation. *Pennsylvania Avenue National Historic Site.* Hearings, Eighty-ninth Congress, second session, on H. J. Res. 678 . . . March 21, 1966. Washington, D.C.: U.S. Government Printing Office, 1966. 117 pp.

U. S. Congress. House. Committee on Interior and Insular Affairs. Subcommittee on National Parks and Recreation. *Preservation of Historical and Archeological Data.* Hearings, Ninety-second Congress, second session, on H.R. 735 . . . September 11 and 12, 1972. Washington, D.C.: U.S. Government Printing Office, 1972. 113 pp.

U.S. Congress. House. Committee on Interior and Insular Affairs. Subcommittee on National Parks and Recreation. *Proposed Pennsylvania Avenue Development Corporation.* Hearings. Ninety-second Congress, second session, on H.R. 10751 . . . April 13 and 14, 1972. Washington, D.C.: U. S. Government Printing Office, 1972. 183 pp.

U. S. Congress. Senate. Committee on Banking and Currency. *Housing and Urban Development Act of 1966; Report, to Accompany S. 3711.* Eighty-ninth Congress, second session, Senate. Report no. 1455. Washington, D.C.: U.S. Government Printing Office, 1966. 40 pp. ◆ Title IV: Preservation of Historic Structures.

U. S. Congress. Senate. Committee on Interior and Insular Affairs. *Pennsylvania Avenue Historic Site Commission; Report to Accompany S. J. Res. 116.* Eighty-ninth Congress, second session, Senate. Report no. 1205. Washington, D.C.: U. S. Government Printing Office, 1966. 20 pp.

U. S. Congress. Senate. Committee on Interior and Insular Affairs. *Preservation of Historic Properties; Report to Accompany S. 3035, July 7, 1966.* Eighty-ninth Congress, second session, Senate. Report no. 1363. Washington, D.C.: U.S. Government Printing Office, 1966. 20 pp.

U.S. Congress. Senate. Committee on Interior and Insular Affairs. *A Program for the Preservation of Additional Historic Properties Throughout the Nation; Report to Accompany H.R. 14896.* Ninety-first Congress, second session, Senate. Report no. 91-781. Washington, D.C.: U. S. Government Printing Office, 1970. 18 pp.

U. S. Congress. Senate. Committee on Interior and Insular Affairs. Subcommittee on Parks and Recreation. *Pennsylvania Avenue Commission.* Hearing, Eighty-ninth Congress, second session, on S. J. Res. 116, joint resolution to provide for the administration and development of Pennsylvania Avenue as a National Historical Site, April 4, 1966. Washington, D.C.: U. S. Government Printing Office, 1966. 62 pp., map.

U. S. Congress. Senate. Committee on Interior and Insular Affairs. Subcommittee on Parks and Recreation. *Pennsylvania Avenue National Historic Site.* Hearing, Ninety-second Congress, second session, on S. 715 . . . S. 4002 . . . (and) H. R. 10751 . . . September 21, 1972. Washington, D.C.: U. S. Government Printing Office, 1972. 245 pp., maps.

U. S. Congress. Senate. Committee on Interior and Insular Affairs. Subcommittee on Parks and Recreation. *Preservation of Historic Properties.* Hearing, Eighty-ninth Congress, second session, on S. 3035 and S. 3098, June 8, 1966. Washington, D.C.: U. S. Government Printing Office, 1966. 35 pp.

U. S. Congress. Senate. Committee on Interior and Insular Affairs. Subcommittee on Parks and Recreation. *Preservation of Historical and Archeological Data and Preservation of Historic Monuments.* Hearings, Ninety-second Congress, first session, on S. 1245 . . . (and) S. 1152 . . . June 10, 1971. Washington, D.C.: U. S. Government Printing Office, 1971. 75 pp., illus.

U. S. Laws, Statutes, etc. *An Act for the Preservation of American Antiquities.* Public Law 59-209, 34 Stat. 225, June 8, 1906. Washington, D.C.: U. S. Government Printing Office, 1906. 1 p. ◆ Basic federal law, providing for the protection of historic or prehistoric remains, or any antiquity on federal lands; establishing criminal sanctions for unauthorized destruction or appropriation of antiquities; and authorizing the scientific investigation of antiquities on federal lands.

U. S. Laws, Statutes, etc. *Act to Amend Surplus Property Act of 1944 to Revise Restriction on Conveyance of Surplus Land for Historic Monument Purposes.* Public Law 87-90, 75 Stat. 211, July 20, 1961. Washington, D.C.: U.S. Government Printing Office, 1961. 1 p.

U. S. Laws, Statutes, etc. *An Act to Amend the Act of October 15, 1966 (80 Stat. 915), as Amended, Establishing a Program for the Preservation of Additional Historic Properties Throughout the Nation, and for Other Purposes.* Public Law 93-54, 87 Stat. 139, July 1, 1973. Washington, D.C.: U. S. Government Printing Office, 1973. 1 p. ◆ Authorizes appropriations through 1976, continues the Advisory Council on Historic Preservation to December 31, 1985, and funds United States participation in the International Centre.

U. S. Laws, Statutes, etc. *An Act to Amend the Act of October 15, 1966 (80 Stat. 915) Establishing a Program for the Preservation of Additional Historic Properties Throughout the Nation and for Other Purposes.* Public Law 91-243, 84 Stat. 204, May 9, 1970. Washington, D.C.: U. S. Government Printing Office, 1970. 2 pp. ◆ Extends historic properties preservation program; increases membership in the Advisory Council on Historic Preservation; authorizes United States membership in the International Centre.

U. S. Laws, Statutes, etc. *An Act to Establish a Program for the Preservation of Additional Historic Properties Throughout the Nation and for Other Purposes.* Public Law 89-665, 80 Stat. 915, October 15, 1966. Washington, D.C.: U.S. Government Printing Office, 1966. 5 pp. ◆ Declares a national policy of historic preservation, including the encouragement of state and private efforts; defines the term historic preservation as the protection, rehabilitation, restoration and reconstruction of districts, sites, buildings, structures, and objects significant in American history, architecture, archeology or culture; directs expansion of the National Register of Historic Places to include cultural resources of state and local as well as national significance; establishes the Advisory Council on Historic Preservation; and provides certain procedures to be followed by federal agencies in the event of a proposal that might affect National Register properties.

U. S. Laws, Statutes, etc. *An Act to Facilitate the Preservation of Historic Monuments, and for Other Purposes.* Public Law 92-362, 84 Stat. 503-504, August 4, 1972. Washington, D.C.: U.S. Government Printing Office, 1972. 1 p. ◆ Amends the Federal Property and Administrative Services Act of 1949 as amended (40 U.S.C. 484) 63 Stat. 385 and 84 Stat. 1084; repeals section 13 (h) of Surplus Property Act of 1944 (50 U.S.C. App. 1622h); enables the General Services Administration to permit states and local bodies to receive title to surplus federal structures of historic and architectural merit.

U. S. Laws, Statutes, etc. *Act to Further Policy Enunciated in the Act of October 26, 1949 (63 Stat. 927) to Facilitate Public Participation in Preservation of Sites, Buildings and Objects of National Significance or Interest by Providing for National Trust for Historic Preservation in the United States.* Public Law 83-160, 67 Stat. 228, July 28, 1953. Washington, D.C.: U. S. Government Printing Office, 1953. 1 p. ◆ Amends the provision for number and terms of office of the general trustees of the National Trust.

U. S. Laws, Statutes, etc. *Act to Provide for Preservation of Historic American Sites, Buildings, Objects and Antiquities of National Significance.* Public Law 74-292, 49 Stat. 666, August 21, 1935. Washington, D.C.: U. S. Government Printing Office, 1935. 3 pp. ◆ Authorizes programs that are known as the Historic American Buildings Survey, the Historic American Engineering Record, and the National Survey of Historic Sites and Buildings; authorizes the preservation of properties of national historical or archeological significance; authorizes the designation of national historic landmarks; authorizes interagency, intergovernmental and interdisciplinary efforts for the preservation of cultural resources.

U. S. Laws, Statutes, etc. *Act to Provide for Preservation of Historical and Archeological Data (Including Relics and Specimens) Which Might Otherwise be Lost as Result of Construction of Dams.* Public Law 86-523, 74 Stat. 220, June 27, 1960. Washington, D.C.: U. S. Government Printing Office, 1960. 2 pp. ◆ Reservoir Salvage Act, providing for the recovery and preservation of historical and archeological data that might be lost or destroyed as a result of the construction of dams, reservoirs and attendant facilities and activities.

U. S. Laws, Statutes, etc. *Demonstration Cities and Metropolitan Development Act of 1966.* Public Law 89-754, 80 Stat. 1255, November 3, 1966. Washington, D.C.: U. S. Government Printing Office, 1966. 42 pp. ♦ To assist comprehensive city demonstration programs for rebuilding slum and blighted areas and for providing the public facilities and services necessary to improve the general welfare of the people who live in those areas; to assist and encourage planned metropolitan development; and for other purposes. Title VI—Preservation of Historic Structures: preservation of historic structures as part of urban renewal projects, local grant-in-aid credit for relocation and restoration of historic structures, grants to the National Trust for Historic Preservation to cover restoration costs, urban planning grants for surveys of historic structures; Title VII—Open Space Land, Urban Beautification, and Historic Preservation (amends Title VII of the Housing Act of 1961): grants for historic preservation.

U. S. Laws, Statutes, etc. *Department of Transportation Act.* Public Law 89-670, 80 Stat. 931, October 15, 1966. Washington, D.C.: U. S. Government Printing Office, 1966. 21 pp. ♦ Section 4(f): provides that the Secretary shall not approve any program or project which requires the use of any land from a historic site of national, state or local significance unless there is no feasible and prudent alternative to the use of such land, and such program includes all possible planning to minimize harm to such historic sites resulting from such use. It applies to all activities, including highways, aviation, urban mass transit, railroads, rivers, harbors, and coastal waterways. National Register properties automatically are entitled to protection; non-Register properties qualify if determined significant by local landmarks commissions.

U. S. Laws, Statutes, etc. *Joint Resolution Authorizing the Secretary of the Interior to Provide for the Commemoration of the One Hundredth Anniversary of the Establishment of Yellowstone National Park, and for Other Purposes.* Public Law 91-332, 84 Stat. 427, July 10, 1970. Washington, D.C.: U. S. Government Printing Office, 1970. 3 pp. ♦ National Parks Centennial Year, 1972, Proclamation: establishes the Commission, functions, personnel, reports to Congress, termination, disposition of books, relics, etc., and appropriation. Provides for the preparation of a suitable plan for commemoration of the 100th anniversary of the beginning of the worldwide national park movement; coordination of activities of agencies and organizations involved in the Centennial; and provision to host services for a world conference on national parks in 1972.

U. S. Laws, Statutes, etc. *Laws Relating to the National Park Service, the National Parks, and Monuments.* Compiled by Hillory A. Tolson, Attorney, Branch of Lands and Uses, National Park Service. Washington, D.C.: U. S. Government Printing Office, 1933. ♦ Also: Supplement I, July 1933-April 1944. Washington, D.C.: U. S. Government Printing Office, 1944, 207 pp.

U. S. Laws, Statutes, etc. *National Environmental Policy Act of 1969.* Public Law 91-190, 83 Stat. 852, January 1, 1970. Washington, D.C.: U. S. Government Printing Office, 1970. 5 pp. ♦ To preserve important historic, cultural and natural aspects of the nation's heritage and to protect the environment by requiring federal agencies to assess the effect that changes they propose could have on the country's resources, with the effect expressed in the preparation of environmental impact statements by the federal agencies.

U. S. Laws, Statutes, etc. *To Further the Policy Enunciated in the Historic Sites Act (49 Stat. 666) and to Facilitate Public Participation in the Preservation of Sites, Buildings and Objects of National Significance or Interest and Providing a National Trust for Historic Preservation.* Public Law 81-408, 63 Stat. 927, October 26, 1949. Washington, D.C.: U. S. Government Printing Office, 1949. 3 pp. ♦ Creates the National Trust as a charitable, educational, and nonprofit corporation to receive donations of sites, buildings and objects; to preserve and administer them for the public benefit; to accept, hold and administer gifts of money, securities or other property for the purpose of carrying out the preservation program.

U. S. President. *Proclamations and Orders Relating to the National Park Service Up to January 1, 1945.* Compiled by Thomas Alan Sullivan, Attorney, Office of the Chief Counsel, National Park Service. Washington, D.C.: U. S. Government Printing Office, 1947. 331 pp., maps. ♦ Issued by the President and the Secretary of the Interior and contains the basic legal authority for operation of the service as of 1945.

Preservation Law: State and Local

Guidelines for State and Local Programs

National Trust for Historic Preservation. *A Guide to State Programs.* 1972 ed. Washington, D.C.: The Trust, 1972. 200 pp., paper. ◆ Information for each state is divided into two sections: preservation framework, giving the basis for the state program, the state's laws relating to preservation, and various state preservation programs and relationships with other state offices; and preservation programs, outlining the programs undertaken by the state in response to preservation legislation. Rev. ed. in preparation.

U. S. Advisory Council on Historic Preservation. *Guidelines for State Historic Preservation Legislation.* Historic Preservation Workshop, National Symposium on State Environmental Legislation, March 15-18, 1972. Washington, D.C.: The Council, 1972. 61 pp., bibliog. footnotes, paper. ◆ Guidelines to promote a higher and more uniform standard of performance within the nationwide historic preservation movement. Includes outlines for a state historic preservation agency, conservation of archeological resources, protection of underwater historic properties, state advisory council, state historical trust, enabling legislation for local preservation activities, procedures to guide state agencies, and an appendix on tax incentives.

Citizen Participation

Adler, Leopold, II. "Economic Incentives," *Historic Preservation,* 23:2 (April-June 1971), pp. 25-28. ◆ An example of citizen action in Savannah, Georgia.

American Association of University Women. *Tool Catalog: Techniques and Strategies for Successful Action Programs.* Washington, D.C.: The Association, 1972. 248 pp., illus., index.

American Society of Planning Officials. *Public Hearings, Controversy, and the Written Response.* Planning Advisory Service Information Report no. 240. Chicago: The Society, 1968. 11 pp., paper. ◆ Emphasis on the theory

of the public hearing and useful guide for practice.

Citizens Advisory Committee on Environmental Quality. *Citizens Make the Difference: Case Studies of Environmental Action.* Washington, D.C.: for sale by Superintendent of Documents, U. S. Government Printing Office, 1973. 71 pp., photos, maps.

Clary, David A. "Preserving the Environment: Participating in the Review Process," *History News,* 28:2 (February 1973), Technical Leaflet no. 8 (new series).

Guitar, Mary Anne. *Property Power: How to Keep the Bulldozer, the Power Lines and the Highwaymen Away from Your Door.* Garden City, N.Y.: Doubleday & Co., Inc. 1972. 322 pp., bibliog., appendices, index. ◆ How to protect property from encroachment. Appendices include a typical land trust certificate, useful local ordinances, sample easement.

Hillman, Ernest, Jr. "Marshaling Public Opinion and Public Support," *Historic Preservation,* 15:1 (1963), pp. 22-25.

Huenefeld, John. *The Community Activist's Handbook: A Guide to Organizing, Financing, and Publicizing Community Campaigns.* Boston: Beacon Press, 1970. 160 pp.

Ikard, Frank N. "How to Approach Your Congressman." Reprinted from *Congressional Action,* February 22, 1963. 2 pp.

MacBeth, Angus, and Peter W. Sly. "Federal-Aid Highways: Public Participation in the Administration Stages, or, How to Hold Up the Highwaymen." Reprinted from *The Concrete Opposition,* March 1972. 6 pp. ◆ Describes federal laws and regulations that apply to any highway project built with federal funds; notes of recent federal court decisions; source of background materials for citizen groups wanting to participate in public hearings or contested highway proposals.

New York (State). *State of New York Local Planning and Zoning, 1969: A Manual of Powers and Procedures for Citizens and Governmental Officials.* Albany, N.Y.: Office of Planning Coordination, 1969. 132 pp., paper. ◆ Includes provision for historic and aesthetic area protection, and an appendix on "Historic Preservation and Capital Program: General Municipal Law."

Stipe, Robert E. "Civic Action and Historic Zoning." Reprinted from *Popular Government,* June-July 1963, 20-24. ◆ Surveying and delineating historic areas in city plans, their contribution to urban economic, social and cultural well-being.

Udall, Morris K. "The Right to Write: Some Suggestions on Writing Your Congressman." Reprinted from *Congressman's Report,* January 20, 1967. 4 pp.

U. S. Environmental Protection Agency, Office of Public Affairs. *Don't Leave It All to the Experts: The Citizen's Role in Environmental Decision Making.* Washington, D.C.: U. S. Government Printing Office, 1972. 20 pp., drawings, bibliog. ♦ How to present organization's point of view to the public, committees, courts or the press, and how to organize and focus one's standpoint and back it up through lobbying, funding, the press, broadcasting, public hearing, and court.

U. S. Environmental Protection Agency, Office of Public Affairs. *Groups That Can Help: A Directory of Organizations.* Washington, D.C.: U. S. Government Printing Office, 1972. 12 pp.

Ziegler, Arthur P., Jr. "Revolving Funds," *Historic Preservation,* 23:2 (April-June 1971), pp. 29-33. ♦ An example of citizen participation in funding in Savannah, Georgia, and Pittsburgh, Pennsylvania.

Preservation Commissions

Boston Redevelopment Authority. *Back Bay Residential District: Guidelines for Exterior Rehabilitation and Restoration.* Sponsored by the Boston Redevelopment Authority, Back Bay Federation for Community Development, and Neighborhood Association of the Back Bay. Boston: The Authority, n.d. 36 pp., photos, maps, bibliog., paper. ♦ Includes a description of the district and the commission.

Flint, Peggy. *The New Haven Preservation Trust: A Ten Years' War, 1962-1972.* New Haven, Conn.: New Haven Preservation Trust, 1972. 32 pp., photos, drawings, paper.

Hale, Richard W., Jr. "Cooperation in Preservation in Massachusetts," *Historic Preservation,* 17:4 (July-August 1965), pp. 152-155. ♦ Description of the work of the Massachusetts Historical Commission.

Holmes, Mrs. Nicholas H., Jr. "The Mobile Historic Preservation Commission: Preservation, Progress, and Urban Renewal," *History News,* 23:4 (April 1968), pp. 71-73.

Maryland Historical Trust. *Purposes, Accomplishments and Plans of the Maryland Historical Trust.* Annapolis, Md.: The Trust, n.d. 8 pp., illus., paper.

Massachusetts Historical Commission. *Local Historical Commissions: Procedures and Duties.* Rev. ed. Boston: The Commission, 1972. 7 pp., mimeo.

Nantucket Historic Districts Commission. *Guidebook for the Old and Historic Districts of Nantucket and Siasconset.* Nantucket, Mass.: Poets Corner Press, 1967. 49 pp., photos, drawings, maps, appendices. ♦ Appendices include drawings of architectural details; types of work in the district for which no application for approval is required; the act establishing the commission.

New York (City). Landmarks Preservation Commission. *Greenwich Village Historic District Designation Report.* New York: 1969. 2 vols., maps. ♦ Includes policies of the Landmarks Preservation Commission.

New York (City). Landmarks Preservation Commission. *SoHo-Cast Iron Historic District Designation Report.* New York: The Commission, 1973. 231 pp., map. ♦ Includes policies of the Landmarks Preservation Commission.

Philadelphia. Historical Commission. *The Philadelphia Historical Commission: Organization and Procedures.* Philadelphia, Pa.: The Commission, 1968? 1 vol., illus.

Pyke, John S., Jr. *Landmark Preservation.* 2nd ed. New York: Citizens Union Research Foundation, 1972. 32 pp., photos, drawings, diagrams, appendix, bibliog., paper. ♦ Includes the challenge and economics of preservation, types of preservation programs, the work of the New York City Landmarks Preservation Commission, and elements of an effective program. The appendix lists where to go for assistance.

Scott, Mellier Goodin. *The States and the Arts: The California Arts Commission and the Emerging Federal-State Partnership.* Berkeley, Calif.: Institute of Governmental Studies, University of California, 1971. 129 pp., bibliog., paper.

Weinberg, Robert C. "Preservation, at Long Last," *American Institute of Architects Journal,* 47:5 (Mary 1967), pp. 114-115. ♦ Brief history of the New York Landmarks Preservation Commission, its trials and errors.

Legal Techniques in Local Historic Preservation

Zoning

American Society of Planning Officials. *Certificates of Compliance.* Planning Advisory Service Information Report no. 220. Prepared by Richard F. Counts, Jr. Chicago: The Society, 1967. 16 pp., paper.

American Society of Planning Officials. *A Glossary of Zoning Definitions.* Planning Advisory Service Information Report no. 233. Prepared by Frederick H. Bair, Jr. Chicago: The Society, 1968. 27 pp.

Anderson, Robert M. *American Law of Zoning: Zoning, Planning, Subdivision Control.* Rochester, N.Y.: Lawyers Co-operative Pub. Co., 1968. 4 vols., 879 pp., Supplement 1971.

Babcock, Richard F. *The Zoning Game: Municipal Practices and Policies.* Madison, Wis.: University of Wisconsin Press, c1966, 1969. 202 pp., bibliog. notes, index, paper.

Dukeminier, J. J., Jr. "Zoning for Aesthetic Objectives: A Reappraisal," *Law and Contemporary Problems,* 20 (April 1955), pp. 218-237.

Haar, Charles M. *Land-Use Planning: A Casebook on the Use, Misuse, and Re-Use of Urban Land.* 2nd ed. Boston: Little, Brown & Co., 1971. 788 pp., illus. ◆ Includes zoning law.

Mandelker, Daniel R. *The Zoning Dilemma: A Legal Strategy for Urban Change.* Indianapolis, Ind.: Bobbs-Merrill Co., 1971. 196 pp., maps, tables, bibliog., index.

New York (City). City Planning Commission. *Special Permit, Pursuant to Section 74-71 of the Zoning Resolution Involving Modification of Use Regulations Applicable to a Designated Landmark (8 Cadman Plaza West).* CP-22348, June 27, 1973, Calendar no. 14. New York: The Commission, 1973. 2 pp.

Stipe, Robert E. "Easement vs. Zoning: Preservation Tools," *Historic Preservation,* 20:2 (April-June 1968), pp. 78-86.

Turnbull, H. Rutherford. "Aesthetic Zoning and Property Values." Reprinted from *Wake Forest Law Review,* 7:2 (March 1971), pp. 230-253. 23 pp., bibliog. footnotes, paper.

Historic Districts and Areas

"Area Preservation and the Beacon Hill Bill," *Old-Time New England,* 46:4 (April-June 1956), pp. 106-110.

Boston Redevelopment Authority. *Back Bay Residential District: Guidelines for Exterior Rehabilitation and Restoration.* Sponsored by the Boston Redevelopment Authority, Back Bay Federation for Community Development, and Neighborhood Association of the Back Bay. Boston: The Authority, n.d. 36 pp., photos, maps, short bibliog., paper. ◆ Includes topographical history and a description of the district and commission.

Cambridge, Massachusetts. *Historic Districts Study Committee: Final Report.* Cambridge, Mass.: 1962. 92 pp., maps.

Codman, John. *Historic Zoning: How to Secure It for Your Community.* Prepared for Beacon Hill Civic Association. Boston: Beacon Hill Civic Association, 1956. 31 pp., appendix, paper.

Codman, John. "A Law for the Preservation of a Historic District," *Historic Preservation,* 14:2 (1962), p. 78. ◆ Suggestions on writing and securing legislation and a listing of what historic legislation will do for a community. Also in *Planning 1964* (Chicago: American Society of Planning Officials, 1964), pp. 207-208.

Delaney, Barbara S.; Robert L. Raley; and Molly A. Ten Broeck. "Preservation 1968," *Antiques,* 93:4 (April 1968), pp. 511-517. ◆ Focus on three preservation districts: Benefit Square, Providence; Old Brandywine Village, Inc., and Tredyffrin Township, Pennsylvania.

Feiss, Carl. "Criteria for Historic District Selection," *Historic Preservation,* 14:2 (1962), pp. 67-73.

Gilbert, Frank B. "Try Historic Districts . . . in Order to Save Significant Portions of Your City from the Bulldozer," *American City,* 83:8 (August 1968), pp. 81-82. ◆ Gives as an example the Brooklyn Heights District, New York City.

Griffin, Frances. *Old Salem: An Adventure in Historic Preservation.* Winston-Salem, N.C.: Old Salem, Inc., 1970. 74 pp., photos, maps, appendix, paper. ◆ Covers the experiences with historic zoning and gives the texts of the historic zoning ordinances.

Jacobs, Stephen W. "A Current View of Area Preservation." Reprinted from American Institute of Architects *Journal,* December 1964. 6 pp., drawing.

Massachusetts. Legislative Research Bureau. *Report Submitted by the Legislative Research Council Relative to the Establishment of Historic Districts Within the Commonwealth, January 25, 1957.* Boston: Wright & Potter Printing Co., legislative printers, 1957. 44 pp., bibliog.

Massachusetts Historical Commission. *Guidelines for the Establishment of Historic Districts.* Rev. ed. Boston: The Commission, 1972. 28 pp., appendices, paper. ◆ Appendices include suggested guidelines for a preliminary report, consideration for a draft ordinance or bylaw, historic districts in Massachusetts, bibliography, Historic Districts Act of 1960.

Montague, Robert L., III, and Tony P. Wrenn. "Santa Fe Victorious—Validates Constitutionality of Its Historic Zoning Ordinance Under Attack for Two Years." Commentary from *Planning for Preservation: Legislative and Economic Trends in Historic Preservation* (Chicago: American Society of Planning Officials, 1964). Reprinted in *Historic Preservation,* 16:5 (September-October 1964), pp. 174-177.

Montgomery County, Pennsylvania. Planning Commission. *Model Ordinance for Historic District Zoning.* Prepared by Frederic T. Dannerth and Howard J. Grossman. Norristown, Pa.: The Commission, 1964. 15 pp.

Nantucket Historic Districts Commission. *Guidebook for the Old and Historic Districts of Nantucket and Siasconset.* Nantucket, Mass.: Poets Corner Press, 1967. 49 pp., photos, drawings, maps, appendices.

New York (City). Landmarks Preservation Commission. *Greenwich Village Historic District Designation Report.* New York: The Commission, 1969. 2 vols., maps.

New York (City). Landmarks Preservation Commission. *SoHo-Cast Iron Historic District Designation Report.* New York: The Commission, 1973. 231 pp., map.

Norfolk, Virginia, Department of City Planning. *Preserving Norfolk's Heritage: Proposed Zoning for Historic and Cultural Conservation.* Norfolk, Va.: The Department, 1965. 40 pp., illus., bibliog.

Pennsylvania. Historical and Museum Commission. *Manual: Establishment of Historic Districts in Pennsylvania.* Harrisburg: The

Commission, 1967. 27 pp. ◆ Includes state law and a model ordinance.

Providence. Development Council, Planning Division. *Historic District Zoning.* Local Planning Bulletin no. 11. Providence, R.I.: 1959. 19 pp. ◆ Three sections include historic district zoning ordinance, model historic district ordinance, and act passed by the state legislature.

Providence. Ordinances, etc. *An Ordinance Amending Chapter 544 of the Ordinances of the City of Providence, Entitled "An Ordinance Zoning the City of Providence and Establishing Use, Height and Area Regulations" as Approved September 21, 1951, as Amended by Adding Article VI-A, Entitled "Historic District Zoning."* Approved August 5, 1960. Providence, R. I.: 1960. 8 pp., map. ◆ Includes Historic Area Zoning Map of Historic College Hill District.

Reed, Thomas J. "Land Use Controls in Historic Areas." Reprinted from *Notre Dame Lawyer,* 44:3 (February 1969). 51 pp., paper.

San Antonio. Community Renewal Program. *San Antonio Historic Survey 1972: Appendix.* Prepared by O'Neill, Perez, Lance, Larcade, architects. San Antonio, Tex.: City Planning Department, 1972. 60 pp., charts, bibliog. ◆ Includes map and resource index, and text of laws.

Schenectady County Historical Society, Schenectady, New York. "Schenectady's Historic District," Schenectady County Historical Society *Bulletin,* 7:1 (September 1963), entire issue. 23 pp., photos, map.

Stipe, Robert E. "Civic Action and Historic Zoning." Reprinted from *Popular Government,* June-July 1963, pp. 20-24. 5 pp., photos. ◆ Surveying and delineating historic areas in city plans.

Tennessee. State Planning Commission. *Historic Zoning: A New Tool for Tennessee Communities.* Publications no. 334. Nashville, Tenn.: The Commission, 1965. 1 vol., unpaged.

Weisman, Leslie. *Flight from Suburbia: West Canfield Historic District.* Detroit: University of Detroit Press, 1973. unpaged, illus., bibliog., paper.

White, Harry E., Jr. "A Discussion of Historic Districts Legislation: The Police Power, Eminent Domain, and the Preservation of Historic Property." Reprinted from *Columbia Law Review,* 63 (April 1963), pp. 708-732. 24 pp., bibliog. footnotes, leaflet.

Architectural Controls

American Society of Planning Officials. *Architectural Control.* Planning Advisory Service Information Report no. 6. Chicago: The Society, 1949. ◆ Survey of architectural controls in 40 municipalities at that time, descriptions of controls, excerpts from ordinances.

American Society of Planning Officials. *Height Regulation in Residential Districts.* Planning Advisory Service Information Report no. 237. Prepared by Frederick H. Bair, Jr. Chicago: The Society, 1968. 12 pp., illus., paper.

American Society of Planning Officials. *New Developments in Architectural Control.* Planning Advisory Service Information Report no. 96. Chicago: The Society, 1957. 25 pp., paper.

Anderson, Robert M. "Architectural Controls." Reprinted from *The Syracuse Law Review,* Fall 1960, pp. 26-49. 23 pp., bibliog. footnotes, paper.

Chicago. Department of Urban Renewal. *Preserving the Architectural Character of a Neighborhood: A Preliminary Study.* Chicago: The Department, 1964. 67 pp., illus., bibliogs. ◆ Contents include design opportunities; legal techniques; architectural techniques; detailed aspects of legal approach, e.g., regulatory measures, convenants, taxation.

Codman, John. *Preservation of Historic Districts by Architectural Control.* Chicago: American Society of Planning Officials, 1956. 35 pp., paper.

Cohn, Sidney. *Architectural Control in Northern Europe: A Comparative Analysis.* Chapel Hill, N.C.: University of North Carolina, 1968. 235 pp., bibliog.

Cohn, Sidney. *Architectural Control in Northern Europe.* Exchange Bibliography no. 64. Monticello, Ill.: Council of Planning Librarians, 1969. 9 pp., paper.

Savannah. *Historic Preservation Plan for the Central Area, General Neighborhood Renewal Area.* Savannah, Ga.: Savannah, 1968? 32 pp., illus.

Property Valuation

Chicago. Department of Urban Renewal. *Preserving the Architectural Character of a Neighborhood: A Preliminary Study.* Chicago: The Department, 1964. 67 pp., illus. bibliogs. ◆ Contents include details of legal approach through regulatory measures, covenants, taxation.

Cobble Hill Association, Brooklyn, N.Y. "Plus or Minus in Cobble Hill," *Historic Preservation,* 17:3 (May-June 1965), pp. 116-119.

Crouch, William H. "Pretrial Conference Checklist of Factors Affecting Valuation." Reprinted from *The Appraisal Journal,* October 1964, pp. 523-530. 8 pp., leaflet. ◆ Involves cases of eminent domain.

"Factors Affecting Property Valuation," *Historic Preservation,* 17:3 (May-June 1965), pp. 108-111.

"How to Make Slums," *Economic News,* April-May 1963. Reprinted in *Historic Preservation,* 15:2 (1963), pp. 62-64. ◆ Suggests that one way to prevent slums is to levy taxes on land value only and not on improvements to buildings.

Levey, Irving L. *Condemnation in U.S.A.* New York: Clark Boardman Co., Ltd., 1969. 1100 pp., looseleaf. ◆ Contains procedures, forms, statutes relating to cases of eminent domain.

Nash, William W. *Residential Rehabilitations: Private Profits and Public Purposes.* Series in Housing and Community Development. New York: McGraw-Hill Book Co., 1959. 272 pp., table, maps, bibliog., appendices, index.

National Trust for Historic Preservation. "Dollars and Sense: Preservation Economics." Reprinted from *Historic Preservation,* 23:2 (April-June 1971), pp. 15-33. ◆ Articles cover economic determinants, real estate values, economic incentives, revolving funds.

Turnbull, H. Rutherford. "Aesthetic Zoning and Property Values." Reprinted from *Wake Forest Law Review,* 7:2 (March 1971), pp. 230-253. 23 pp., bibliog. footnotes, paper.

Wall, Louis S. *The Feasibility of Tax Credits as Incentives for Historic Preservation.* Report of a study done through a grant from the National Endowment for the Humanities. Washington, D.C.: National Trust for Historic Preservation, 1972. 111 pp. ◆ Unpublished; available at National Trust for Historic Preservation library.

Wrenn, Tony P. "Real Estate Realities," *Historic Preservation,* 15:2 (1963), pp. 53-59. ◆ Effect of historic districting ordinances and architectural controls on real estate values.

Transfer of Development Rights

Costonis, John J. "The Chicago Plan: Incentive Zoning and the Preservation of Urban Landmarks." Reprinted from *Harvard Law Review,* 85:3 (January 1972), pp. 574-634. 60 pp., bibliog. footnotes, paper.

Costonis, John J. "Preservation of Urban Landmarks: The Chicago Plan: A Proposal for Safeguarding the Architectural Heritage of American Cities." Reprinted from *The Architectural Forum,* March 1972. 3 pp., paper. ◆ Discusses the transfer of development rights.

Costonis, John J. *Space Adrift: Landmark Preservation and the Marketplace.* Urbana, Ill.: University of Illinois Press, 1974. 224 pp., illus., tables, drawings.

Costonis, John J. *Space Adrift: Saving Urban Landmarks Through the Chicago Plan.* Urbana, Ill.: Published for the National Trust for Historic Preservation by University of Illinois Press, 1974. 207 pp., photos, graphs, charts, tables, bibliog., index, paper. ◆ A study supported by a HUD demonstration grant to the National Trust for Historic Preservation, published as the paperback edition of the University of Illinois Press volume cited above.

Gilbert, Frank B. "Saving Landmarks: The Transfer of Development Rights," *Historic Preservation,* 22:3 (July-September 1970), pp. 13-17. ◆ Discusses the transfer of air development rights in New York City law.

Miller, Hugh C. *The Chicago School of Architecture: A Plan for Preserving a Significant Remnant of America's Architectural Heritage.* Washington, D.C.: National Park Service, 1973. 38 pp., illus., bibliog., paper. ◆ Discusses the Chicago Plan of development rights transfer.

New York (City). City Planning Commission. *Special Permit, Pursuant to Section 74-79 of the Zoning Resolution Involving the Transfer of Development Rights from a Landmark Site (311 East 58th Street).* CP-22151, November 29, 1972, Calendar no. 58. New York: The Commission, 1972. 3 pp.

Okamoto, Rai Y. *Urban Design Effects of Landmark Preservation Through Development Rights Transfers.* Washington, D.C.: National Trust for Historic Preservation, 1972. 28 pp., drawings, paper. ◆ Special report on file in the National Trust for Historic Preservation library prepared as support material for Costonis volume, *Space Adrift . . . .*

Real Estate Research Corporation. *Economic Analysis of the Transfer of Development Rights in Historic Preservation.* Washington, D.C.: National Trust for Historic Preservation, 1972. 69 pp., drawings, charts, paper. ◆ Special report on file in the National Trust for Historic Preservation library prepared as support material for Costonis volume, *Space Adrift . . . .*

Wright, Robert R. *The Law of Airspace.* Indianapolis, Ind.: Bobbs-Merrill Co., 1968. 575 pp., table of cases, bibliog., index. ◆ History, law, policies, and problems of using airspace.

NOTES

The Chicago Plan. The plan provides for the sale of the unused development potential of landmark buildings for use on nonlandmark sites, transferring the cost of preservation from the owner or the city to the development process itself (transfer of development rights).

Easements and Open Space

Biddle, James. "Easements and the Trust," *Preservation News,* 13:1 (January 1973), p. 5.

Brenneman, Russell L. *Private Approaches to the Preservation of Open Land.* New London, Conn.: Conservation and Research Foundation, Inc., c1967, 1969. 133 pp., bibliog. footnotes, appendices.

Cole, John N. " 'From the People Up'," *Yankee,* 38:1 (January 1974), pp. 86-93. ◆ Development and use of conservation easements and the work of the Maine Coast Heritage Trust; also notes on how the Connecticut River Watershed Council uses the conservation easement.

Connecticut. Department of Environmental Protection. *Land: The Most Enduring Gift.* Hartford, Conn.: The Department, 1972? 24 pp., drawings, appendices, paper. ◆ Discusses Connecticut's conservation and preservation easements, scenic transfers in trust, outright conveyances, reservations of life estates, 'reverter' clauses, testamentory gifts, endowments, monetary gifts, tax allowances, restrictions, and other forms of state open-land control.

Gilchrist, Martin C. "Strategies for Preserving Scenic Rivers: The Maryland Experience," *Landscape Architecture,* 62:1 (October 1971), pp. 35-42. ◆ From the report, *Scenic Rivers in Maryland,* prepared by the Maryland Department of State Planning in cooperation with the Scenic Rivers Review Board.

Guitar, Mary Anne. *Property Power: How to Keep the Bulldozer, the Power Lines and the Highwaymen Away from Your Door.* Garden City, N.Y.: Doubleday & Co., 1972. 322 pp., bibliog., index, appendices. ◆ Appendices include a typical land trust certificate, useful local ordinances, sample easement.

Nelson, Gaylord. "Scenic Easements and Preservation," *Historic Preservation,* 17:4 (July-August 1965), pp. 132-135.

Schmertz, Mildred F., ed. *Acquisition, Creation and Design of Open Space for People.* An Illustrated Anthology of Papers Presented at the 1970 International Conference of the Commission on Town Planning of the Union Internationale des Architects. Washington, D.C.: American Institute of Architects, 1970. 111 pp., photos, plans, maps, bibliog., index.

Stipe, Robert E. "Easement vs. Zoning: Preservation Tools," *Historic Preservation,* 20:2 (April-June 1968), pp. 78-86.

Vermont. Division of Historic Sites. *Historic Preservation Through Land Use Legislation.* Montpelier, Vt.: The Division, 1973. 24 pp., prints, suppl. state statutes and four maps, bibliog., paper. ◆ Ties historic preservation with the environmental movement, as being part of the broader picture.

Virginia. Laws, Statutes, etc. *Park and Open Space Laws Applying to the Cities, Towns and Counties of Virginia; A Compendium of Enabling Provisions Extracted from the Code of Virginia for the Convenience of Local Government Officials in Determining Their Authority under Virginia General Law.* Richmond, Va.: Commission of Outdoor Recreation, 1968. 24 pp.

Virginia Historic Landmarks Commission. *Open-Space Easements.* Richmond, Va.: The Commission, (ca. 1970). 4 pp., photos, sample deed of easement, paper.

Whyte, William H., Jr. *Securing Open Space for Urban America: Conservation Easements.* Technical Bulletin 36. Washington, D.C.: Urban Land Institute, 1959. 67 pp., illus.

View Protection

American Society of Planning Officials. *The Disposal of Junked Cars.* Planning Advisory Service Information Report no. 201. Chicago: The Society, 1965. 24 pp., photos, bibliog., paper. ◆ Background of auto disposal and review of public regulations.

Appleyard, Donald; Kevin Lynch; and John R. Myer. *The View from the Road.* Joint Center for Urban Studies Publication. Cambridge, Mass.: M.I.T. Press, 1964. 64 pp., illus., bibliog.

Beal, Frank. *Elimination of Nonconforming Signs.* Planning Advisory Service Information Report no. 209. Chicago: American Society of Planning Officials, 1966. 19 pp., paper.

California. Interdepartmental Committee on Scenic Highways. *The Scenic Route: A Guide for the Designation of an Official Scenic Highway.* Sacramento, Calif.: Transportation Agency, Superintendent of Public Works, 1965? 54 pp., photos, drawings, map, appendix of laws, paper. ◆ Deals with such considerations as initial legislation, procedures, criteria for corridor delineation, standards for corridor protection, and effectuation, controls and fiscal policy

California Roadside Council. *Signs in California.* San Francisco, Calif.: The Council, 1972. 32 pp., photos, paper. ◆ Handbook on ways to rid communities of one form of visual pollution.

Fonoroff, Alan. *The Preservation of Roadside Scenery Through the Police Power.* Montpelier, Vt.: Vermont Central Planning Office, 1966. 33 pp., illus.

Howlett, Bruce, and Frederick J. Elmiger. *Power Lines and Scenic Values in the Hudson River Valley.* 3rd printing, rev. Tarrytown, N.Y.: Hudson River Valley Commission of New York, 1969. 23 pp., drawings, diagrams, paper.

National Industrial Pollution Control Council. *Junk Car Disposal: Sub-Council Report, October, 1970.* Prepared for the Secretary of Commerce. Washington, D.C.: U. S. Government Printing Office, 1970. 54 pp., photos, charts, maps, appendices, paper.

Parke, Margot. *View Protection Regulations.* Planning Advisory Service Information Report no. 213. Chicago: American Society of Planning Officials, 1966. 20 pp., illus., plans.

3

Urban Development and Redevelopment

"A city is not civilized without its past." Again, this is the voice of Ada Louise Huxtable, serving as the national conscience. Trouble is, of course, that most cities have never learned the lesson or—and this is frequently even more shattering—they have learned it the hard way, after the event, as it were.

In spite of the federal legislation designed to protect the nation's heritage from adverse use of federal funds, too frequently there is only lip service offered, and sometimes downright hostility, at the local level. What it comes down to sometimes is that local preservation interests must make themselves experts on their rights and powers. More and more help is being offered by state and even national agencies, but it is on the local group that the principal burden falls. Sometimes and in some states they can get aid from municipal and county planning departments. This is especially true when those departments are preparing studies of environmental and scenic resources or historic inventories with state assistance.

In *Preserving Historic America* it is pointed out: "Urban renewal is a local program, locally conceived, planned and carried out. It is a concerted effort by the city, using its public and private resources to remedy and prevent urban blight and decay and to carry out a continuing program of planned conservation, rehabilitation and redevelopment of both residential and nonresidential areas." True enough, but one is reminded of the reaction of the old mayor of a Vermont city, who when a woman appeared in shorts on his Main Street for the first time, simply said, "We have went too fur!"

It would seem that only a concerned citizenry can prevent a city from going too far. In this (and indeed in the chapters that follow) there is a solid and growing body of books and articles designed to help those who are seeking to help themselves in their own communities.

Included are sources on the growth and development of American communities, how urban planning and design works, and the relationship between urban renewal and historic preservation. Federal programs designed to assist our cities and towns have included effective tools for historic preservation, but it is up to the public to acquaint themselves with the operation and educate their local officials.

Urban Studies

Abrams, Charles, and Robert Kolodny. *The Language of Cities: A Glossary of Terms.* New York: Viking Press, Inc., 1971. 365 pp., index.

Bacon, Edmund N. *Design of Cities.* Rev. ed. New York: Viking Press, 1972. 336 pp., illus., maps, diagrams.

Callow, Alexander B., Jr., comp. *American Urban History: An Interpretive Reader with Commentaries.* New York: Oxford University Press, 1969. 674 pp., bibliog. references, paper.

Conference on Social Statistics and the City, Washington, D.C., 1967. *Social Statistics and the City: Report.* David M. Heer, ed. Cambridge, Mass.: Joint Center for Urban Studies of the M.I.T. and Harvard University Press, 1968. 186 pp., bibliog. footnotes, paper.

Geddes, Patrick. *Cities in Evolution: An Introduction to the Town Planning Movement and to the Study of Civics.* Reprint of 1915 ed. New York: H. Fertig, 1968. 409 pp., illus., maps, plans, bibliog. ◆ Also: paperback published by Harper & Row, New York, 1971.

Green, Constance McLaughlin. *The Rise of Urban America.* New York: Harper & Row, Colophon Books, c1965, 1967. 208 pp., bibliog., paper.

Hauser, Philip M., and Leo F. Schnore, eds. *The Study of Urbanization.* New York: John Wiley & Sons, Inc., 1965. 554 pp., bibliog. ◆ Series of papers by the Committee of the Social Science Research Council appraising the study of urbanization in such fields as geography, political science, economics, history, anthropology, and sociology.

Jacobs, Jane. *The Death and Life of Great American Cities.* New York: Random House, Vintage Books, 1961. 458 pp., index, paper.

Jacobs, Jane. *The Economy of Cities.* New York: Random House, 1969. 268 pp., diagrams, index, paper.

Lynch, Kevin. *The Image of the City.* Publications of the Joint Center for Urban Studies. Cambridge, Mass.: The M.I.T. Press, c1960, 1966. 194 pp., photos, drawings, diagrams, maps, paper.

McKelvey, Blake. *The Emergence of Metropolitan America, 1915-1966.* New Brunswick, N.J.: Rutgers University Press, 1968. 311 pp., illus., maps, bibliog. references.

McKelvey, Blake. *The Urbanization of America, 1860-1915.* New Brunswick, N. J.: Rutgers University Press, c1963, 1969. 370 pp., photos, prints, chapter notes, bibliog., index.

Mumford, Lewis. *The City in History: Its Origins, Its Transformations, and Its Prospects.* New York: Harcourt, Brace & World, a Harbinger Book, 1961. 675 pp., photos, prints, maps, bibliog., index, paper. ◆ Extensive bibliography with some editorial annotations.

Mumford, Lewis. *The Culture of Cities.* New York: Harcourt Brace Jovanovich, Inc., a Harvest Book, c1938, 1970. 586 pp., photos, maps, bibliog., index, paper.

Reps, John W. *The Making of Urban America: A History of City Planning in the United States.* Princeton, N.J.: Princeton University Press, 1965. 574 pp., maps, plans, photos.

Reps, John W. *Town Planning in Frontier America.* Princeton, N.J.: Princeton University Press, c1965, 1969. 473 pp., prints, diagrams, maps, bibliog., index, paper.

Saalman, Howard, *Haussman: Paris Transformed.* New York: George Braziller, Inc., 1971. 128 pp., illus., bibliog., paper.

Schlesinger, Arthur Meier, Sr. *The Rise of the City: 1878-1898.* A History of American Life, vol. 10. Arthur M. Schlesinger, Sr., and Dixon Ryan Fox, eds. Chicago, Ill.: Quadrangle Books, c1933, 1971. 494 pp., photos, prints, maps, bibliog., index. paper.

Scientific American. *Cities.* New York: Alfred A. Knopf, Inc., 1965. 211 pp., map, bibliog., paper.

Strauss, Anselm L., comp. *The American City: A Sourcebook of Urban Imagery.* Chicago: Aldine Publishing Co., 1968. 530 pp., illus., bibliog.

Tunnard, Christopher. *The City of Man: A New Approach to the Recovery of Beauty in American Cities.* 2nd ed. New York: Charles Scribner's Sons, 1970. 424 pp., illus., plans, maps, bibliog. references.

Tunnard, Christopher, and Henry Hope Reed. *American Skyline: The Growth and Form of Our Cities and Towns.* New York: New American Library, Mentor Books, c1953, 1956. 224 pp., photos, drawings, bibliog., index, paper.

U. S. Congress. Senate. Committee on Government Operations. *Metropolitan America: A Selected Bibliography.* Prepared for the Subcommittee on Intergovernmental Relations of the Committee on Government Operations, U. S. Senate. Washington, D.C.: U. S. Government Printing Office, 1964. 34 pp.

U. S. National Archives and Records Service. *Washington: The Design of the Federal City.* By Lorraine Schmidt. Washington, D.C.: National Archives, 1972. 80 pp., illus. ◆ Survey of the history of urban planning in Washington through map and pictorial holdings in the National Archives.

Warner, Sam Bass, Jr. *The Private City: Philadelphia in Three Periods of Its Growth.* Philadelphia: University of Pennsylvania, 1968. 236 pp., illus., maps, bibliog. footnotes.

Whalen, Richard J. *A City Destroying Itself: An Angry View of New York.* New York: Apollo Editions, Inc., 1966. 127 pp., illus., paper.

Urban/Suburban Planning

American Institute of Planners, and American Society of Consulting Planners. *Selecting a Professional Planning Consultant: A Recommended Procedure for Selecting a Professional Planning Consultant and Services and Fees of Planning Firms.* Washington, D.C.: American Institute of Planners, 1971. 5 pp., leaflet.

American Society of Planning Officials. *Public Hearings, Controversy, and the Written Response.* Planning Advisory Service Information Report no. 240. Chicago: The Society, 1968. 11 pp., paper. ◆ Emphasis on the theory of the public hearing and useful guide for practice.

American Society of Planning Officials. *Vest Pocket Parks.* Planning Advisory Service Information Report no. 229. Prepared by Piero Faraci. Chicago: The Society, 1967. 15 pp., illus., bibliog.

Amery, Colin; Mark Girouard; and Dan Cruickshank. "Save the Garden," *Architectural Review,* 152:905 (July 1972), pp. 16-32. ◆ Reviews all factors involved in saving Covent Garden; its history, roads and transportation, housing, alternative uses, economics, environmental space, storage, and rights of local merchants, habitants, and developers.

Anderson, Robert M. *American Law of Zoning: Zoning, Planning, Subdivision Control.* Rochester, N.Y.: Lawyers Co-operative Pub. Co., 1968. 4 vols., 879 pp., Supplement 1971.

Bair, Frederick H., Jr., and Virginia Curtis, eds. *Planning Cities: Selected Writings on Principles and Practice.* Chicago: American Society of Planning Officials, 1970. 499 pp., illus., bibliog. references. ◆ Includes sections on zoning suggestions for historic and cultural conservation, land-use regulations, planning principles.

Baker, John D. "Anonymity and American Architecture." *Historic Preservation,* 24:3 (July-September 1972), pp. 12-17. ◆ Suggests stripping away anonymity from good architects and linking their identity with their buildings.

Bard, Albert S. *Aesthetics and City Planning.* New York: Citizens Union Research Foundation, 1957. 15 pp. ◆ Revision and expansion of an article in *The American Journal of Economics and Sociology,* 15:3 (April 1956).

Bestor, George C., and Holway R. Jones. *City Planning: A Basic Bibliography of Sources and Trends.* 3rd ed. Sacramento, Calif.: California Council of Civil Engineers and Land Surveyors, 1966. 195 pp. ◆ A standard reference to over 2,000 vital books, reports, and articles.

Bourne, Larry S. *Private Redevelopment of the Central City: Spatial Processes of Structural Change in the City of Toronto.* Department of Geography Research Paper no. 112. Chicago: Department of Geography, University of Chicago, 1967. 199 pp., maps, tables, graphs, bibliog., appendices, paper.

Buchanan, Sir Colin M. *The State of Britain.* London: Faber, 1972. 87 pp. ◆ Discusses the problems of modern urban planning and how to assess the amenities of traditional town life versus the facilities of technological progress in the urban dilemma.

Cambridge Seven Associates. *Report to the U. S. Commission of Fine Arts on the Environmental Design of Streets in Washington, D.C.* Cambridge, Mass.: Cambridge Seven Associates, Inc., n.d. 44 pp., plates, photos, drawings, diagrams, maps, paper.

Carnes, Charles N., and C. M. Smart. *City Appearance and the Law: A Manual to Assist in the Development of Ordinance-based Visual Improvement Programs in Smaller Cities.* Fayetteville, Ark: City Planning Division, University of Arkansas, 1971. 140 pp.

Chadwick, George F. *The Park and the Town: Public Landscape in the 19th and 20th Cen-*

turies. New York: Praeger Publishers, 1966. 388 pp., illus., plans, bibliog.

Clawson, Marion. *Suburban Land Conversion in the United States: An Economic and Governmental Process.* Baltimore: Published for Resources for the Future by Johns Hopkins Press, 1971. 406 pp., illus., bibliogs. ♦ Shows how the free-for-all process of suburban land conversion works and how the process creates the sprawl, high costs, and racial segregation of the suburbs.

Clay, Grady. "The Cityscape," *Historic Preservation,* 15:1 (1963), pp. 14-18.

Cleveland. City Planning Commission. *The Fine Arts Guide: A Guide for Submitting Projects Involving Aesthetics to the Cleveland City Planning Commission Through Its Fine Arts Advisory Committee.* 2nd rev. ed. Cleveland: 1966. 26 pp., maps.

Cole, Margaret van Barneveld. *The Urban Aesthetic: Evolution of a Survey System.* St. Louis?: 1960. 130 pp., illus. ♦ Illustration and verification of a study on identification of values in city design with a four-block sample survey in San Francisco.

"Congressional Struggles with Coastal-Zone and Land-Use Policy," *C F Letter,* August 1972, entire issue.

Council of Europe. Council for Cultural Cooperation. *Active Maintenance of Monuments, Groups, and Areas of Buildings of Historical or Artistic Interest Within the Context of Regional Planning; Preservation and Rehabilitation of Groups and Areas of Buildings of Historical or Artistic Interest.* Symposium D, The Hague, 22-27 May 1967; Report. Strasbourg: 1967. 107 pp., illus.

Crosby, Theo. *The Necessary Monument: Its Future in the Civilized City.* Greenwich, Conn.: New York Graphic Society, Ltd., 1970. 128 pp., prints, diagrams, photos, appendices, bibliog. ♦ Discusses the architectural monument in terms of the monument reborn, the monument in balance, the monument destroyed; and also in terms of social connection, urban development and city planning, problems of identity.

Cullen, Gordon. *The Concise Townscape.* New York: Van Nostrand Reinhold Co., c1961, 1971. 199 pp., photos, drawings, index, paper. ♦ Illustrated manual analyzing visual aspects of landscape details, exterior spaces, building materials and structures in urban and village context.

Darling, Frank Fraser, and John P. Milton, eds. *Future Environments of North America.* Being the record of a conference convened by the Conservation Foundation in April, 1965, at Airlie House, Warrenton, Virginia. Garden City, N.Y.: Natural History Press, c1966. 767 pp., bibliogs. ♦ See chapter by Christopher Tunnard, "Preserving the Cultural Patrimony."

"A Disruption in Greenwich Village, an Interview with Hugh Hardy," *Historic Preservation,* 24:3 (July-September 1972), pp. 36-42. ♦ Relationship of old and new architecture in the case of replacing an 1844 Greek Revival townhouse in Greenwich Village which was demolished by an explosion.

Dober, Richard P. *Environmental Design.* New York: Van Nostrand Reinhold Co., 1969. 278 pp., illus., maps, plans.

Eckbo, Garrett. *Urban Landscape Design.* New York: McGraw-Hill, 1964. 248 pp., illus., plans, bibliog.

Environment and Change: The Next Fifty Years. Commissioned and edited by William R. Ewald, Jr., on behalf of the American Institute of Planners. Bloomington, Ind.: Indiana University Press, 1968. 397 pp., bibliog., appendices.

Euston, Hugh Denis Charles Fitzroy. "The Future of Historic Town Centres in Urban Replanning," Town Planning Institute *Journal,* 49 (July-August 1963), pp. 215-221.

Ewald, William R., Jr. *Street Graphics: A Concept and a System.* Legal analysis by Daniel R. Mandelker. Washington, D.C.: American Society of Landscape Architects Foundation, 1971. 176 pp., illus., bibliog. ♦ Signs and graphics useful in commercial areas of historic districts. Intended for use with the movie "Street Graphics," coproduced by W. R. Ewald, Jr., and Filmhouse, Inc.

Fein, Albert. *Frederick Law Olmsted and the American Environmental Tradition.* New York: George Braziller, Inc., 1972. 180 pp., photos, prints, diagrams, maps, bibliog., index, paper. ♦ Review of Olmsted's work and ideas and how they can enrich environmental and social planning today.

Feiss, Carl. *Community Architecture: An Appeal to Action.* Washington, D.C.: American Institute of Architects Urban Design Committee, 1962. 16 pp., bibliog. ♦ Discusses major conversion taking place in the focus of comprehensive architecture of whole communities.

Fleming, Ronald Lee. "A Call for Visual Relevance," *Historic Preservation*, 25:3 (July-September 1973), pp. 24-25.

Gibberd, Frederick. *Town Design.* 5th ed. rev. New York: Praeger Publishers, Inc., 1967. 372 pp., illus., plans.

Gilliam, Harold. *Between the Devil and the Deep Blue Bay: The Struggle to Save San Francisco Bay.* San Francisco, Calif.: The Chronicle Publishing Co., Chronicle Books, 1969. 151 pp., illus., maps, paper.

Great Britain. Ministry of Housing and Local Government. *Preservation Policy Group: Report to the Minister of Housing and Local Government, May, 1970.* London: Her Majesty's Stationery Office, 1970. 55 pp., paper. ◆ Includes new legislation, report on four towns, recommendations for additional legislation, publicity and education, new uses for old buildings, traffic, technical advice, finance.

Greenfield, Albert M., & Company, Inc. *A Technical Report on Neighborhood Conservation: Improved Techniques for Using Small Parcels of Land Resulting from Selective Clearance (Demonstration Project Penna. D-2). Interim Report No. 2: New Town Houses for Washington Square East.* Prepared for the Redevelopment Authority of the City of Philadelphia by Albert M. Greenfield & Co., inc., with the Institute for Architectural Research of the University of Pennsylvania. Philadelphia, Pa.: 1964. 213 pp., illus., maps.

Griswold, Ralph E. "The Landscape Setting," *Historic Preservation*, 13:1 (1961), pp. 15-22.

Haar, Charles M. *Land-Use Planning: A Casebook on the Use, Misuse and Re-use of Urban Land.* 2nd ed. Boston: Little, Brown & Co., 1971. 788 pp., illus.

Halprin, Lawrence, *Cities.* Cambridge, Mass.: M. I. T. Press, 1972. 240 pp., illus., paper. ◆ A landscape architect looks at elements of design, texture and form in the details that constitute the visual appeal of cities.

Howlett, Bruce, and Frederick J. Elmiger, *Power Lines and Scenic Values in the Hudson River Valley.* 3rd printing, rev. Tarrytown, N.Y.: Hudson River Valley Commission of New York, 1969. 23 pp., drawings, diagrams, paper.

International City Manager's Association. *Principles and Practice of Urban Planning.* Edited by William I. Goodman and Eric C. Freund. 4th ed. Washington, D.C.: The

Association, 1968. 621 pp., bibliog., list of contributors.

International Federation for Housing and Planning, Standing Committee on "Historic Urban Areas." *Historic Urban Areas: Venice Meeting Acts.* Publication no. 1. Torino, Italy: Urbanistica, 1965? 115 pp., illus., maps, plans.

Jacobs, Stephen W., and Barclay G. Jones. *City Design Through Conservation: Methods for the Evaluation and Utilization of Aesthetic and Cultural Resources.* Berkeley, Calif.: The University of California, 1960. 2 vols., illus., plans, maps, bibliog. footnotes. ◆ Limited distribution of 100 copies to libraries. Revised edition in preparation.

Johnson, Philip C.; Harmon H. Goldstone; John W. Lawrence; and Paul Muldawer. "Contemporary Building in Historic Districts," *Historic Preservation*, 23:1 (January-March 1971), pp. 17-36. ◆ Includes critique of new auditorium in Charleston; New York City Landmarks Preservation Commission cases and examples; review of contemporary designs in historic context in Washington, D.C., Boston, and New Haven; criteria for design in historic areas.

Joint Committee on Design Control. *Planning and Community Appearance: Report.* Prepared with the cooperation of the Regional Plan Association, Henry Fagin and Robert C. Weinberg, eds. New York: Published for the Joint Committee by Regional Plan Association, 1958. 159 pp., photos, bibliog., paper.

Jones, Barclay Gibbs. *The Historic Monument in City Planning.* Eugene, Ore.: Society of Architectural Historians, Pacific Section, 1958. 13 pp., mimeo. ◆ Paper presented at the spring meeting, April 12, 1958.

Kentucky. Division of Development Information. *Directory of Technical Assistance and Information Services for Community Development.* Frankfort, Ky.: Kentucky Program Development Office, 1969. 1 vol., various pagings, maps.

Kingsbury, Felicia D. "Town Planning Methods Applied to Preservation," *Old-Time New England*, 41:4 (Spring 1951), pp. 92-95.

Land-Use Policies. Papers presented at the land-use policies short course held at the 1970 American Society of Planning Officials National Planning Conference. Chairman, John W. Reps; editor, Virginia Curtis. Chicago:

American Society of Planning Officials, 1970. 74 pp., bibliog. references.

League of Kansas Muncipalities. *A Guide to Community Design: Aesthetics and Architectural Control.* Topeka, Kans.: The League, 1973. 34 pp. ◆ A manual to acquaint local officials with use of governmental power to preserve, restore, and promote beauty in communities, and the need for aesthetic regulations.

Lunny, Robert M. *Historic Preservation and Municipal Planning.* Federation Planning Information Report, Vol. 2, No. 2. Newark, N.J.: New Jersey Federation of Planning Officials, 1967. 11 pp., mimeo.

Lynch, Kevin. *Site Planning.* 2nd ed. Cambridge, Mass.: M.I.T. Press, c1962, 1971. 348 pp., illus., diagrams, bibliog.

McHarg, Ian L. *Design With Nature.* Garden City, N.Y.: Natural History Press, published for the American Museum of Natural History, c1969, 1971. 197 pp., illus., maps, bibliog. footnotes, paper.

McQuade, Walter, comp. *Cities Fit to Live In, and How We Can Get Them; Recent Articles on the Urban Environment.* Urban Environment, no. 1. New York: Macmillan Co., 1971. 152 pp., illus., maps, plans, bibliog. references, paper.

Mandelker, Daniel R. *Managing Our Urban Environment: Cases, Text and Problems.* 2nd ed., rev. Indianapolis, Ind.: Bobbs-Merrill Company, 1971. 1194 pp., illus., bibliog. ◆ A casebook of legal logic for planning office as well as classroom.

Meshenberg, Michael J. *Environmental Planning: A Selected Annotated Bibliography.* Planning Advisory Service Information Report no. 263-4. Chicago: American Society of Planning Officials, 1970. 2 vols., illus., maps, bibliog. ◆ Volume 1: Environmental Information for Policy Formulation; Volume 2: A Selected Annotated Bibliography.

Miller, Hugh C. *The Chicago School of Architecture: A Plan For Preserving a Significant Remnant of America's Architectural Heritage.* Washington, D.C.: U. S. National Park Service, 1973. 38 pp., illus., bibliog., paper. ◆ Discusses the "Chicago Plan" of development rights transfer.

Miner, Ralph W., Jr. *Conservation of Historic and Cultural Resources.* Chicago: American Society of Planning Officials, 1969. 56 pp.,

photos, bibliog., paper. ◆ The report defines historic and cultural conservation, traces the changing emphases of the preservation movement, and outlines an approach to a comprehensive program through surveys, legal techniques, public and private options.

Minnesota. State Planning Agency. *A Regional Planning and Development System for Minnesota: Report to the Governor and the Legislature.* St. Paul: 1969. 8 pp.

Modernizing Urban Land Policy. Edited by Marion Clawson. Baltimore, Md.: Published for Resources for the Future by Johns Hopkins University Press, 1973. 248 pp., tables, graphs, bibliog., appendix, index. ◆ Papers presented at a Resources for the Future Forum, Washington, D.C., April 13-14, 1972.

National Trust for Historic Preservation. *County Planning: How the English Do It.* Report of an Investigative Workshop in England for the Boards of Supervisors of Fauquier and Loudoun Counties, Virginia, January 15-22, 1972. Sponsored by the National Trust for Historic Preservation and The National Association of Counties. Washington, D.C.: The Trust, 1972. 40 pp., illus., paper.

The New City. Edited by Donald Canty. New York: Published for Urban America, Inc. by Praeger, 1969. 180 pp., illus., maps. ◆ Papers selected from conferences held in 1969 by the National Committee on Urban Growth Policy.

New York (City). Housing and Redevelopment Board. *Neighborhood Conservation in New York City.* New York: The Board? 1966. 183 pp., illus., maps, bibliog. footnotes. ◆ A community-directed, ongoing neighborhood improvement program using new methods of neighborhood rehabilitation, preservation and family assistance.

New York (City). Museum of Modern Art. *The New City: Architecture and Urban Renewal.* Catalog of an exhibition held January 23 through March 13, 1967, at the Museum of Modern Art. New York: 1967. 46 pp., illus., maps, plans, paper. ◆ Four projects commissioned by the Museum of Modern Art to explore possible solutions to such problems as housing and renewal, the development of misused land, and modifications of existing layout of streets and parks. Texts also summarize twentieth century theory and practice in city planning.

New York State Council on Architecture. *Inventory of New York State Agencies Re-*

sponsible for Design, Planning and Construction: Phase 2 – Methods and Procedures. Prepared by Daniel Sullivan. New York: The Council, 1973. 121 pp., appendix, paper.

Owings, Nathaniel Alexander. The American Aesthetic. 1st ed. New York: Harper & Row, 1969. 198 pp., photos, diagrams, maps, index.

Papageorgiou, Alexandros Demetrios Nikolaou. Continuity and Change: Preservation in City Planning. Preface by Frederick Gutheim. Translated by Gerald Onn. New York: Praeger Publishers, 1971. 185 pp., photos, diagrams, maps, bibliog. ◆ History and significance of historic urban centers, critical survey and role of historic centers in future settings, and rehabilitation of historic urban centers.

Pawley, Martin. Architecture Versus Housing. New York: Praeger Publishers, 1971. 128 pp., photos, charts, diagrams, bibliog., index, paper.

Reilly, William K., ed. The Use of Land; A Citizen's Policy Guide to Urban Growth. Task force report sponsored by The Rockefeller Brothers Fund. New York: Thomas Y. Crowell Co., 1973. 318 pp., photos, tables, graphs, bibliog., index.

Richards, J. M., and Abraham Rogatnick. "Venice: Problems and Possibilities," Architectural Review, 149:891 (May 1971), pp. 258-324, special issue. 67 pp., photos, prints. ◆ Diversity of topics relative to saving an entire city.

Rowland, Howard S. The New York Times Guide to Federal Aid for Cities and Towns. New York: Quadrangle Books, 1972. 1243 pp.

Rudofsky, Bernard. Streets for People: A Primer for Americans. 1st ed. Garden City, N.Y.: Doubleday & Company, 1969. 351 pp., illus., music, bibliog., paper.

Schmertz, Mildred F., ed. Acquisition, Creation and Design of Open Space for People. An Illustrated Anthology of Papers Presented at the 1970 International Conference of the Commission on Town Planning of the Union Internationale des Architects. Washington, D.C.: American Institute of Architects, 1970. 111 pp., photos, plans, maps, bibliog., index.

Schwartz, Ralph. "A Ford Foundation Project in New York City." Historic Preservation, 21:1 (January-March 1969), pp. 36-40. ◆ Planning and development of Turtle Bay area on Manhattan's East Side.

Scott, Mellier Goodin. The Future of San Francisco Bay. Berkeley, Calif.: Institute of Governmental Studies, University of California, 1963. 125 pp., illus., bibliog.

Sharp, Thomas. Town and Townscape. London: John Murray, 1968. 156 pp., photos, maps, index. ◆ Analysis of English urban settings, visual and spatial qualities and problems of traffic and modern building.

Simonds, John Ormsbee. Landscape Architecture: The Shaping of Man's Natural Environment. New York: McGraw-Hill, 1961. 244 pp., illus.

Steele, R. Spencer. "Old Homes in the Community," New York State Federation of Official Planning Organizations, Planning Institute Papers (1964), pp. 17-23.

Stewart, Ian R. Nineteenth Century American Public Landscape Design. Exchange Bibliography no. 68. Monticello, Ill.: Council of Planning Librarians, 1969. 20 pp. ◆ Bibliography covering public parks movement, city planning, landscape architecture and design, municipal reform, from 1840 to 1910.

Thiry, Paul, ed. "Washington in Transition," American Institute of Architects Journal, 39:1 (January 1963), pp. 23-118, special issue. ◆ Includes a review of historic city plans and current proposals, historic areas, parks and open space, urban renewal, transportation, memorials and monuments, historic preservation in city and village, administration, planning aims, and bibliography.

Tunnard, Christopher. "Planning and Replanning of American Cities," Historic Preservation, 16:1 (1964), pp. 8-9.

Tunnard, Christopher, and Boris Pushkarev. Man-made America: Chaos or Control: An Inquiry into Selected Problems of Design in the Urbanized Landscape. New Haven, Conn.: Yale University Press, 1963. 479 pp., illus., maps, bibliog., paper. ◆ See Part VI, "Something for the Future: The Preservation of Visible History," pp. 401-440.

The Ultimate Highrise: San Francisco's Mad Rush Toward the Sky. Edited by Bruce Brugmann and Greggar Sletteland. 1st ed. San Francisco, Calif.: The San Francisco Bay Guardian, 1971. 255 pp., illus., tables, bibliog. references. ◆ Research and documentation of San Francisco skyscrapers and their adverse effect on the economy.

U. S. Council on Environmental Quality. The Quiet Revolution in Land Use Control.

Washington, D.C.: U. S. Government Printing Office, 1971. 327 pp., appendices.

U. S. Department of Housing and Urban Development. Library. *Neighborhood Conservation and Property: A Bibliography.* Washington, D.C.: U. S. Government Printing Office, 1969. 78 pp. ◆ Lists publications dealing with various phases of housing and property rehabilitation including appraisals, condemnation and eminent domain, code enforcement, financing, grievance procedures, land use, non-residential rehabilitation, urban renewal. Also includes a list of films, training aids, and courses.

U. S. Department of Transportation. Federal Highway Adminstration. *Economic and Social Effects of Highways.* Washington, D.C.: The Department, 1971. 373 pp., bibliog., index. ◆ Information on more than 200 studies of the social and economic effects of highways in two parts: narrative discussion of the studies, and abstracts of the studies.

U. S. Environmental Protection Agency. *Toward a New Environmental Ethic.* Washington, D.C.: U. S. Government Printing Office, 1971. 25 pp., photos, paper.

U. S. Federal Highway Administration. Environment Development Division. *Highway Environment Reference Book.* Prepared with special assistance from the Office of Public Affairs. Washington, D.C.: U. S. Federal Highway Administration, 1970 (i.e. 1971). 92 pp., bibliogs.

U. S. Housing and Home Finance Agency, Office of Metropolitan Development. *National Survey of Metropolitan Planning.* Prepared by the U.S. Housing and Home Finance Agency for the Subcommittee on Intergovernmental Relations of the Committee on Government Operations, U. S. Senate. Washington, D.C.: U. S. Government Printing Office, 1963. 1 vol., various pagings.

U. S. National Commission on Urban Problems. *Building the American City: Report.* Praeger Special Studies in U. S. Economics and Social Development. New York: Praeger, 1969. 500 pp., illus., bibliog. footnotes.

U. S. National Park Service. *Man–Nature––City: The Urban Ecosystem.* Urban Ecology Series no. 1. Washington, D.C.: U. S. Government Printing Office, 1971. 21 pp., photos, drawings, maps, booklet.

U. S. President's Council on Recreation and Natural Beauty. *From Sea to Shining Sea: A Report on the American Environment, Our Natural Heritage.* Washington, D.C.: U. S. Government Printing Office, 1968. 304 pp., photos, bibliog., index, paper. ◆ Issued in cooperation with the Citizens' Advisory Committee on Recreation and Natural Beauty. Includes historic preservation, pp. 55-56, 68-71; and annotated bibliography and names and addresses of helpful organizations, Part IV.

Whyte, William H. *The Last Landscape.* Garden City, N.Y.: Doubleday & Co., 1968. 376 pp., illus., maps, paper.

Woodbury, Coleman, ed. *The Future of Cities and Urban Redevelopment.* Chicago: University of Chicago Press, 1953. 764 pp., bibliog. footnotes.

Woodbury, Coleman, ed. *Urban Redevelopment Problems and Practices.* Chicago: University of Chicago Press, 1953. 525 pp., illus., bibliog.

Wright, Russell. *Manual for Incorporating Historic Preservation Objectives in the Highway Planning Process.* Washington, D.C.: National Trust for Historic Preservation and Department of Transportation, 1972. 100 pp., bibliog., glossary. ◆ Prepared by the author under a grant from the Department of Transportation administered by the National Trust for Historic Preservation. Draft on deposit at the National Trust library; publication by the Department pending.

NOTES AND PERIODICALS

American Institute of Planners, 1776 Massachusetts Avenue, N.W., Washington, D.C. 20036. Founded in 1917, it now has thirty-two local chapters. It is a professional society of individuals who are engaged in comprehensive planning on city, county, regional, state, and national levels and who are employed as public officials, private consultants, or by private agencies. Committees include Continuing Education, International, Jury of Awards, Status of Planners in the Federal Government, and Women's Rights. Its departments are City Planning and Management, Environment, Information Systems, Metropolitan and Regional Planning, Planning Education, and Urban Design. It publishes *AIP Newsletter,* monthly; *American Institute of Planners Journal* (cited below); *Planners Notebook,* bimonthly; *Conference Proceedings,* annual; handbook and roster, biennial; and background papers and reports.

American Institute of Planners Journal. 1925, bimonthly, membership/subscription. American Institute of Planners, 1776 Massachusetts Avenue, N.W., Washington, D.C. 20036.

American Society of Planning Officials, 1313 East 60th Street, Chicago, Illinois 60637. Founded in 1934 to foster the best techniques and decisions for the planned development of communities and regions. It serves as a clearinghouse for information; instituted Planning Advisory Service in 1949 for research and inquiry-answering; conducts consulting services; holds workshops; and maintains an extensive library. It publishes *Planning* (formerly *ASPO Newsletter,* cited below); *Planning* (also called *Planning Yearbook),* conference papers (cited below); Planning Advisory Service Information Reports, monthly; Land-Use Controls Publications Service (includes *Zoning Digest* and *Land-Use Controls Annual,* cited below).

Center for Urban Development Research, Cornell University, 726 University Avenue, Ithaca, New York 14850. Summer Institute on Historic Preservation Planning; one week seminar, in cooperation with the College of Architecture, Art and Planning, the Graduate School of Business and Public Administration, and the National Trust for Historic Preservation, covering the means of safeguarding our design heritage and its use as a resource in planning for the future. Topics include preservation theory, social benefits of preservation, urban history as a basis for preservation, designing for preservation, survey techniques, evaluation techniques for sites and structures, economics of area preservation, legal aspects of preservation, private and government programs, and organizing for preservation. The course is intended for laymen as well as architects, planners, historians, and other professionals.

Federal Design Matters. January 1974, quarterly, subscription. Superintendent of Documents, U. S. Government Printing Office, Attn.: Mail List, Washington, D.C. 20402. Newsletter from the National Endowment for the Arts covering news and information on architecture, graphics, visual communication, interior and industrial design, landscape architecture, visual arts from federal agencies and private domestic sources. Copies free to federal administrators and designers; subscription to nonfederal design professionals and the public.

Historic Urban Plans, Box 276, Ithaca, New York 14850. Reproductions of major American city maps. Catalogue available.

Housing and Planning References. 1948, bimonthly, free to libraries, subscription to individuals. U. S. Department of Housing and Urban Development, U. S. Government Printing Office, Washington, D.C. 20402. Selective list of publications and articles of use to HUD workers; includes historic preservation as a section.

International Federation for Housing and Planning, General Secretariat, 43 Wassenaarseweg, The Hague, Netherlands 24 45 57. Founded in 1913 as a nongovernmental organization to study and promote throughout the world the improvement of housing and the theory and practice of urban, regional, and national planning within the context of related disciplines with a view to securing higher standards of housing, the improvement of urban and rural settlements, and a better distribution of population. It now numbers members and collaborators in over sixty-five countries, and has been granted consultative status by the United Nations Economic and Social Council, the World Health Organization, and UNESCO. It maintains relations with other international organizations dealing with problems in housing, planning, or related fields. Corporate and individual members include governmental departments, voluntary associations for housing, planners institutes, architects, and municipal officials. It provides for world congresses, international congresses, standing committees, and working groups. Its services include contacts for members, a specialized library, inquiry and information service. It publishes a *Bulletin* (monthly), Congress reports, separate reports and publications of standing committees, monographs.

Land-Use Controls Annual. Winter 1971-72, annual, included in subscription to *Zoning Digest.* Land-Use Controls Publications Service, American Society of Planning Officials, 1313 East 60th Street, Chicago, Illinois 60637.

Planning (formerly **ASPO Newsletter**). 1935, monthly, membership. American Society of Planning Officials, 1313 East 60th Street, Chicago, Illinois 60637.

Planning (also called **Planning Yearbook**). 1909, annual, subscription. American Society of Planning Officials, 1313 East 60th Street, Chicago, Illinois 60637.

U. S. Department of Transportation and National Trust for Historic Preservation. "Techniques for Incorporating Historic Preservation Objectives into the Highway Planning Process," a study prepared by Russell Wright for publication in 1974. The study enlisted the active participation and assistance of state and local transportation planners, preservationists, and community leaders. It is intended for use as a guide for planners whose projects may impinge upon historic sites, architecture, or artifacts. See Wright, Russell (cited above).

Zoning Digest. 1948, 10-12/yr., subscription includes *Land-Use Controls Annual.* Land-Use Controls Publications Service, American Society of Planning Officials, 1313 East 60th Street, Chicago, Illinois 60637. ♦ Appellate court decisions and articles by zoning experts.

Government and Urban Renewal

Carlson, David B. "Urban Renewal: A New Face on the American City," *Architectural Forum,* 119:2 (August 1963), pp. 80-85. ♦ Reviews the progress of urban renewal programs in 24 American cities, concluding that dollars won out over design.

Chicago. Department of Urban Renewal. *Preserving the Architectural Character of a Neighborhood: A Preliminary Study.* Chicago: The Department, 1964 67 pp., illus., bibliogs. ♦ Contents include design opportunities; legal techniques; architectural techniques; detailed aspects of legal approaches such as regulatory measures, covenants, taxation; appendix.

Collins and Dutot. *The Appearance of Parking – Washington, D.C.* Prepared for the Commission of Fine Arts. Washington, D.C.: U.S. Commission of Fine Arts, 1966. 20 pp., photos, drawings, diagrams, paper.

Frieden, Bernard J. *The Future of Old Neighborhoods: Rebuilding for a Changing Population.* Cambridge, Mass.: M.I.T. Press, 1964. 209 pp., illus. ♦ Gradual rebuilding of city neighborhood areas with New York City, Los Angeles, and Hartford as case studies.

Greenfield, Albert M., & Company, Inc. *A Technical Report on Neighborhood Conservation: Improved Techniques for Using Small Parcels of Land Resulting from Selective Clearance (Demonstration Project Penna. D-2). Interim Report No. 2: New Town Houses for Washington Square East.* Prepared for the Redevelopment Authority of the City of Philadelphia by Albert M. Greenfield & Co., Inc., with the Institute for Architectural Research of the University of Pennsylvania. Philadelphia, Pa.: 1964. 213 pp., illus., maps.

Greer, Scott. *Urban Renewal and American Cities: The Dilemma of Democratic Intervention.* Indianapolis, Ind.: Bobbs-Merrill, Inc. c1965, 1966. 201 pp., bibliog., paper.

Hanford, Lloyd D., Sr. "Build America Better: Conservation-Centered Urban Renewal," *Historic Preservation,* 16:5 (September-October 1964), pp. 180-183.

"Historic Preservation via Urban Renewal," *Journal of Housing,* 19 (August 10, 1962), pp. 296-315.

Huxtable, Ada Louise. *Will They Ever Finish Bruckner Boulevard?* New York: Macmillan Co., 1970. 268 pp., illus., paper. ♦ Collection of addresses, essays, and lectures on urban beautification, urban renewal, architecture.

Johnson, Thomas F.; James R. Morris; and Joseph G. Butts. *Renewing America's Cities.* Washington, D.C.: Institute for Social Science Research, 1962. 130 pp., illus., bibliog.

Meyerson, Martin, and Edward C. Banfield. *Politics, Planning and the Public Interest: The Case of Public Housing in Chicago.* Glencoe, Ill.: The Free Press, 1955. 353 pp., illus., paper.

New York (City). Museum of Modern Art. *The New City: Architecture and Urban Renewal.* Catalog of an exhibition held January 23 through March 13, 1967, at the Museum of Modern Art. New York: 1967. 46 pp., illus., maps, plans, paper. ♦ Four projects commissioned by the Museum to explore possible solutions to such problems as housing and renewal, the development of misused land, and modifications of existing layout of streets and parks. Text also summarizes twentieth century theory and practice in city planning.

New York (State). Office of Planning Coordination. *New York State Development Plan – 1.* Albany, N.Y.: The Office, 1971. 128 pp., photos, drawings, charts, graphs, tables, maps, bibliog., index, paper.

Rettie, Dwight. "The Department of Housing and Urban Development," *Historic Preservation,* 20:1 (January-March 1968), pp. 16-21.

♦ One of three articles on federal responsibility in historic preservation.

Reynolds, James F. "Historic Preservation and Urban Renewal in Providence," *Historic Preservation*, 16:1 (1964), pp. 33-36.

Rochester, N.Y. *Third Ward Urban Renewal Project, Rochester, New York: Urban Renewal Plan.* Rochester: 1966. 43 pp. ♦ Includes a section on special provisions for buildings of significance or architectural merit.

Snow, Barbara. "Preservation Notes: Urban Renewal — Wolf in Sheep's Clothing?" *Antiques,* 82:1 (July 1962), p. 86. ♦ Old Philadelphia and Society Hill areas.

Snow, Barbara, ed. "Preservation and Urban Renewal: Is Co-existence Possible?" *Antiques,* 84:4 (October 1963), pp. 442-453. ♦ Series of articles by historic preservation experts.

"Special Issue-Government and Preservation," *Preservation News,* 9:5 (May 1969), entire issue. 12 pp., photos, graphs, tables.

Stewart, Robert G. "Urban Renewal and Historic Preservation in St. Louis, Missouri," *History News,* 16:5 (March 1961), pp. 66-67.

U. S. Department of Housing and Urban Development. *Preserving Historic America.* Washington, D.C.: U. S. Government Printing Office, 1966. 80 pp., photos, drawings, diagrams, maps, bibliog. ♦ Focus on urban renewal as a tool for historic preservation, giving examples of local experiences with urban renewal programs, the Urban Planning Assistance Program, the Urban Renewal Demonstration Grant Program, the Open-Space Land Program and Urban Beautification Program, and other federal aid for preservation.

U. S. Department of Housing and Urban Development. *Program Guide to Model Neighborhoods in Demonstration Cities.* Title I of the Demonstration Cities and Metropolitan Development Act of 1966. Washington, D.C.: U.S. Government Printing Office, 1967. 51 pp., appendices. ♦ See Part III-T, "Preservation of Natural and Historic Sites."

U. S. Urban Renewal Administration. *Historic Preservation Through Urban Renewal: How Urban Renewal Works, Two Areas of Emphasis, Broad Requirements, Preservation and Renewal in Action.* Prepared by Margaret Carroll. Washington, D.C.: U. S. Government Printing Office, 1963. 28 pp., illus., paper. ♦ Discusses role of urban renewal and cites examples of programs in twelve cities.

"Urban Renewal Ramble," *Historic Preservation,* 13:4 (1961), pp. 149-159.

Von Eckardt, Wolf. *Bulldozers and Bureaucrats: Cities and Urban Renewal.* A New Republic Pamphlet. Washington, D.C.: New Republic, 1963. 65 pp.

Wentworth, Mrs. Eric. "An Amendment to the Rescue," *Historic Preservation,* 17:5 (September-October 1965), pp. 176-177. ♦ Discusses Kennedy-Tower amendment to the Federal Housing Act of 1965, providing that federal funds may be used for moving, new foundation, and site preparation of historic buildings in urban renewal developments. Cites case of Plymouth Heritage Trust.

Wilson, James Q., ed. *Urban Renewal: The Record and the Controversy.* Publications of the Joint Center for Urban Studies. Cambridge, Mass.: M.I.T. Press, c1966, 1967. 683 pp., illus., plans, bibliog., paper.

4

Preservation Research and Planning

Early in the history of the National Trust for Historic Preservation a letter was received from a local preservation organization that went something like this: "We have acquired the John Doe House, an early nineteenth century building of unusual distinction. We have restored it and furnished it, and it is open to the public daily. Now will you help us to do the research?"

Happily, the preservation movement has progressed rapidly beyond that point, but there are still some who do not understand that the strong base on which all preservation activity must stand is the art and science of research. It is the beginning of all planning activity.

This chapter deals with the materials that will help both the professional and the amateur to lay out a comprehensive preservation program for the structures with which they are dealing. It includes sections on sources for research in architecture and archeology, the traditional disciplines, and in industrial archeology, which concerns itself with the industrial and engineering structures of our past.

And there are numerous manuals and handbooks to aid researchers, both professional and volunteer, in conducting surveys and inventories of historic sites and areas.

The production of inventories has been stimulated briskly by the provisions of the Historic Preservation Act of 1966. All states sharing in the federal largess find themselves confronted with the need to survey and inventory, and in so doing they reach down to both urban and rural grass roots. *The National Register of Historic Places,* the official schedule of national, state, and local properties worth saving, is the most comprehensive collection of information of historic sites and structures in the United States.

The sections on "Surveys and Inventories" and "Master Plans and Case Studies" are arranged geographically for reader convenience and include the United States, the states, the territories, and Canada, Great Britain, and other. The principal value is that one may see how proper research led to a comprehensive survey which provided the basis for a detailed master plan, whether it was for a single building, a district, or a state.

Research and planning tell you not only which road to take but what is at the end of the road.

Research for Preservation

Architecture

American Association of Architectural Bibliographers. *Papers.* Vol I- , 1965- Charlottesville, Va.: University Press of Virginia, 1965- . Nine vols. to date, annual.

Andrews, Wayne. *Architecture in America: A Photographic History from the Colonial Period to the Present.* New York: Atheneum Publishers, 1960. 179 pp., illus.

Arnold, James. *The Shell Book of Country Crafts.* 1st Amer. ed. New York: Hastings House, 1969. 358 pp., photos, drawings, bibliog., museum list, index. ♦ Description of over three dozen crafts including many involving building construction and furnishing.

Baker, John D. "Anonymity and American Architecture," *Historic Preservation,* 24:3 (July-September 1972), pp. 12-17. ♦ Suggests stripping away anonymity from good architects and linking their identity with their buildings.

Barnard, Julian. *Victorian Ceramic Tiles.* London: Studio Vista, 1972. 184 pp., photos, bibliog., glossary, listing of English and American manufacturers, index. ♦ Description of development, manufacture, and design of decorative tiles, largely in England.

Brunskill, R. W. *Illustrated Handbook of Vernacular Architecture.* New York: Universe Books, c1970, 1971. 230 pp., photos, drawings, diagrams, charts, maps, glossary, appendices, bibliog., index.

Bullock, Orin M., Jr. "Architectural Research." In *The Restoration Manual: An Illustrated Guide to the Preservation and Restoration of Old Buildings* (Norwalk, Conn.: Silvermine Publishing Co., 1966), pp. 33-77.

Clifton-Taylor, Alec. *The Pattern of English Building.* New ed. London: Faber and Faber, Ltd., 1972. 466 pp., photos, figures, glossary, bibliog., maps, indexes, paper. ♦ Comprehensive survey of history and use of traditional building materials of England, largely domestic. Also available from Watson-Guptill, New York.

Cliver, E. Blaine, and Tony P. Wrenn. *The Dranesville Tavern: An Architectural Analysis.* Fairfax, Va.: Fairfax County History Commission, 1970. 81 pp., photos, drawings, color codes, map, plans, appendices, paper. ♦ Indicates what clues to look for in determining changes in a building's character.

Columbia University. Libraries. Avery Architectural Library. *Avery Index to Architectural Periodicals.* Boston: G. K. Hall, 1963. 12 vols. with supplements.

Columbia University. Libraries. Avery Architectural Library. *Avery Obituary Index of Architects and Artists.* Boston: G. K. Hall, 1963. 338 pp.

Columbia University. Libraries. Avery Architectural Library. *Catalog of the Avery Memorial Architectural Library of Columbia University.* Rev. and enl. ed. Boston: G. K. Hall, 1968. 19 vols. with supplements.

Condit, Carl W. *American Building: Materials and Techniques from the First Colonial Settlement to the Present.* Chicago History of American Civilization Series no. 25. Chicago: University of Chicago Press, 1969. 329 pp., photos, prints, drawings, diagrams, bibliog., paper and hardcover. ♦ The focus is on the materials and techniques of construction, rather than the cosmetics, of American buildings. The four parts deal with colonial building development, the agricultural republic, rise of the industrial republic, and industrial and urban expansion in the twentieth century.

Condit, Carl W. *American Building Art: The Nineteenth Century.* New York: Oxford University Press, 1960. 371 pp., photos, prints, drawings, diagrams, notes, bibliog., index.

Condit, Carl W. *American Building Art: The Twentieth Century.* New York: Oxford University Press, 1961. 427 pp., photos, drawings, diagrams, tables, notes, bibliog., index.

Davey, Norman. *A History of Building Materials.* New York: Drake Publishers, 1970. 260 pp., photos, drawings. ♦ An important history of building materials.

"Early Roofing Materials," *Bulletin of APT,* II: 1-2 (1970), pp. 18-88.

Fitch, James Marston. *American Building, 1: The Historical Forces That Shape It.* 2nd ed., rev. and enl. Boston: Houghton Mifflin Co., c1947, 1966. 350 pp., photos, prints, drawings, diagrams, bibliog. notes, index, paper and hard-cover. ♦ A comprehensive view of architecture in the United States, taking into account the materials, the needs, the technical equipment, esthetic theory, and creative genius that shaped saltbox and skyscraper.

Fitch, James Marston. *American Building, 2: The Environmental Forces That Shape It.* 2nd ed., rev. and enl. Boston: Houghton Mifflin Co., 1972. 349 pp., photos, drawings, diagrams, charts, graphs, tables, bibliog., index.

Fitchen, John. *The New World Dutch Barn: A Study of Its Characteristics, Its Structural System, and Its Probable Erectional Procedures.* Syracuse, N.Y.: Syracuse University Press, 1968. 178 pp., photos, diagrams, maps, pictorial glossary, bibliog., index.

Giedion, Siegfried. *Mechanization Takes Command: A Contribution to Anonymous History.* 1948. Reprint. New York: W. W. Norton & Co., 1969. 743 pp., photos, prints, diagrams, bibliog. footnotes, index, paper. ◆ Basic work on effects of industrialization, especially as it relates to development of mechanical systems in buildings.

Hamlin, Talbot Faulkner. *Greek Revival Architecture in America: Being an Account of Important Trends in American Architecture and American Life Prior to the War Between the States.* 1944. Reprint. New York: Dover Publications, 1964. 439 pp., photos, prints, diagrams, appendices, bibliog., index, paper. ◆ Includes extensive bibliography. Also available from Peter Smith, Gloucester, Massachusetts.

Hansen, Hans Jurgen, ed. *Architecture in Wood: A History of Wood Building and Its Techniques in Europe and North America.* New York: Viking Press, 1971. 288 pp., photos, drawings, bibliog., index.

Harris, John, and Jill Lever. *Illustrated Glossary of Architecture, 850-1830.* New York: Clarkson N. Potter, 1966. 79 pp., illus., plans.

Harvey, Nigel. *A History of Farm Buildings in England and Wales.* Newton Abbot, England: David & Charles, 1970. 277 pp., photos, figures, bibliog., index. ◆ Historical development of farm buildings from Roman occupation to modern times.

Hewett, Cecil Alec. *The Development of Carpentry, 1200-1700: An Essex Study.* New York: Augustus M. Kelley, 1969. 232 pp., photos, drawings, glossary, bibliog. references, appendices, index. ◆ An aid in the dating of timber buildings and study of jointing techniques in English timber buildings.

Hitchcock, Henry-Russell. *American Architectural Books: A List of Books, Portfolios, and Related Subjects Published in America Before 1895.* Minneapolis: University of Minnesota Press, c1946, 1962. 130 pp., list of holders, bibliog., index. ◆ Lists architectural design books and carpenter's manuals printed in America for use as a guide for the designs of American buildings after 1775.

Hudson, Kenneth. *Building Materials.* London: Longman Group Ltd., 1972. 122 pp., illus., bibliog., gazetteer, appendix. ◆ Basic history of building materials in England.

Hudson, Kenneth. *The Fashionable Stone.* 1st U. S. ed. Park Ridge, N.J.: Noyes Press, c1971, 1972. 120 pp., illus., appendices, bibliog., index. ◆ An account of the history, use and development of Bath and Portland stone in English buildings.

Innocent, C. F. *The Development of English Building Construction.* 1916. Reprint. New introduction and bibliography by Sir Robert de Z. Hall. 1st ed., new impression. Newton Abbot, England: David & Charles, 1971. 294 pp., illus., map, plan, bibliog. ◆ History of building practices, materials and elements as applied to folk building in England.

Iredale, David. *This Old House.* Discovering Books Series. Tring, Herts., England: Shire Publications, 1968. 64 pp., photos, drawings, maps, plans. ◆ An archivist describes how to research the history of houses.

Isham, Norman Morrison. *Early American Houses: and, A Glossary of Colonial Architectural Terms.* DaCapo Press Series in Architecture and Decorative Art, vol. 10. 1928; 1939. Reprint. New York: DeCapo Press, 1967. 61, 37 pp., photos, drawings, diagrams, glossary, index.

Johns Hopkins University. John Work Garrett Library. *The Fowler Architectural Collection of the Johns Hopkins University.* Catalogue compiled by Laurence Hall Fowler and Elizabeth Baer. Baltimore: Evergreen House Foundation, 1961. 383 pp., 30 plates, bibliog.

Johnston, Norman B. *The Human Cage: A Brief History of Prison Architecture.* New York: Published for the American Foundation, Institute of Corrections by Walker, 1973. 68 pp., illus., bibliog., paper.

Jordy, William H. *American Buildings and Their Architects: Vol. 3 - Progressive and Academic Ideals at the Turn of the 20th Century.* Garden City, N.Y.: Doubleday & Co., 1971. 420 pp., photos, notes, glossary, index. ◆ See also volumes 1 and 2 by William H. Pierson.

Jordy, William H. *American Buildings and Their Architects: Vol. 4 – The Impact of European Modernism in the Mid-Twentieth Century.* Garden City, N.Y.: Doubleday & Co., 1972. 469 pp., photos, notes, glossary, index. ◆ See also volumes 1 and 2 by William H. Pierson.

Koyl, George S. *American Architectural Drawings: A Catalog of Original and Measured Drawings of the United States of America to December 31, 1917.* Comp. and ed. by George S. Koyl. Philadelphia: American Institute of Architects, Philadelphia Chapter, 1969. 5 vols., drawings.

Little, Nina Fletcher. "On Dating New England Houses: Part I — The Seventeenth Century, Floor Plans and Framing," *Antiques,* 47:3 (March 1945), pp. 155-157. ◆ See also: "Part II—Interiors: Seventeenth Century and Transitional Period," *Antiques,* 47:4 (April 1945), pp. 228-231; "Part III—The Great Georgian Period, 1735-1780," *Antiques,* 47:5 (May 1945), pp. 273-275; "Part IV—The Adam Period, 1780-1820," *Antiques,* 47:6 (June 1945), pp. 334-336.

Long, Amos. *Farmsteads and Their Buildings.* Lebanon, Pa.: Applied Arts Publishers, 1972. 40 pp., photos. ◆ A study of farm buildings and building practices in southeastern and central Pennsylvania.

McKaig, Thomas H. *Building Failures: Case Studies in Construction and Design.* New York: McGraw-Hill Book Co., 1962. 261 pp., plans, bibliog., index. ◆ Case studies assembled to help architects, engineers, and contractors build more safely. Includes concrete failures, steel failures, miscellaneous construction failures, foundation failures, old buildings and overload, minor and incipient failures.

Massey, James C. *Sources for American Architectural Drawings in Foreign Collections: A Preliminary Survey Carried Out Under a Grant from the Ford Foundation.* Washington, D.C.: Historic American Buildings Survey, 1969. 140 pp., illus., plans.

Meeks, Carroll Louis Vanderslice. *The Railroad Station: An Architectural History.* New Haven, Conn.: Yale University Press, 1956. 203 pp., illus., table of trainsheds, drawings, maps, diagrams, bibliog. ◆ Basic architectural history of the railroad station.

Mercer, Henry C. *The Dating of Old Houses.* Doylestown, Pa.: The Bucks County Historical Society, 1923. 28 pp., illus. ◆ See also: *Old-*

Time New England, 14:4 (April 1924), pp. 170-190.

Michelson, Peter. "The Investigation of Old Rural Buildings." Offprint from *Dansk Folkemuseum & Frilandsmuseet: History and Activities,* 1966, pp. 51-76. ◆ Description of techniques used to record history of old farm buildings.

Nelson, Lee H. "Nail Chronology as an Aid to Dating Old Buildings," rev. ed., *History News,* 24:11 (November 1968), Technical Leaflet no. 48 (new series).

New York State Historic Trust. *Nineteenth Century Tin Roofing and Its Use at Hyde Hall.* By Diana S. Waite. Albany: The Trust, 1971. 56 pp., photos, drawings, diagrams, bibliog. footnotes and additional bibliog., paper.

New York State Historic Trust and The Society for Industrial Archeology. *Iron Architecture in New York City: Two Studies in Industrial Archeology.* Edited by John G. Waite. Albany, N.Y.: The Trust and The Society, 1972. 82 pp., photos, prints, diagrams, map, appendix of architectural drawings and chronology. ◆ Section 1, "The Edgar Laing Stores, 1849," by John G. Waite; Section 2, "The Cooper Union, 1853-1859," compiled by William Rowe III.

Newton, Norman T. *Design on the Land: The Development of Landscape Architecture.* Cambridge, Mass.: Belknap Press of Harvard University Press, 1971. 714 pp., illus., map, plans, bibliog.

Park, Helen O'Brien. *A List of Architectural Books Available in America Before the Revolution.* Art and Architecture Bibliographic Series No. 1. Los Angeles, Calif.: Hennessey & Ingalls, Inc., 1973. 80 pp., illus. ◆ Provides a basis for determining sources of much American architectural design. See also: Cambridge, Mass.: The Fogg Art Museum, Harvard University, 1958. 13 pp., mimeo. Compiled for course work. See also: *Journal of the Society of Architectural Historians,* 20 (October 1961), pp. 115-130.

The Penguin Dictionary of Architecture. By John Fleming, Hugh Honour, and Nikolaus Pevsner; with drawings by David Etherton. Baltimore: Penguin Books, c1966, 1967. 247 pp., illus., diagrams, paper.

Peterson, Charles E. "Pioneer Prefabs in Honolulu," *AIA Journal,* 60:3 (September 1973), pp. 42-47. ◆ Discusses export of the first precut frames to Hawaii by the Russians in

Alaska in 1809. Condensed from an article in *The Hawaiian Journal of History,* 5 (1971).

Peterson, Charles E. "The Technology of Early American Building (TEAB)," *Newsletter of APT,* 1:1 (April 1969), entire issue. ◆ An outline of early building technology, including personnel, design, materials, and construction prior to 1860.

Pierson, William Harvey. *American Buildings and Their Architects: Vol. 1–The Colonial and Neo-Classical Styles.* Garden City, N.Y.: Doubleday & Co., 1970. 503 pp., photos, prints, diagrams, maps, glossary, bibliog. notes, index. ◆ Volume 2, nineteenth century to Chicago World's Fair, in preparation. See also volumes 3 and 4 by William H. Jordy.

Pillsbury, Richard, and Andrew Kardos. *A Field Guide to the Folk Architecture of the Northeastern United States.* Geography Publications at Dartmouth, no. 8. Hanover, N.H.: Department of Geography, Dartmouth College, 1970? 99 pp., photos, drawings, maps, glossary, bibliog., appendix, paper. ◆ Classification of house types in the Northeast dating from the eighteenth and nineteenth centuries.

Pothorn, Herbert. *Architectural Styles.* New York: Viking Press, 1971. 187 pp., photos, drawings, glossary, charts.

Rempel, John I. *Building with Wood, and Other Aspects of Nineteenth-Century Building in Ontario.* Toronto: University of Toronto Press, 1967. 287 pp., photos, drawings, diagrams, charts, bibliog., index.

Riggs, John Beverley. *Documentary Sources for Historic Preservation: Manuscripts.* Washington, D.C.: National Trust for Historic Preservation, n.d. 4 pp., bibliog., leaflet.

Roberts, H. V. Molesworth. "Recording Dates of Buildings," *Journal of the Society of Architectural Historians,* 12:3 (October 1953), pp. 23-26. ◆ Discusses the pitfalls of "factual" dates, and indicates methods of proper recording.

Roos, Frank J., Jr. *Bibliography of Early American Architecture: Writings on Architecture Constructed Before 1860 in Eastern and Central United States.* Rev. ed. Urbana, Ill.: University of Illinois Press, 1968. 389 pp.

Saylor, Henry H. *Dictionary of Architecture.* New York: John Wiley & Sons, Inc., c1952, 1967. 221 pp., drawings, paper.

Shurtleff, Harold R. *The Log Cabin Myth: A Study of the Early Dwellings of the English Colonists of North America.* Edited by Samuel Eliot Morrison. 1939. Reprint. Gloucester, Mass.: Peter Smith, 1967. 243 pp., photos, prints, drawings, bibliog. footnotes. ◆ One of the few works dealing with the earliest house forms in America.

Smith, H. R. Bradley. "Chronological Development of Nails." Supplement to *Blacksmith's and Farrier's Tools at Shelburne Museum.* Museum Pamphlet Series no. 7. Shelburne, Vt.: Shelburne Museum, 1966. 10 pp., diagrams, paper.

Smith, J. T., and E.M. Yates. "On the Dating of English Houses from External Evidence." Reprinted from *Field Studies,* 2:5 (1968), pp. 537-577. 40 pp., drawings, diagrams.

Sturgis, Russell, ed. *A Dictionary of Architecture and Building: Biographical and Descriptive.* By Russell Sturgis and many architects, painters, engineers, and other expert writers, American and foreign. 1901-02. Reprint. Detroit: Gale Research Co., 1966. 3 vols., photos, drawings, diagrams, bibliog. ◆ Best source for the definition of architectural terms.

U. S. Office of Archeology and Historic Preservation, Division of History. *Preliminary Bibliographical Inventory of Park Historical and Architectural Studies.* Compiled by Gary Christopher and Dorothy Junkin. Washington, D.C.: National Park Service, 1971. 169 pp., o.p. ◆ Although out of print, it is a valuable bibliography of all National Park Service research reports related to history and restoration.

Waite, Diana S., ed. *Architectural Elements: The Technological Revolution.* American Historical Catalog Collection, vol. 17. Princeton, N. J.: The Pyne Press, 1973. 160 pp., paper and hard-cover. ◆ Documentary source on the development of modern American architecture, indicating the wide range of ready-made structural and decorative elements including iron, stone, and wooden columns, mantels, bannisters, balconies, and trim generally available for use in homes and public buildings.

Ware, Dora, and Betty Beatty. *A Short Dictionary of Architecture.* 3rd rev. and enl. ed. New York: Fernhill House, Ltd., c1953, 1961. 135 pp., illus., bibliog.

West, Trudy. *The Timber-Frame House in England.* New York: Architectural Book Publishing Co., 1971. 222 pp., photos, drawings, diagrams, appendix, index. ◆ Contents include history and styles of timber-frame structures, restoration, preservation, moving the building, and appendix of professional and trade organizations.

Withey, Henry F., and Elsie Rathburn Withey. *Biographical Dictionary of American Architects, Deceased.* 1956. Reprint. Los Angeles, Calif.: Hennessey & Ingalls, Inc., 1970. 678 pp.

Wood, Charles B. "A Survey and Bibliography of Writings on English and American Architectural Books Published Before 1895." Reprinted from the *Winterthur Portfolio, II* (1965), pp. 127-137. 11 pp., bibliog., paper.

NOTES AND PERIODICALS

AIA Journal (formerly American Institute of Architects *Journal*). 1944, monthly, subscription. American Institute of Architects, Octagon, 1735 New York Avenue, N.W., Washington, D.C. 20006.

American Association of Architectural Bibliographers, Fayerweather Hall, University of Virginia, Charlottesville, Virginia 22904. Founded in 1954 to further interest in, knowledge of, and research for, architectural bibliography. It sponsors research for publication, and publishes *Papers,* annual.

American Institute of Architects, Octagon, 1735 New York Avenue, N.W., Washington, D.C. 20006. Founded in 1857 to serve the needs of and improve the capability of the nation's architects and to be of service to the safety of the general public. It conducts "War on Community Ugliness," annually; sponsors educational programs; maintains a library and a comprehensive architectural slide collection; and publishes *AIA Journal* (cited above), *AIA Memo,* monthly newsletter, a directory, and a descriptive leaflet.

American Society of Landscape Architects, 2013 Eye Street, N.W., Washington, D. C. 20006. Founded in 1899, the Society serves professional landscape architects through twenty-two regional chapters. It seeks to strengthen existing and proposed courses in landscape architecture as the official accrediting agency, offers counsel to new schools, encourages state registration of landscape architects, maintains a traveling exhibition of works of landscape architects. Its committees are urban parks and recreation; city, regional, and national planning; civil service; housing redevelopment; national and state parks and forests; national capital; public roads; controlled access highways and parkways; research; exhibitions; and education. It publishes *Landscape Architecture* (cited below), and holds an annual meeting and convention.

Architecture Canada (formerly Royal Architectural Institute of Canada *Journal*). 1924, monthly, subscription. Royal Architectural Institute of Canada, 160 Eglinton Avenue E, Toronto 315, Canada.

Journal of the Society of Architectural Historians. 1941, quarterly, membership. Society of Architectural Historians, Room 716, 1700 Walnut Street, Philadelphia, Pennsylvania 19103.

Landscape Architecture. 1910, quarterly, membership. American Society of Landscape Architects, Schuster Building, 1500 Bardstown Road, Louisville, Kentucky 40205.

Newsletter of the Society of Architectural Historians. 1957, bimonthly, membership. James C. Massey, Editor, 614 South Lee Street, Alexandria, Virginia 22314.

Royal Institute of British Architects Journal. 1893, monthly, membership/subscription. Royal Institute of British Architects, 66 Portland Place, London, W1N 4 AD, England.

Society of Architectural Historians, Room 716, 1700 Walnut Street, Philadelphia, Pennsylvania 19103. Founded in 1940 for architects, city planners, educators, etc., interested in architecture and the preservation of buildings of historical and aesthetic significance. It sponsors tours of the United States and Europe, and publishes a *Journal of the Society of Architectural Historians* (cited above) and a *Newsletter of the Society of Architectural Historians* (cited above).

Archeology

Bass, George F. *Archaeology Under Water.* Harmondsworth: Penguin Books, 1970. 183 pp., illus., maps, bibliog., index, paper. ◆ Also available in hard-cover, New York, Praeger, 1966. 224 pp., illus., maps, bibliog.

Brew, J. O. "Salvage Archaeology and History Preservation," American Council of Learned Societies *Newsletter,* 20:4 (May 1969). Reprinted in *Museum News,* 48:2 (October

1969), pp. 20-26. ◆ Discusses the survey and excavation on sites and areas endangered by technological development, and a brief history of salvage archaeology.

Clarke, David L. *Analytical Archaeology.* London: Methuen (distr. in U.S. by Barnes & Noble, Division of Harper & Row), 1968. 684 pp., illus., bibliog., maps.

Committee for the Recovery of Archaeological Remains. *The Inter-Agency Archaeological Salvage Program After Twelve Years.* Columbus, Mo.: University of Missouri, 1958. 24 pp., illus.

Conference on Historic Site Archaeology. *Papers.* Vol. 1–, May 1967–. Edited by Stanley South. Raleigh N.C.: The Conference, 1967–. Seven volumes to date, paper.

Conference on Underwater Archaeology, St. Paul, 1963. *Diving Into the Past: Theories, Techniques, and Application of Underwater Archaeology.* The proceedings of a Conference on Underwater Archaeology, sponsored by the Minnesota Historical Society, St. Paul, April 26-27, 1963. Edited by June D. Holmquist and Ardis H. Wheeler. St. Paul: Minnesota Historical Society, 1964. 111 pp., photos, drawings, diagrams, bibliog., index. ◆ A pioneer work on techniques, legal ramifications, and problems of underwater archaeology. Includes sections on historic research and identification and conservation of artifacts, and an extensive bibliography.

Cotter, John L., comp. *Handbook for Historical Archaeology—Part I.* Philadelphia, Pa.: The Author, 1968. 75 pp., illus., bibliog.

Deetz, James. *Invitation to Archaeology.* Garden City, N.Y.: Natural History Press for the American Museum of Natural History, 1967. 150 pp., illus., bibliog., paper.

"The First Practical Application of the Subterrene." Reprinted from *The Atom,* May 1973. 4 pp., photos. ◆ Describes an experimental program with archeological ruins at a National Park Service site conducted by the Los Alamos Scientific Laboratory of the University of California at Los Alamos, New Mexico.

Hammond, Philip C. *Archaeological Techniques for Amateurs.* Princeton, N.J.: Van Nostrand, 1963. 329 pp., drawings, diagrams, forms, bibliog., index.

Heizer, Robert F., ed. *The Archaeologist at Work: A Source Book in Archaeological Method and Interpretation.* New York: Harper & Row, Publishers, 1959. 520 pp., photos, drawings, diagrams, charts, graphs, maps, bibliog., index.

Heizer, Robert F., ed. *A Guide to Archaeological Field Methods.* 3rd rev. ed. Palo Alto, Calif.: National Press Books, c1958, 1966. 162 pp., photos, drawings, diagrams, charts, forms, maps, bibliog., index, paper.

Heizer, Robert F., and John A. Graham, eds. *A Guide to Field Methods in Archaeology: Approaches to the Anthropology of the Dead.* New rev. ed. Palo Alto, Calif.: National Press Books, 1967. 274 pp., illus., bibliog.

Hulan, Richard, and Stephen S. Laurence. *A Guide to the Reading and Study of Historic Site Archaeology.* Museum Brief no. 5. Columbia, Mo.: Published for the Conference on Historic Site Archaeology by the Museum of Anthropology, University of Missouri, 1970. 127 pp., paper. ◆ Bibliography, with editorial comment in the introduction to each chapter, of the best and most authoritative books and articles on historical archaeology available to the general reader, the student, and the professional.

International Museum Office. *Manual on the Technique of Archaeological Excavation.* Paris: The Office, 1940. 231 pp., illus.

Kenyon, Kathleen M. *Beginning in Archaeology.* Rev. ed., with sections on American archaeology by Saul D. and Gladys D. Weinberg. New York: Frederick A. Praeger, c1961, 1966. 228 pp., photos, diagrams, charts, bibliog., index, paper.

McGimsey, Charles R., III. *Public Archeology.* Studies in Archeology. New York: Seminar Press, 1972. 265 pp. ◆ A guide to encouraging and enlisting support for archeology programs, techniques for insuring legislative protection of endangered sites, and legal bases that characterize current state and federal archeological programs. It also describes financial support and administrative arrangement for programs.

McGimsey, Charles R., III; Hester A. Davis; and Carl Chapman. *These Are the Stewards of the Past.* Columbia, Mo.: University of Missouri, Extension Division, 1970. 23 pp., photos. ◆ Issued by the Steering Committee of the Mississippi Alluvial Valley Archaeological Program, it includes a directory of state archeologists and anthropologists and agencies that can assist.

New York (State) University. State Education Department. Office of State History. *Diving Into History: A Manual of Underwater Archeology for Divers in New York State.* By Paul J. Scudiere. Albany, N.Y.: The University, 1969. 33 pp., photos, drawings, diagrams, bibliog., paper.

Noel Hume, Ivor. *A Guide to Artifacts of Colonial America.* 1st ed. New York: Alfred A. Knopf, 1970. 323 pp., illus., bibliog.

Noel Hume, Ivor. *Historical Archaeology.* New York: Alfred A. Knopf, 1969. 335 pp., photos, diagrams, charts, bibliog. ◆ A comprehensive guide for amateurs and professionals to the techniques and methods of excavating historical sites. The book treats preparation for digging, how to proceed, different types of sites, recording and presenting the story, treatment, study and storage.

Peterson, Mendel. *History Under the Sea: A Manual for Underwater Exploration.* Rev. ed. Washington, D.C.: Smithsonian Institution Press, 1969. 208 pp., illus., maps, bibliog. ◆ A handbook on underwater archaeology with a section devoted to the problems and solutions of conserving materials from a marine environment.

Petsche, Jerome. *Bibliography of Salvage Archaeology in the United States.* With a foreword by Joan M. Brew. Publications in Salvage Archaeology no. 10. Lincoln, Neb.: 1968. 168 pp. ◆ Projects are part of the River Basin Surveys program of the Museum of Natural History, Smithsonian Institution. The bibliography is available from the Missouri Basin Project, Smithsonian Institution, 1835 P Street, Lincoln, Nebraska 68508.

Place, Robin. *Down to Earth: A Practical Guide to Archaeology.* New York: Philosophical Library, c1954, 1955. 173 pp., illus.

Place, Robin. *Introduction to Archaeology.* New York: Philosophical Library, 1968. 168 pp., photos, drawings, diagrams, charts, bibliog. references, index.

"The Problems with Preservation." Reprinted from *The Atom,* January-February 1973. 6 pp., photos. ◆ Describes the subterrene program at National Park Service sites and other ruins stabilization proposals. Reprinted by the Los Alamos Scientific Laboratory, University of California, Los Alamos, New Mexico 87544.

Rackl, Hanns-Wolf. *Diving Into the Past: Archaeology Under Water.* Translated by Ronald J. Floyd. New York: Charles Scribner's Sons, 1968. 292 pp., photos, drawings, diagrams, maps, bibliog., index, paper.

"Symposium on Salvage," *Archaeology,* 14:4 (Winter 1961), special issue.

United Nations Educational, Scientific and Cultural Organization. *Field Manual for Museums.* Museums and Monuments no. XII. Paris: UNESCO, 1970. 171 pp., photos, diagrams, drawings, forms, bibliogs., paper.

United Nations Educational, Scientific and Cultural Organization. *Underwater Archaeology: A Nascent Discipline.* Museums and Monuments no. XIII. Paris: UNESCO, 1971. 340 pp., figures, illus., maps.

Webster, Graham. *Practical Archaeology: An Introduction to Archaeological Fieldwork and Excavation.* London: Adam & Charles Black, 1963. 176 pp., photos, drawings, index, bibliog. footnotes.

Wheeler, Sir Robert E.M. *Archaeology From the Earth.* Baltimore: Penguin Books, Inc., 1961. 252 pp., illus., maps, tables, bibliog., paper. ◆ Contains information on the interlocking role between the archaeologist and conservator, setting up a lab in the field, and the equipment and supplies needed, plus specific methods for treating material.

Williams, R. E., and J. E. Griggs. *Use of the Rock-Melting Subterrene for Formation of Drainage Holes in Archaeological Sites.* Informal Report No. LA-5370-MS. Los Alamos, N.M.: Los Alamos Scientific Laboratory of the University of California, 1973. 8 pp., photos, diagrams. ◆ Reports on the technique of boring holes in the earth to drain water from archeological ruins. The experimental subterrene program was conducted at two National Park Service sites in New Mexico and was sponsored by the National Science Foundation.

Woodall, J. Ned. *An Introduction to Modern Archaeology.* Cambridge, Mass.: Schenkman Publishing Co., 1972. 96 pp., bibliog., paper.

Yale University, Institute of Human Relations. *Outline of Cultural Materials.* By George P. Murdock and others. Behavior Sciences Outlines, Vol. 1. 3rd rev. ed. New Haven, Conn.: Human Relations Area Files, 1950. 162 pp., paper.

NOTES AND PERIODICALS

American Antiquity. 1935, quarterly, membership. Society for American Archaeology, 1703 New Hampshire Avenue, N.W., Washington, D.C. 20009.

American Journal of Archaeology. 1885, quarterly, subscription. Archaeological Institute of America, 260 W. Broadway, New York, New York 10013.

Archaeological Institute of America, 260 W. Broadway, New York, New York 10013. Founded in 1879 as a scientific society of archaeologists and others interested in archaeological study and research. It founded five schools of archaeology: American School of Classical Studies in Athens (1881), School of Classical Studies of the American Academy in Rome (1895); American Schools of Oriental Research, Jerusalem (1900), and Baghdad (1921); School of American Research (1907), headquartered in Santa Fe, New Mexico. It publishes *Archaeology* (cited below); *American Journal of Archaeology* (cited above); *Monographs,* irregular; and *Bulletin,* annual.

Archaeology. 1948, quarterly, subscription. Archaeological Institute of America, 260 W. Broadway, New York, New York 10013.

Conference on Historic Site Archaeology, Stanley South, Chairman, The Institute of Archeology and Anthropology, University of South Carolina, Columbia, South Carolina 29208. The Conference was organized in 1959 to present papers emphasizing artifact analysis. Since 1960 the papers presented at the annual Conference have been published with participants being urged to emphasize analysis and synthesis in their presentations. Members of the Conference are eligible to submit a manuscript for judging for the John M. Goggin Award for method and theory in historical archaeology. Membership in the Conference is open to archaeologists, historians, architects, students, and others interested in historical archaeology. It publishes *Papers,* annually.

Historical Archaeology. 1967, annual, membership. Society for Historical Archaeology, Roderick Sprague, Secretary-Treasurer, Department of Sociology/Anthropology, University of Idaho, Moscow, Idaho 83843.

Man in the Northeast. 1971, semiannual, subscription. Man in the Northeast, Inc., Howard R. Sargent, Editor, Box 589, Center Harbor, New Hampshire 03226.

Society for American Archaeology, 1703 New Hampshire Avenue, N.W., Washington, D.C. 20009. Founded in 1935 for the purpose of stimulating scientific research in the achaeology of the New World by creating closer professional relations among archaeologists. Membership is open to professionals, nonprofessionals, and students interested in archaeology. It publishes *American Antiquity* (cited above); *Memoirs,* irregular; *Archives of Archaeology,* irregular; and *Abstracts of New World Archaeology.*

Society for Historical Archaeology, Mackinac Island State Park Commission, Stevens T. Mason Building, Lansing, Michigan 48926. Founded in 1967 to bring together persons interested in scholarship on specific historic sites, as well as the development of generalizations concerning historical periods and cultural dynamics. The main focus is the era since the beginning of the exploration of the non-European world by Europeans. It publishes *Newsletter,* quarterly; *Historical Archeology* (cited above).

Industrial Archeology

American Society of Civil Engineers. Committee on History and Heritage of American Civil Engineers. *A Biographical Dictionary of American Civil Engineers.* ASCE Historical Publication no. 2. New York: 1972.163 pp. ♦ Collection of brief biographies of American civil engineers; an important reference work.

Bracegirdle, Brian. *The Archaeology of the Industrial Revolution.* London: Heinemann, 1973. 207 pp., photos. ♦ Covers the entire range of structures that could be included under industrial archeology, and includes explanations of industrial processes.

Cossons, Neil, ed. *Industrial Archaeologist's Guide, 1971-73.* Edited by Neil Cossons and Kenneth Hudson. New York: Fernhill House, Ltd., c1971, 1972. 201 pp., photos, drawings, diagrams, maps, charts, bibliog., list of addresses.

Crosby, Theo. *The Necessary Monument: Its Future in the Civilized City.* Greenwich, Conn.: New York Graphic Society, Ltd., 1970. 128 pp., prints, diagrams, photos, bibliog., appendices. ♦ Discusses three architectural monuments: Paris Opera, Tower Bridge, and Pennsylvania Station.

Ferguson, Eugene S. *Bibliography of the History of Technology.* Cambridge, Mass.: The

70

Society for the History of Technology, 1968. 347 pp., ♦ The basic bibliography on the history of technology.

Giedion, Siegfried. *Mechanization Takes Command: A Contribution to Anonymous History.* 1948. Reprint. New York: W. W. Norton & Co., 1969. 743 pp., photos, prints, diagrams, bibliog. footnotes, index, paper. ♦ Basic work on the effects of industrialization, especially as it relates to the development of mechanical systems in buildings.

Gies, Joseph. *Bridges and Men.* New York: Grosset & Dunlap, c1963, 1966. 343 pp., photos, prints, diagrams, bibliog., appendix, index, paper. ♦ A basic nonscholarly history of bridges.

Harris, Robert. *Canals and Their Architecture.* New York: Frederick A. Praeger, Inc., 1969. 223 pp., photos, drawings, appendices, bibliog., maps, index. ♦ Well illustrated with mostly English examples.

Hindle, Brooke. *Technology in Early America: Needs and Opportunities for Study.* With a directory of artifact collections by Lucius Ellsworth. Chapel Hill, N.C.: University of North Carolina Press for the Institute of Early American Culture at Williamsburg, Va., 1966. 145 pp., directory, bibliog. footnotes, index, paper. ♦ An interpretive essay and extensive bibliography surveying the chronology and characteristics of American technology before 1850.

Historic American Buildings Survey. *The New England Textile Mill Survey: Selections from the Historic American Buildings Survey Number Eleven.* Edited by Ted Sande. Washington, D.C.: HABS, Division of Historic Architecture, Office of Archeology and Historic Preservation, 1971. 176 pp., photos, drawings, charts, maps, case studies, bibliog., paper. ♦ Limited edition, now out of print.

Hudson, Kenneth. *A Guide to the Industrial Archaeology of Europe.* 1st Amer. ed. Madison, N.J.: Fairleigh Dickinson University Press, 1971. 186 pp., plates, illus.

Hudson, Kenneth. *Handbook for Industrial Archaeologists: A Guide to Fieldwork and Research.* New York: Fernhill House, Ltd., 1967. 84 pp., photos, diagrams, drawings, bibliog.

Hudson, Kenneth. *Industrial Archaeology: An Introduction.* 2nd rev. ed. New York: Fernhill House, Ltd., c1963, 1966. 184 pp., photos, bibliog., gazetteer, index.

Jacobs, David, and Anthony E. Neville. *Bridges, Canals and Tunnels: The Engineering Conquest of America.* New York: American Heritage Publishing Co., Inc. (distr. by Van Nostrand), 1968. 159 pp., plates, photos, prints, diagrams, maps, appendix, bibliog., index. ♦ Well illustrated history of American civil engineering by topics.

Klingender, Francis Donald. *Art and the Industrial Revolution.* Rev. and ext. ed.; edited and revised by Arthur Elton. London: Evelyn Adams & Mackay, 1968. 222 pp., illus., bibliog. references.

Pannell, John Percival Masterman. *The Techniques of Industrial Archaeology: The Industrial Archaeology of the British Isles.* Clifton, N.J.: Augustus M. Kelley, Publisher, 1967. 191 pp., plates, maps, diagrams, plans, bibliog.

Reynolds, John. *Windmills and Watermills.* New York: Praeger Publishers, 1970. 196 pp., bibliog., glossary, illus. ♦ Basic description of mill types and construction with many illustrations including isometric drawings.

Richards, James Maude. *The Functional Tradition in Early Industrial Buildings.* London: The Architectural Press, 1958. 200 pp., illus.

Rix, Michael. *Industrial Archaeology.* General Series no. 65. London: The Historical Association, 1967. 25 pp., photos, diagrams, bibliog., paper.

Smith, Norman Alfred Fisher. *Victorian Technology and Its Preservation in Modern Britain: A Report Submitted to the Leverhulme Trust.* Leicester: Leicester University Press, 1970. 74 pp., appendices, paper. ♦ Also available from Humanities Press, New York.

Straub, Hans. *A History of Civil Engineering: An Outline from Ancient to Modern Times.* English translation by Erwin Rockwell. Cambridge, Mass.: M.I.T. Press, 1964. 258 pp., chronological table, illus., bibliog., paper. ♦ A basic history.

Tyler, John D. "Industrial Archaeology and the Museum Curator," *Museum News,* 47:5 (January 1969), pp. 30-32.

Vogel, Robert M. "Industrial Archaeology—A Continuous Past," *Historic Preservation,* 19:2 (April-June 1967), pp. 68-75.

Vogel, Robert M., ed. *A Report of the Mohawk-Hudson Area Survey: A Selective Recording Survey of the Industrial Archeology of the Mohawk and Hudson River Valleys in the Vicinity of Troy, New York, June-September 1969.* Conducted by Historic American Engineering Record. Smithsonian Studies in History and Technology no. 26. Washington, D.C.: Smithsonian Institution Press, 1973. 210 pp., photos, drawings, appendix.

Zimiles, Murray, and Martha Zimiles. *Early American Mills.* New York: Clarkson N. Potter, Inc., 1973. 290 pp., illus.

NOTES AND PERIODICALS

Industrial Archaeology: The Journal of the History of Industry and Technology. 1964, quarterly, subscription. Dr. John Butt, Editor, University of Strathclyde, Department of History, McCarie Building, Richmond Street, Glasgow C.1, Scotland. ◆ Formerly the *Journal of Industrial Archaeology.* Issues of journal, vols. 1966-68, published in hardbound form by Augustus M. Kelley, 1968. The publication carries an annual review of literature on industrial archaeology and industrial history.

Society for Industrial Archeology, Vance Packard, Treasurer, William Penn Memorial Museum, Pennsylvania Historical and Museum Commission, P.O. Box 1026, Harrisburg, Pennsylvania 17108. Formed in 1971 to promote the study of the physical remains of North America's industrial and technological heritage by encouraging field investigations, recording, and research, and to disseminate and assist in the exchange of information on aspects of industrial archeology through publications, meetings, and by other means. Membership is open to all who have an interest in the field. Publications include Society for Industrial Archeology *Newsletter* (cited below), and *Occasional Publications,* begun in April 1973. In 1972 the Society extracted and distributed a compilation of places related to its interests that were listed on the Advisory List to the National Register of Historic Places in order to encourage the preservation of industrial sites.

Society for Industrial Archeology *Newsletter.* 1972, bimonthly, membership. Robert M. Vogel, Editor, Society for Industrial Archeology, Room 5020, National Museum of History and Technology, Smithsonian Institution, Washington, D.C. 20560.

Surveys and Manuals

Survey Manuals

Alabama Historical Commission, Survey Committee. *How to Conduct a Survey of His-*toric Buildings and Sites. Montgomery, Ala.: The Commission, 1968. 8 pp., drawings, diagrams.

Bowyer, Jack. *Guide to Domestic Building Surveys.* 2nd ed. London: The Architectural Press, 1972. 174 pp., technical drawings, photos, bibliog. ◆ How to conduct a survey and what to look for in recording buildings.

Brown, Theodore M. "The Importance and Use of Surveys," *Historic Preservation,* 15:4 (1963), pp. 126-129.

Cole, Margaret van Barneveld. *The Urban Aesthetic: Evolution of a Survey System.* St. Louis?: 1960. 130 pp., illus. ◆ Illustration and verification of a study on identification of values in city designs with a four-block sample survey in San Francisco.

Council of Europe. Council for Cultural Cooperation. *Criteria and Methods for a Protective Inventory: Preservation and Development of Groups and Areas of Buildings of Historical or Artistic Interest.* Symposium A, Barcelona, 17-19 May 1965; Report. Strasbourg (?): 1965. 49 pp., mimeo.

"Criteria for Inventorying Scenic Highways and Parkways," *Historic Preservation,* 17:4 (July-August 1965), pp. 136-137.

Fazio, Michael W., and Clyde Patterson. *A Landmark Survey Methodology: Lisbon, Ohio, May, 1971.* Kent, O.: Ohio Arts Council and Kent State University, 1971. 16 pp., photos, drawings, maps, bibliog., forms, paper.

Feiss, Carl. "Survey, Evaluation and Registration." In *Historic Preservation Tomorrow: Revised Principles and Guidelines for Historic Preservation in the United States, Second Workshop, Williamsburg, Virginia* (Williamsburg, Va.: National Trust for Historic Preservation and Colonial Williamsburg, 1967), pp. 7-14.

Hale, Richard W. "Points to Consider in Surveying." In *Historic Preservation Tomorrow: Revised Principles and Guidelines for Historic Preservation in the United States, Second Workshop, Williamsburg, Virginia* (Williamsburg, Va.: National Trust for Historic Preservation and Colonial Williamsburg, 1967), Appendix, pp. 37-38.

Historic American Buildings Survey. *Recording Historic Buildings: The Historic American Buildings Survey.* Compiled by Harley J. McKee. Washington, D.C.: U. S. National Park Service, 1970. 165 pp., photos, drawings, diagrams, tables, bibliog. ◆ The basic text on techniques for recording buildings by drawing, photography, and documentation.

Jacobs, Stephen W. "Stable Values in a Changing World: Historic Preservation in City Planning and Urban Renewal." Reprinted from *Journal of Architectural Education*, 15:1 (Spring 1960), pp. 7-14. 24 pp. ◆ Discusses the role of surveys.

McKee, Harley J., comp. *Amateur's Guide to Terms Commonly Used in Describing Historic Buildings Following the Order Used by the Historic American Buildings Survey.* Rev. and enl. ed. for the New York State Historical Association 23rd Annual Seminars on American Culture, June 28-July 11, 1970. Rochester: The Landmarks Society of Western New York, c1967, 1970. 14 pp., drawings.

Maryland Historical Trust. *MHT Worksheet for National Register Nominations: Instructions and Samples.* MHT Guides to Historic Preservation Activity no. 2. Annapolis, Md.: The Trust, n.d. 22 pp., paper.

Maryland Historical Trust. *Photographing Historic Landmarks.* MHT Guides to Historic Preservation Activity no. 1. Annapolis, Md.: The Trust, n.d. 6 pp., paper.

Maryland Historical Trust. *Researching Maryland Buildings.* MHT Guides to Historic Preservation Activity no. 3. Annapolis, Md.; The Trust, n.d. 15 pp., paper.

Massachusetts. Historical Commission. *Guide to Inventory Techniques.* Boston: The Commission, 1970. 22 pp., drawings, maps, forms, appendix.

Massachusetts. Historical Commission. *Procedures Manual for an Inventory of the Historical Assets of the Commonwealth, Part I: Sites and Structures.* Boston: The Commission, 1966. 15 pp., photos, drawings, forms, map, bibliog., paper. ◆ Part II not published.

Massachusetts. Historical Commission. *Procedures Manual for an Inventory of the Historical Assets of the Commonwealth, Part III: Burial Grounds.* Boston: The Commission, 1968. 8 pp., photos, drawings, forms, bibliog., paper.

Massey, James C. *The Architectural Survey.* Washington, D.C.: National Trust for Historic Preservation, n.d. 19 pp., photos, drawings, form, bibliog., leaflet. ◆ Brief version published in *Historic Preservation,* 16:6 (November-December 1964), pp. 216-219.

Massey, James C. *How to Organize an Architectural Survey.* Washington, D.C.: National Trust for Historic Preservation, n.d. 7 pp., bibliog., leaflet. ◆ Prepared for the Preservation for the Bicentennial kit.

Massey, James C. "Preservation Through Documentation," *Historic Preservation,* 18:4 (July-August 1966), pp. 148-151. ◆ Program of recording buildings by the Historic American Buildings Survey.

Miner, Ralph W. "Historic Building Evaluation Checklist"; "Historic Area Evaluation Checklist." In *Conservation of Historic and Cultural Resources* (Chicago: American Society of Planning Officials, 1968), Appendices A and B.

Miner, Ralph W. "Preliminary Survey"; "Comprehensive Inventory and Evaluation"; and "Area Analysis." In *Conservation of Historic and Cultural Resources* (Chicago: American Society of Planning Officials, 1968), pp. 16-22.

Mitchell, William R., Jr. *Handbook for Historic Preservation in Georgia: A Guide for Volunteers.* Atlanta, Ga.: Georgia Historical Commission, 1971. 34 pp., photo, print, forms, bibliog., paper.

Morton, Terry Brust. "The Published Architectural Survey," *Historic Preservation,* 16:3 (1964), pp. 102-107.

National Trust for Historic Preservation. *How to Evaluate Historic Sites and Buildings.* A report by the Committee on Standards and Surveys. Rev. ed. Washington, D.C.: The Trust, 1971. 2 pp., leaflet. ◆ The basic statement on criteria in the field.

New York (State). Office of Parks and Recreation, Division for Historic Preservation. *Historic Resources Survey Manual.* Rev. ed. Albany, N.Y.: The Division, 1974. 76 pp., photos, drawings, maps, bibliog., paper. ◆ Model manual designed to be used by volunteer groups or individuals. Methods of organizing local survey teams and the components of surveys are described.

Roberts, H.V. Molesworth. "Recording Dates of Buildings," *Journal of the Society of Architectural Historians,* 12:3 (October 1953), pp. 23-26. ◆ Discusses the pitfalls of supposedly "factual" dates and indicates methods of proper recording.

Sykes, Meredith, and Ann Falkner. *Canadian Inventory of Historic Building: Training Manual.* 2nd ed. Ottawa, Canada: National Sites Service, National and Historic Parks Branch, Department of Indian Affairs and Northern Development, 1971. 57 pp., drawings, diagrams, glossary, paper. ♦ Description of how to interpret the inventory forms.

U.S. Office of Archeology and Historic Preservation. *How to Complete National Register Forms.* Washington, D.C.: National Park Service, National Register of Historic Places, September 1972. 64 pp., appendices, paper. ♦ Explanations of the purpose and criteria of the National Register, nomination procedures, and processing nominations are given. Instructions for completing the forms are covered in detail, and the appendices include sample forms, copies of the laws relating to the National Register, and the State Preservation Officers list.

Surveys and Inventories

Historic American Buildings Survey. *Catalog of the Measured Drawings and Photographs of the Survey in the Library of Congress, March 1, 1941.* Bibliography and Reference Series No. 416. New York: Burt Franklin, Publisher, c1941, 1971. 470 pp. ♦ Also available from National Technical Information Service, 5285 Port Royal Road, Springfield, Va. 22151.

Historic American Buildings Survey. *Catalog of the Measured Drawings and Photographs of the Survey in the Library of Congress, Comprising Additions Since March 1, 1941.* Washington, D.C.: National Park Service, 1959, 1968. Unpaged, photos, drawings, diagrams, paper. ♦ Also available from National Technical Information Service (address above).

Historic American Buildings Survey. *A Check List of Subjects: Additions to Survey Material Deposited in the Library of Congress Since Publication of the HABS Supplement January 1950-January 1963.* Washington, D.C.: National Park Service, Division of Architecture, Historic American Buildings Survey, 1963. 32 pp., mimeo.

Historic American Buildings Survey. *The New England Textile Mill Survey: Selections From the Historic American Buildings Survey Number Eleven.* ♦ Edited by Ted Sande. Washington, D.C.: HABS, Division of Historic Architecture, Office of Archeology and Historic Preservation, 1971. 176 pp., photos, drawings, charts, maps, case studies, bibliogs., paper. ♦ Limited edition, now out of print.

The National Register of Historic Places, 1972. 2nd ed. Washington, D.C.: National Park Service, 1973. 603 pp., illus. ♦ The official schedule of the nation's cultural property —national, state, and local—worth saving. The current edition lists over 3,500 buildings, structures, objects, sites, and districts.

Sarles, Frank B., and Charles E. Shedd. *Colonials and Patriots: Historic Places Commemorating Our Forebears, 1700-1783.* National Survey of Historic Sites and Buildings, vol. 6. Washington, D.C.: U.S. Department of the Interior, National Park Service, 1964. 286 pp., photos, prints, maps, bibliog., index.

U.S. National Park Service. *Advisory List to the National Register of Historic Places, 1969.* Washington, D.C.: U.S. Government Printing Office, 1970. 311 pp., paper.

U. S. National Park Service. *Areas Administered by the National Park Service and Related Properties as of January 1, 1970.* Washington, D.C.: U.S. Government Printing Office, 1970. 140 pp., charts, paper.

U.S. National Park Service. *Explorers and Settlers: Historic Places Commemorating the Early Exploration and Settlement of the United States.* National Survey of Historic Sites and Buildings, vol. 5. Washington, D.C.: For sale by the Superintendent of Documents, U.S. Government Printing Office, 1968. 506 pp., photos, prints, maps, bibliog., index. ♦ Also available from Finch Press, Ann Arbor, Michigan.

U.S. National Park Service. *Founders and Frontiersmen: Historic Places Commemorating Early Nationhood and the Westward Movement, 1783-1828.* National Survey of Historic Sites and Buildings, vol. 7. Washington, D.C.: For sale by the Superintendent of Documents, U.S. Government Printing Office, 1967. 410 pp., photos, prints, maps, bibliog., index. ♦ Also available from Finch Press, Ann Arbor, Michigan.

U.S. National Park Service. *Prospector, Cowhand, and Sodbuster: Historic Places Associated with the Mining, Ranching, and Farming Frontiers in the Trans-Mississippi West.* National Survey of Historic Sites and Buildings, vol. 11. Washington, D.C.: For sale by the Superintendent of Documents, U.S. Government Printing Office, 1967. 320 pp., photos, prints, maps, bibliog., index. ◆ Also available from Finch Press, Ann Arbor, Michigan.

U.S. National Park Service. *Soldier and Brave: Historic Places Associated with Indian Affairs and the Indian Wars in the Trans-Mississippi West.* New ed. National Survey of Historic Sites and Buildings, vol. 12. Washington, D.C.: U. S. Government Printing Office, 1971. 453 pp., photos, prints, maps, bibliog., index.

CALIFORNIA

American Institute of Architects, Northern California Chapter. *Historic California: Sonoma-Benicia.* Prepared by the American Institute of Architects, Northern California Chapter; the East Bay Chapter, the Society of Architectural Historians P.S.; and the California Heritage Council. San Francisco?: n.p., 1960. 21 pp., illus.

American Institute of Architects. San Diego Chapter. *A.I.A. Guide to San Diego.* San Diego, Calif.: American Institute of Architects, n.d. Folder, photos, maps, index.

California. Department of Parks and Recreation. *California Historical Landmarks.* Sacramento: 1972. 134 pp., illus., maps.

Gebhard, David; Roger Montgomery; Robert Winter; John Woodbridge; and Sally Woodbridge. *A Guide to Architecture in San Francisco and Northern California.* Santa Barbara, Calif.: Peregrine Smith, Inc., 1973. 557 pp., illus., maps, glossary, index, paper. Survey of California architecture from Big Sur to the Oregon border.

Gebhard, David, and Robert Winter. *A Guide to Architecture in Southern California.* Los Angeles, Calif.: Los Angeles County Museum of Art, 1965. 164 pp., plates, maps, bibliog., paper.

Monterey Savings and Loan Association, Monterey, California. *Monterey's Adobe Heritage.* Monterey, Calif.: 1965. 1 vol., unpaged, photos, drawings.

Olmsted, Roger R. *Here Today: San Francisco's Architectural Heritage.* San Francisco: Chronicle Books, 1968. 334 pp., illus., maps. ◆ An historic sites project of the Junior League of San Francisco, Inc., with text by Roger R. Olmsted and T.H. Watkins.

Smith, Gerald A.; L. Burr Belden; and Arda M. Haenszel. "San Bernardino County Registered State Historical Landmarks," *San Bernardino County Museum Association Quarterly,* XVII:1 (Fall 1972), entire issue. 74 pp.

Western Heritage, Inc. *Old Sacramento: Inventory of Historical Buildings.* Prepared by Western Heritage, Inc. for State of California, Resources Agency, Department of Parks and Recreation, Division of Beaches and Parks. Historical Report No. 2. Sacramento: 1962. 62 pp., illus., paper.

Woodbridge, John Marshall, comp. *Buildings of the Bay Area: A Guide to Architecture of the San Francisco Bay Region.* Compiled by John Marshall Woodbridge and Sally Byrne Woodbridge. New York: Grove Press, 1960. 1 vol. unpaged, drawings, illus., maps.

COLORADO

Jackson, Olga. *Architecture: Colorado.* Edited by George Thorson. Denver, Colo.: Colorado Chapter of the American Institute of Architects, 1966. 96 pp., illus.

CONNECTICUT

Historic American Buildings Survey. *New Haven Architecture.* Selections no. 9. Washington, D.C.: National Park Service, 1970. 159 pp., illus., maps, plans, bibliog., o.p.

DELAWARE

Eberlein, Harold Donaldson. *Historic Houses and Buildings of Delaware.* 2nd ed. By Harold Donaldson Eberlein and Cortlandt Van Dyke Hubbard. Dover, Del.: Public Archives Commission, c1962, 1963? 227 pp., illus., maps, plans.

DISTRICT OF COLUMBIA

Eberlein, Harold Donaldson. *Historic Houses of George-Town and Washington City.* By Harold Donaldson Eberlein and Cortlandt Van Dyke Hubbard. Richmond, Va.: Dietz Press, 1958. 480 pp., illus., map, bibliog.

Historic American Buildings Survey. *District of Columbia Catalog: A List of Measured Drawings, Photographs, and Written Documentation in the Survey.* Edited by Nancy K. Beinke. Washington, D.C.: Historic American Buildings Survey, Office of Archeology and Historic Preservation, National Park Service, 1968. 47 pp., illus., o.p.

Historic American Buildings Survey. *Washington, D.C. Architecture–Market Square.* Selections from the Historic American Buildings Survey no. 8. Washington, D.C.: National Park Service, 1969. 151 pp., illus., o.p.

Jacobsen, Hugh Newell, ed. *A Guide to the Architecture of Washington, D.C.* New York: Published for the Washington Chapter, American Institute of Architects by Frederick A. Praeger, Publishers, 1965. 212 pp., photos, prints, maps, index, paper. ◆ Revised edition in preparation.

U. S. Congress. House. Committee on the District of Columbia. *Registration of Historic Landmarks in the District of Columbia; Report to Accompany H.R. 10939, August 25, 1967.* Ninetieth Congress, first session, House of Representatives Report no. 612. Washington, D.C.: U. S. Government Printing Office, 1967. 18 pp.

U. S. National Capital Planning Commission. *Downtown Urban Renewal Area Landmarks, Washington, D.C.* Prepared by the National Capital Planning Commission in cooperation with the District of Columbia Redevelopment Land Agency. Washington, D.C.: U. S. Government Printing Office, 1970. 118 pp., illus., plans, maps, bibliog., paper.

FLORIDA

American Institute of Architects. Florida South Chapter. *A Guide to the Architecture of Miami.* Miami, Fla.: c1963. 64 pp., illus.

Newton, Earle Williams, ed. *Historic Architecture of Pensacola.* Pensacola, Fla.: Pensacola Historical, Restoration and Preservation Commission, 1969. 36 pp., illus., plans.

GEORGIA

Lower Savannah Regional Planning and Development Commission. *A Survey of Historical Sites in the Lower Savannah Region.* Aiken, S.C.: The Commission, 1971. 129 pp., photos, maps.

HAWAII

Historic Buildings Task Force. *Old Honolulu: A Guide to Oahu's Historic Buildings.* Honolulu: The Task Force, 1969 (i.e. 1970). 70 pp., illus., maps.

Maui Historical Society. *Lahaina Historical Guide: Describing the Landmarks of Its Days as Playground of the Alii, Capital of the*

Hawaiian Kingdom, Anchorage of the Pacific Whaling Fleet, Producer of Sugar and Pineapple. 2nd ed. Honolulu: Printed by the Star-Bulletin Printing Co., 1964. 53 pp., illus., map.

ILLINOIS

Historic American Buildings Survey. *Historic American Buildings Survey: Chicago and Nearby Illinois Areas, List of Measured Drawings, Photographs and Written Documentation in the Survey 1966.* Compiled and edited by the Historic American Buildings Survey, Eastern Office, Design and Construction, National Park Service, Department of the Interior. J. William Rudd, comp. Park Forest, Ill.: The Prairie School Press, 1966. 52 pp., photos, drawings, diagrams, index, paper.

Koeper, Frederick. *Illinois Architecture from Territorial Times to the Present: A Selective Guide.* Chicago: University of Chicago Press, 1968. 304 pp., illus., paper.

INDIANA

Historic American Buildings Survey. *Indiana Catalog: A List of Measured Drawings, Photographs, and Written Documentation in the Survey.* Compiled by William P. Thompson; edited by Nancy K. Beinke. Prelim. ed. Washington, D.C.: National Park Service, 1971. 54 pp., drawing, mimeo.

KANSAS

Kansas State Historical Society. *A Survey of Historic Sites and Structures in Kansas.* Topeka, Kans.: The Society, 1957. 66 pp., photos.

KENTUCKY

City-County Planning Commission (Lexington and Fayette Co., Ky.). *Historical Survey: Rural Settlements in Fayette County.* Lexington, Ky.: 1971. 12 pp., maps, bibliog.

Kentucky Heritage Commission. *Statewide Survey of Historic Sites: Commonwealth of Kentucky.* Frankfort, Ky.: The Commission, 1971. 432 pp., maps, appendices, forms, bibliog.

Old Louisville. Louisville, Ky.: University of Louisville, 1961. 68 pp., illus., map. ◆ Three parts cover the architecture, the people, and architectural conservation.

LOUISIANA

American Institute of Architects. New Orleans Chapter. Guide Book Committee. *A Guide to the Architecture of New Orleans, 1699-1959.* By Samuel Wilson, Jr., chairman. New York: Reinhold Publishing Corp., c1959. 76 pp., illus.

New Orleans Architecture. Text by Samuel Wilson, Jr., and Bernard Lemann. Compiled and edited by Mary Louise Christovich, Roulhac Toledano, and Betsy Swanson. Gretna, La.: Friends of the Cabildo (distr. by Pelican Publishing Co.), 1971- . ◆ First two of a five-part series: vol. 1—*The Lower Garden District* (1971), 160 pp., plates, photos, bibliog., index; vol. 2—*The American Sector* (1973), 243 pp., plates, photos, bibliog., inventory of architects, index.

MAINE

Greater Portland Landmarks. *Portland.* Portland, Me.: Greater Portland Landmarks, 1973. 236 pp., photos, glossary. ◆ History of the city's architecture and contributions made by its leading citizens.

MARYLAND

Historic American Buildings Survey. *Records of Historic Maryland Buildings.* Rev. ed. Washington, D.C.: National Park Service, 1969. 35 pp., mimeo.

MASSACHUSETTS

Boston Society of Architects. *Boston Architecture.* Produced and edited by Donald Freeman. Cambridge, Mass.: M.I.T. Press, 1970. 1 vol., unpaged, photos, diagrams, maps, bibliog., index, paper.

Cambridge, Mass. Historical Commission. *Survey of Architectural History in Cambridge:* Report 1—*East Cambridge* (1965); Report 2—*Mid-Cambridge* (1967); Report 3—*Cambridgeport* (1971); Report 4—*Old Cambridge* (1973). Boston: M.I.T. Press for Cambridge, Mass. Historical Commission, 1965- . Photos, prints, drawings, diagrams, maps, bibliog., paper. ◆ Report 1—o.p. Report 5—*Northwest Cambridge,* in preparation, last in the series.

Historic American Buildings Survey. *Massachusetts Catalog: List of Measured Drawings, Photographs, and Written Documentation in the Survey 1964.* John C. Poppeliers, ed. Boston: Massachusetts Historical Commission, 1965. 69 pp., photos, diagrams, index, paper, o.p.

Massachusetts. Bureau of Transportation Planning and Development. *Historic Sites Study: Report.* Developed with the Massachusetts Historical Commission, Massachusetts Department of Commerce and Development, et al., through the Eastern Massachusetts Regional Planning Project. Department of Public Works Publication no. 748. Boston: The Bureau, 1968. 40 pp., illus. ◆ Demonstration city, Boxford, Massachusetts.

Massachusetts. Historical Commission. *Massachusetts Historic Landmarks, 1970.* Boston: The Commission, 1970. 28 pp., photos, drawings, bibliog., paper. ◆ See also, 1972 supplement.

Massachusetts. Historical Commission. *Massachusetts Historic Landmarks, 1972 Supplement: Massachusetts Listings, National Landmarks, National Register of Historic Places.* Boston: The Commission, 1972. 15 pp., photos, paper.

Ramirez, Constance Werner. *The Historic Architecture and Urban Design of Nantucket.* Washington, D.C.: Circulated by Smithsonian Institution, 1970. 16 pp., illus., paper.

MICHIGAN

Detroit Architecture: A.I.A. Guide. Katherine Mattingly Meyer, ed. Prepared under the sponsorship of the American Institute of Architects, Detroit Chapter. Detroit: Wayne State University Press, 1971. 202 pp., illus., maps.

Historic American Buildings Survey. *Michigan: List of Measured Drawings, Photographs, and Documentation in the Survey of 1965, and Complete Listings of Michigan's HABS Records.* Harley J. McKee, comp. Lansing, Mich.: Historical Society of Michigan and Detroit Society of Architects, 1965. 65 pp., photos, bibliog. footnotes, o.p.

MINNESOTA

Dunn, David J. *Historic Sites in Olmsted County.* Rochester, Minn.: Olmsted County Historical Society, 1967. 45 pp., illus., map.

Koeper, H. F. *Historic St. Paul Buildings: A Report of the Historic Sites Committee, A Special Citizens Group Named by the St. Paul City*

Planning Board. St. Paul, Minn.: St. Paul City Planning Board, 1964. 116 pp., illus.

Minneapolis. Planning Commission. *Toward a New City: A Preliminary Report on Minneapolis' Urban Design Pilot Study.* A joint study by the Planning Commission, Minneapolis Chapter, American Institute of Architects, and the Minneapolis School of Arts, with the assistance of the Walker Art Center, the Minnesota Institute of Arts, and the University of Minnesota. Minneapolis, Minn.: Urban Design Study, Community Renewal Program, 1965. 1 vol., various pagings, illus. ◆ Chapter 4, Survey of Historic Buildings, part I.

MISSOURI

Franzwa, Gregory M. *The Story of Old Ste. Genevieve.* St. Louis, Mo.: Patrice Press, 1967. 169 pp., illus., maps, bibliog.

McCue, George. *The Building Art in St. Louis: Two Centuries, A Guide to the Architecture of the City and Its Environs.* Rev. and enl. ed. St. Louis, Mo.: St. Louis Chapter, American Institute of Architects, 1967. 104 pp., illus., maps, paper.

Missouri. State Historical Society. *Missouri Historic Sites Catalogue.* Edited by Dorothy J. Caldwell. Columbia, Mo.: 1963. 199 pp., illus., maps.

Perry, Milton F., et al., comp. *Mulkey Square, Kansas City, Missouri, 1869-1973: A Survey of the City's First Suburb.* Researched and compiled by Milton F. Perry, James Anthony Ryan, Gayle Eggen, and Patricia Hardy. Kansas City, Mo.: The Museums Council of Mid-America and the Junior League of Kansas City, Missouri, Inc., 1973. 42 pp., photos, drawings, paper.

NEBRASKA

Kolberg, Persijs, and Carl H. Jones. *A Survey of Historic, Architectural, and Archaeological Sites of the Eleven County Eastern Nebraska Urban Region.* Lincoln, Neb.: Nebraska Historical Society, 1971. 119 pp., illus.

Magie, John Q., and Carl H. Jones. *A History and Historic Sites Survey of Johnson, Nemaha, Pawnee, and Richardson Counties in Southeastern Nebraska.* Lincoln, Neb.: Nebraska State Historical Society, 1969. 158 pp., illus., maps, bibliog.

NEW HAMPSHIRE

Giffen, Daniel H. "Historic American Buildings Survey Catalog, Merrimack and Hillsborough Counties, New Hampshire," *Historical New Hampshire,* 22:3 (Autumn 1967), pp. 2-21.

"New Hampshire Catalogue, Historic American Buildings Survey, Records in the Library of Congress," *Historical New Hampshire,* 18:2 (October 1963), pp. 1-17.

Portsmouth, New Hampshire. Community Improvement Program. *An Exterior Architectural and Historical Survey of the South End of Portsmouth, New Hampshire.* Portsmouth, N.H.: The Program, 1972. 32 pp., photos, charts, maps, appendix, bibliog., mimeo.

Strawbery Banke, Inc., Portsmouth, N.H. *Strawbery Banke in Portsmouth, New Hampshire: Official Guidebook and Map.* 3rd rev. ed. Edited by Nancy R. Beck based on genealogical research by Dorothy M. Vaughn and Natalie L. Fenwick, and architectural research by James L. Garvin. Portsmouth, N.H.: c1966, 1971. 83 pp., photos, diagrams, map, bibliog.

NEW MEXICO

Historic Santa Fe Foundation. *Old Santa Fe Today.* 2nd ed., rev. and enl. Albuquerque, N.M.: University of New Mexico Press for the Historic Santa Fe Foundation, 1972. 79 pp., illus., paper.

NEW YORK

American Institute of Architects, New York Chapter. *AIA Guide to New York City.* Norval White and Elliot Willensky, eds. New York: The Macmillan Co., 1967. 464 pp., photos, prints, maps, indexes.

Bailey (Russell D.) and Associates, Utica, N.Y. *A Report on Historic Sites and Buildings in the Hudson River Valley.* Prepared for the Hudson River Valley Commission. Albany, N.Y.: 1965. 232 pp., photos, prints, drawings, maps, Register and Criteria for Historic Landmarks, paper.

Burnham, Alan, ed. *New York Landmarks: A Study and Index of Architecturally Notable Structures in Greater New York.* Middletown, Conn.: Published under the auspices of the

Municipal Art Society of New York by Wesleyan University Press, c1963, 1970. 430 pp., photos, bibliog., indexes.

Dutchess County Planning Board. *Landmarks of Dutchess County, 1683-1867: Architecture Worth Saving in New York State.* New York: New York State Council on the Arts, 1969. 242 pp., illus., maps.

Everest, Allan S. *Our North Country Heritage: Architecture Worth Saving in Clinton and Essex Counties.* Plattsburgh, N.Y.: Tundra Books, 1972. 143 pp., photos, maps, appendices, glossary, bibliog., paper.

Foerster, Bernd. *Architecture Worth Saving in Rensselaer County, New York.* Sponsored by the New York State Council on the Arts. Troy, N.Y.: Rensselaer Polytechnic Institute, 1965. 207 pp., photos, brief bibliog., paper.

Greene County Planning Department. *Environment and Scenic Resources*; and *Historic Building Supplement.* Hudson, N.Y.: Greene County Planning Board, 1971. 39, 24 pp., photos, maps, paper.

The Heritage of New York: Historic-Landmark Plaques of the New York Community Trust. New York: Fordham University Press, 1970. 402 pp., chiefly illus., maps. ♦ Supplement with maps, "Walking-guide to The Heritage of New York."

Historic American Buildings Survey. *New York City Architecture.* Its Selections no. 7. Washington, D.C.: 1969. 96 pp., illus., bibliog., o.p.

Historic Pittsford, Inc. *Architecture Worth Saving in Pittsford, Elegant Village.* Edited by Andrew D. Wolfe. Pittsford, N.Y.: Historic Pittsford, Inc., 1969. 1 vol., unpaged, illus.

Lancaster, Clay. *Old Brooklyn Heights: New York's First Suburb.* Including detailed analyses of 619 century-old houses. 1st ed. Rutland, Vt.: Charles E. Tuttle, 1961. 183 pp., photos, glossary, bibliog. notes, map.

Marcou, O'Leary & Associates, Inc. *Historic Cohoes, Cohoes, New York: A Survey of Historic Resources.* By Marcou, O'Leary & Associates, Inc., Washington, D.C., and Rensselaer Polytechnic Institute. Cohoes, N.Y.?: Marcou, O'Leary & Associates and Rensselaer Polytechnic Institute, 1971. 64 pp., photos, drawings, maps, appendices, bibliog.

Montillon, Eugene D. *Historic Architecture in Broome County, New York, and Vicinity.*

Binghamton, N.Y.: Broome County Planning Department and Broome County Historical Society, 1972. 140 pp., illus., maps.

New York (City). Landmarks Preservation Commission. *Greenwich Village Historic District Designation Report.* New York: The Commission, 1969. 2 vols., maps.

New York (State). Hudson River Valley Commission. *The Hudson: The Report of the Hudson River Valley Commission, 1966.* New York: :The Commission, 1966. 100 pp., photos, maps, drawings, diagrams, graphs, tables, appendices, paper.

New York (State). Office of Planning Coordination, The Metropolitan New York District Office. *Long Island Landmarks.* Albany, N.Y.: New York State Office of Planning Coordination, 1969. 122 pp., photos, maps, appendix, paper. ♦ Appendix—Architectural Landmark Evaluation and Index. Reprinted by the Society for the Preservation of Long Island Antiquities, 1971.

Prokopoff, Stephen S., and Joan C. Siegfried. *The Nineteenth-Century Architecture of Saratoga Springs: Architecture Worth Saving in New York State.* New York: New York State Council on the Arts, 1970. 104 pp., illus.

Rubenstein, Lewis., comp. *Historic Resources of the Hudson: A Preliminary Inventory, January, 1969.* Tarrytown, N.Y.: Hudson River Valley Commission, 1969. 96 pp., drawings, forms, maps, index, paper.

Syracuse University. School of Architecture. *Architecture Worth Saving in Onondaga County.* New York: New York State Council on the Arts, 1964. 202 pp., photos, drawings, diagrams, maps, paper.

Vogel, Robert M., ed. *A Report of the Mohawk-Hudson Area Survey: A Selective Recording Survey of the Industrial Archeology of the Mohawk and Hudson River Valleys in the Vicinity of Troy, New York, June-September 1969.* Conducted by Historic American Engineering Record. Smithsonian Studies in History and Technology no. 26. 210 pp., photos, drawings, appendix.

Wood and Stone: Landmarks of the Upper Mohawk Region. By Virginia B. Kelly, Merrilyn R. O'Connell, Stephen S. Olney, and Johanna R. Reig. Utica, N.Y.: Central New York Community Arts Council, 1972. 120 pp., photos, prints, drawings, maps, landmarks inventory, paper.

OHIO

American Institute of Architects. Cleveland Chapter. *Cleveland Architecture, 1796-1958.* New York: Reinhold Publishing Corp., 1958. 64 pp., illus.

Cincinnati. City Planning Commission. *Inventory and Appraisal of Historic Sites, Buildings and Areas.* Cincinnati, O.: The Commission, 1960. 101 pp., photo, map, mimeo.

Kidney, Walter C. *Historic Buildings of Ohio: A Selection from the Records of the Historic American Buildings Survey, National Park Service.* Historic Buildings of America Series. Pittsburgh, Pa.: Ober Park Associates, Inc., 1972. 130 pp., photos, drawings, diagrams, map, bibliog. notes, index.

Landmark Committee, Dayton, Ohio. *Report, June 1, 1968: A Study and Evaluation of the Significant Structures and Sites of Montgomery County, Ohio.* Dayton, O.: 1968. 74 pp., photos, forms, maps.

Ohio Historical Society. *Ohio Historic Landmarks: Phase 1 of the Ohio Historic Survey.* Columbus, O.: The Society, 1967. 58 pp., photos.

OKLAHOMA

Oklahoma. State University of Agriculture and Applied Science, Stillwater, School of Architecture. *Oklahoma Landmarks: A Selection of Noteworthy Structures.* Prepared by the School of Architecture, Oklahoma State University. Stillwater, Okla.: Department of Publishing and Printing, Oklahoma State University, 1967. 1 vol., unpaged, illus., map.

OREGON

American Institute of Architects. Portland, Oregon Chapter. *A Guide to Portland Architecture.* Portland, Ore.: American Institute of Architects, Portland Chapter, 1968. 74 pp., illus., bibliog., paper.

Vaughan, Thomas, and George A. McMath. *A Century of Portland Architecture.* Portland, Ore.: Oregon Historical Society, 1967. 226 pp., illus., bibliog. references.

PENNSYLVANIA

American Institute of Architects. Philadelphia Chapter. *Philadelphia Architecture.* New York: Reinhold Publishing Corp., 1961. 75 pp., illus.

Bucks County Planning Commission. *Design Resources of Doylestown, Bucks County, Pennsylvania.* Doylestown, Pa.?: The Commission, 1968. 125 pp., photos, drawings, maps, paper. ◆ Includes design resources inventory, historical development, and survey method.

Delaware Valley Regional Planning Commission. *Inventory of Historic Sites.* Principal writer, Hanka Gorska. Philadelphia, Pa.: 1969. 237 pp., plates, illus., maps, bibliog.

Richman, Irwin. *Pennsylvania's Architecture.* Pennsylvania History Studies no. 10. University Park, Pa.: Pennsylvania Historical Association, 1969. 63 pp., photos, prints, map, diagrams, bibliog.

Simon, Grant. "The Philadelphia Historical Commission Survey Resources," *Historic Preservation,* 18:5 (September-October 1966), pp. 190-193.

Van Trump, James D. *Evergreen Hamlet.* The Stones of Pittsburgh no. 4. Pittsburgh, Pa.: Pittsburgh History and Landmarks Foundation, 1967. 4 pp., illus., paper.

Van Trump, James D., and Arthur P. Ziegler, Jr. *Landmark Architecture of Allegheny County, Pennsylvania.* The Stones of Pittsburgh no. 5. Pittsburg, Pa.: Pittsburgh History and Landmarks Foundation, 1967. 294 pp., illus., maps, bibliog.

SOUTH CAROLINA

Historic American Buildings Survey. *Records of Buildings in Charleston and the South Carolina Low Country.* Harley J. McKee, comp. Philadelphia, Pa.: Eastern Office, Design and Construction, National Park Service, 1965. 26 pp., paper.

South Carolina Appalachian Council of Governments. *Historic Places in the South Carolina Appalachian Region: A Survey.* Greenville, S.C.?: The Council, 1971. 132 pp., photos, maps, bibliog., appendix. ◆ Part of a statewide survey compiled from ten districts.

Stoney, Samuel Gaillard. *This Is Charleston: A Survey of the Architectural Heritage of a Unique American City.* Rev. ed. Charleston, S.C.: Carolina Art Association, 1970. 137 pp., illus., maps, paper.

SOUTH DAKOTA

Clay County Historical Society (S.D.). Historic Sites Committee. *Register of Historic*

Sites in Clay County. Vermillion, S.D.: 1972. 55 pp., illus., bibliog. references.

TENNESSEE

Alderson, William Thomas, and Hulan Glyn Thomas. *Historic Sites in Tennessee.* Rev. ed. Nashville, Tenn.: Tennessee Historical Commission in cooperation with the Tennessee Division of Tourist Information, 1967. 1 vol., unpaged, illus., maps.

TEXAS

American Institute of Architects. Dallas Chapter. *The Prairie's Yield: Forces Shaping Dallas From 1840-1962.* New York: Reinhold Publishing Corp., 1962. 72 pp., illus.

American Institute of Architects. San Antonio Chapter. *Historic San Antonio, 1700-1900.* San Antonio, Tex.: 1963. 32 pp., illus., plans, maps in pocket.

Historic American Buildings Survey. *The Galveston Architecture Inventory, 1966-1967.* Sponsored by the Galveston Historical Foundation. Washington, D.C.: Historic American Buildings Survey, Office of Archeology and Historic Preservation, National Park Service, 1967. 2 vols., illus., o.p.

Houston: An Architectural Guide. Houston, Tex.: Houston Chapter, American Institute of Architects, 1972. 168 pp., illus.

Texas State Historical Survey Committee. *The National Register in Texas: 1968-1971.* Austin, Tex.: The Committee, 1972. 27 pp., photos, appendix, index, paper.

UTAH

Goeldner, Paul. *Utah Catalog: Historic American Buildings Survey.* Salt Lake City, Utah: Utah Heritage Foundation, 1969. 76 pp., photos, prints, drawings, diagrams, bibliog. footnotes, index, paper.

VIRGINIA

Dulaney, Paul S. *The Architecture of Historic Richmond.* Charlottesville, Va.: University Press of Virginia, 1968. 208 pp., illus., maps, paper.

Historic Alexandria Foundation. *Historic Chart, Alexandria, Virginia; Showing Historic Buildings and Sites from Oronoco Street to Jefferson Street and Union Street to West Street.* Compiled by Historic Alexandria

Foundation, 1959-1962 (revised in part 1963). Prepared by the Department of City Planning. C.T. Washburn, artist. Alexandria, Va.: (distr. by the Office of the City Clerk), 1963. 20 pp., illus.

Northern Virginia Regional Planning and Economic Development Commission. *Historic Northern Virginia Buildings and Places.* Arlington, Va.: The Commission, 1966. 34 pp., illus., maps, bibliog.

Virginia Historic Landmarks Commission. *Virginia Landmarks Register.* Richmond, Va.: The Commission, 1970. 32 pp., photos, paper.

WASHINGTON

Washington (State). State Parks and Recreation Commission. *Heritage Sites.* Text by Ralph H. Rudeen. Olympia, Wash.: The Commission, 1970. 22 pp., illus.

WISCONSIN

Historic American Buildings Survey. *Wisconsin Architecture: A Catalog of Buildings Represented in the Library of Congress with Illustrations from Measured Drawings.* Narrative by Richard W.E. Perrin. Washington, D.C.: U. S. Government Printing Office, 1966. 80 pp., photos, measured drawings, diagrams, maps, bibliog.

An Historic Structure Inventory for Wisconsin Including the Old World Research Project. Madison, Wis.: State Historical Society of Wisconsin, 1969. 339 pp., illus., maps, bibliog.

Perrin, Richard W. E. *The Architecture of Wisconsin.* Madison, Wis.: State Historical Society of Wisconsin, 1967. 175 pp., illus., bibliog. references.

Perrin, Richard W. E. *Milwaukee Landmarks: An Architectural Heritage, 1850-1950.* Milwaukee Public Museum Publications in History no. 9. Milwaukee, Wis.: Milwaukee Public Museum Press, 1968. 108 pp., photos, drawings, index, paper.

VIRGIN ISLANDS

Historic American Buildings Survey. *Historic Architecture of the Virgin Islands.* Selections from the Historic American Buildings Survey no. 1. Philadelphia, Pa.: The Survey, 1966. 1 vol., unpaged. ◆ Available from National Technical Information Service, 5285 Port Royal Road, Springfield, Virginia 22151.

Gosner, Pamela W. *Plantation and Town: Historic Architecture of the United States Virgin Islands, A Guide.* Durham, N.C.: Moore Publishing Co., 1971. 110 pp., illus., bibliog.

CANADA AND GREAT BRITAIN

Astroff, Vivian. "Taking Stock of Our Old Buildings: Part I," *Habitat,* 14:4-6 (1971), pp. 18-22; "Part II," *Habitat, 15:1 (1972), pp. 40-43.*

Civic Trust. *Index of Conservation Areas.* London: The Trust, 1973. 16 pp. ◆ Complete list of conservation areas designated up to January 1, 1973.

Great Britain. Royal Commission on the Ancient and Historical Monuments and Constructions of England. *Peterborough, New Town: A Survey of the Antiquities in the Areas of Development.* London: Her Majesty's Stationery Office, 1969. 87 pp., photos, drawings, diagrams, maps, index, paper. ◆ Includes archeological and architectural inventory.

Kingston, Ontario. *Buildings of Historic and Architectural Significance.* Vol. I. Kingston, Ontario: City of Kingston, 1971. 104 pp., illus., appendices.

Kingston, Ontario. *Buildings of Architectural and Historic Significance.* Vol. II. Kingston, Ontario: City of Kingston, 1973. 154 pp., photos, drawings, maps.

The Survey of London: *Being the First Volume of the Register of the Committee for the Survey of Memorials of Greater London, Containing the Parish of Bromley-by-bow.* 1900. Reprint. New York: AMS Press, 1971. 53 pp., illus., folding map, bibliog. references. ◆ Edited by C. R. Ashbee, from material collected by members of the Survey Committee. Entire survey reissued in 36 volumes to date by AMS Press.

Master Plans and Case Studies

UNITED STATES—GENERAL

U.S. National Park Service. *The National Park System Plan: Part I–History.* Washington, D.C.: 1970. 164 pp., charts, appendices, paper. ◆ Part II covers natural history.

ALABAMA

Holmes, Mrs. Nicholas H., Jr. "The Mobile Historic Preservation Commission: Preservation, Progress, and Urban Renewal," *History News,* 23:4 (April 1968), pp. 71-73.

Mobile, Alabama. City Planning Commission. *Downtown Mobile: A Plan for the Development of Bienville Center and Central Mobile.* Mobile, Ala.: The Commission, 1967. 39 pp., maps, charts, plans.

Mobile, Alabama. City Planning Commission. *The Plan for Fort Conde Plaza.* Mobile, Ala.: 1971. 19 pp., illus., maps.

Mobile, Alabama. Historic Development Commission. *Preservation with a Purpose: An Outline of How Preservation of Mobile's Traditional Architecture and Development of Mobile's Historic Districts Can Create a Multi-Million Dollar Industry.* Mobile, Ala.: The Commission, 1963. 12 pp., drawings, folding map insert.

Mobile, Alabama. Housing Board. *An Illustrated Plan for the East Church Street Area Historic Project.* Mobile, Ala.: Dewey Crowder Associates, 1964. 1 vol., illus., folding map.

ALASKA

Alaska. Division of Parks. *Alaska Outdoor Recreation and Historic Preservation Report.* Juneau: annual. illus.

ARIZONA

Barrio Historico, Tucson. By Dennis R. Bell and others. Tucson, Ariz.: College of Architecture, University of Arizona, 1972. 171 pp., illus., bibliog.

Garrett, Bill G., and James W. Garrison. *Plan for the Creation of a Historic Environment.* Tombstone, Ariz.: Tombstone Restoration Commission, 1972. 125 pp., photos, drawings, diagrams, maps, plans, tables, appendix.

Van Valkenburgh, Sallie. "The Casa Grande of Arizona as a Landmark on the Desert, a Government Reservation, and a National Monument," *The Kiva,* 27 (1962).

CALIFORNIA

Barrick, S. James. *The Golden Chain of the Mother Lode.* A report of a preliminary survey of the Mother Lode and adjacent areas leading to its preservation for the enjoyment and use of the general public as requested by ACR no. 128, 1959. Sacramento, Calif.: Division of Beaches and Parks, Department of Natural Resources, 1959. 81 pp., illus., maps.

California. Department of Parks and Recreation. *California Coastline Preservation and Recreation Plan.* Prepared by Robert M. Baker. Sacramento, Calif.: The Department, 1971. 123 pp., illus., bibliog.

California. Division of Beaches and Parks. *Old Sacramento: A Report on Its Significance to the City, State, and Nation, with Recommendations for the Preservation and Use of Its Principal Historical Structures and Sites.* Sacramento, Calif.: 1958-1960. 3 parts, illus.

California. Division of Beaches and Parks. *Old Sacramento, State Historic Park Study.* Requested by House Resolution no. 91, Statutes of 1964. Sacramento: 1965. 9 pp., illus., maps. ◆ Project analysis, resources, costs, economic factors, maps and plans.

California. Resources Agency. *The California History Plan.* Vol. 3. Sacramento, Calif.: The Agency, 1973. 41 pp., photos, line drawings, tables.

Candeub, Fleissig & Associates. *Historic Old Sacramento.* Sacramento, Calif.: Redevelopment Agency, City of Sacramento, 1964. 20 pp., illus.

Candeub, Fleissig & Associates. *Old Sacramento Historic Area and Riverfront Park: Technical Report.* Prepared for Redevelopment Agency of the City of Sacramento. Sacramento, Calif.: Candeub, Fleissig & Associates, 1964. 237 pp., plates, maps, bibliog.

Cannon, John G. "Historic Old Sacramento and U. S. Interstate Route 5," *Traffic Quarterly,* 19:3 (July 1965), pp. 405-412.

Moore, Charles W. "The Restoration of Old Monterey," American Institute of Architects *Journal,* 31:3 (March 1959), pp. 21-25. ◆ Discussion of the problem of integrating an historic area with the modern city and handling the tourist traffic.

Sacramento, California. Historic Landmarks Commission. *Old Sacramento, a Reference Point in Time.* By Aubrey Neasham. Sacramento, Calif.: Sacramento Historic Landmarks Commission in cooperation with the Redevelopment Agency of the City of Sacramento, 1965. 19 pp., illus., maps.

San Francisco. Department of City Planning. *Jackson Square.* San Francisco, Calif.: The

Department, 1971. 37 pp., 22 pp. maps and plans, appendix.

San Francisco. Department of City Planning. *The Preservation of Landmarks in San Francisco.* San Francisco, Calif.: The Department, 1966 (i.e. 1967). 24 pp., illus.

San Francisco. Department of City Planning. *The Urban Design Plan for the Comprehensive Plan of San Francisco.* San Francisco, Calif.: The Department, 1971. 155 pp., illus., maps. ◆ Evaluation of physical assets including historic resources and proposals made for preserving and improving environmental design qualities.

COLORADO

Lobato, Rudolph B. *An Architectural and Historic Building Survey: Inventory and Evaluation of Littleton, Colorado.* Littleton, Colo.: City of Littleton and Littleton Area Historical Museum, 1973. 74 pp., photos, plans.

CONNECTICUT

Connecticut Historical Commission. *Historic Conservation: Progress and Prospects.* Hartford, Conn.: The Commission, 1969. 52 pp., photos, maps, appendices, mimeo.

Connecticut Historical Commission. *The State of Connecticut Historic Preservation Plan: 1970 Plan.* Prepared with the assistance of Raymond, Parish, Pine & Plavnick. Hartford, Conn.: The Commission, 1970. 112 pp., photos, map, paper, o.p.

Delaney, Barbara Snow. "The Goodspeed Opera House: Preservation in East Haddam, Connecticut," *Antiques,* 103:6 (June 1973), pp. 1178-1183.

Erickson, Richard B. "A Proposed Marine Heritage Area for Southeastern Connecticut," *Historic Preservation,* 18:1 (January-February 1966), pp. 24-31.

Flint, Peggy. *The New Haven Preservation Trust: A Ten Years' War, 1962-1972.* New Haven, Conn.: New Haven Preservation Trust, 1972. 32 pp., photos, drawings, paper.

Hommann, Mary. *Wooster Square Design: A Report on the Background, Experience and Design Procedures in Redevelopment and Rehabilitation in an Urban Renewal Project.* New Haven: New Haven Redevelopment Authority, 1965. 191 pp., illus., maps, plans.

"Rebuilding: A Charming Folly Restored," *Architectural Forum,* 119:2 (August 1963), pp. 102-107. ♦ Restoration of the Goodspeed Opera House, East Haddam, Connecticut.

DELAWARE

Delaware. Division of Historical and Cultural Affairs. *Preliminary Historic Preservation Plan for Delaware.* Dover, Del.: The Division, 1971. 43 pp., drawings, appendices, loose-leaf.

New Castle County, Delaware Regional Planning Commission. *Historical Buildings and Areas; A County Comprehensive Development Plan Background Study, New Castle County, Delaware.* HUD Grant Study. Wilmington Del.: Advanced Planning Division of the Commission, 1967. 75 pp., illus., maps, bibliog.

New Castle County, Delaware, Regional Planning Commission. *Historical Development: A County Comprehensive Development Plan Background Study, New Castle County, Delaware, April 1966.* Wilmington, Del.: Advanced Planning Division of the Commission, 1966. 61 pp., illus., maps.

DISTRICT OF COLUMBIA

Citizens Association of Georgetown. *Georgetown, 1980: A Program for the Coming Decade.* Washington, D.C.: The Association, 1969. 54 pp., maps, appendices. ♦ Appendices include historic sites and preservation legislation of 1935 and 1966, and condensed history of Georgetown zoning.

de Schweinitz, Dorothea. "Historic Preservation Without Federal Aid: Georgetown, D.C.," *Historic Preservation,* 16:1 (1964), pp. 12-16.

McLeod, Ferrara and Ensign. *Franklin School Building.* Washington, D.C.: The Authors, c1969, 1973. 58 pp., photos, drawings, map. ♦ Restoration proposal including history, condition survey, remodeling scheme, and budget.

"Preservation in Washington, D.C.," *Historic Preservation,* 15:3 (1961), entire issue. 36 pp., photos. ♦ Articles: "A First Lady and a New Frontier, 1800"; "The Art of Architecture and the Capital of a World"; "New (Architectural) Frontier in Washington"; "Washington Megalopolis, Some Current Village Preservation Problems"; "Planning for the Conservation of Landmarks in the Nation's Capital."

U.S. Congress. House. Committee on Interior and Insular Affairs. Subcommittee on National Parks and Recreation. *Federal City Bicenten-*

nial Development Corporation. Hearings, Ninety-first Congress, second session, on H.R. 18677 and H.R. 19097. . . September 17 and 18, 1970. Washington, D.C.: U. S. Government Printing Office, 1971. 157 pp.

U.S. Congress. House. Committee on Interior and Insular Affairs. Subcommittee on National Parks and Recreation. *Pennsylvania Avenue National Historic Site.* Hearings, Eighty-ninth Congress, second session, on H.J. Res. 678 . . . March 21, 1966. Washington, D.C.: U.S. Government Printing Office, 1966. 117 pp.

U.S. Congress. House. Committee on Interior and Insular Affairs. Subcommittee on National Parks and Recreation. *Proposed Pennsylvania Avenue Bicentennial Development Corporation.* Hearings, Ninety-second Congress, second session, on H.R. 10751 . . . April 13 and 14, 1972. Washington, D.C.: U. S. Government Printing Office, 1972. 183 pp.

U. S. Congress. Senate. Committee on Interior and Insular Affairs. *Pennsylvania Avenue Historic Site Commission; Report to Accompany S.J. Res. 116.* Eighty-ninth Congress, second session, Senate. Report no. 1205. Washington, D.C.: U.S. Government Printing Office, 1966. 20 pp.

U.S. Congress. Senate. Committee on Interior and Insular Affairs. Subcommittee on Parks and Recreation. *Pennsylvania Avenue National Historic Site.* Hearing, Ninety-second Congress, second session, on S. 715 . . . S. 4002 . . . (and) H.R. 10751 . . . September 21, 1972. Washington, D.C.: U. S. Government Printing Office, 1972. 245 pp., maps.

U.S. President's Council on Pennsylvania. *Pennsylvania Avenue: Report.* Washington, D.C.: U. S. Government Printing Office, 1964. 56 pp., illus., plans.

FLORIDA

Bateman (Robert S.) & Associates. *The Master Plan: Pensacola Historic District.* Prepared for the Historic Pensacola Preservation Board of Trustees (in cooperation with the Escambia-Santa Rosa County Regional Planning Commission and the Pensacola City Planning Commission). Mobile, Ala: 1971. 36 pp., illus., maps.

Florida. Board of Parks and Historic Memorials. Special Advisory Committee. *The St. Augustine Restoration Plan.* St. Augustine, Fla.: 1959. 23 pp., illus., maps, plans.

Milo Smith and Associates. *The Beach, the Bay, and the City: Tourism at the Crossroads.* Prepared for the Escambia-Santa Rosa Regional Planning Council and Pensacola-Escambia County Development Commission. Pensacola, Fla.: Escambia-Santa Rosa Regional Planning Council, 1971. 69 pp., illus.

St. Augustine Historical, Restoration and Preservation Commission. *San Agustin Antiguo: The Restoration of Old St. Augustine, 1960-66.* St. Augustine, Fla.: 1967? 16 pp., chiefly illus.

St. Augustine Historical, Restoration and Preservation Commission. *The Restoration of St. Augustine, Oldest City in the United States.* St. Augustine, Fla. (?): The Commission, 1961. 31 pp., photos, maps, diagrams.

GEORGIA

Georgia. University. Department of Landscape Architecture. *A Visual Survey and Civic Design Study for Madison, Georgia.* Prepared by the Landscape Architecture Department, University of Georgia, in cooperation with the Northeast Georgia Area Planning and Development Commission. Athens, Ga.: University of Georgia Press, 1964. 78 pp., illus., plans, paper.

Half a Heritage. Savannah, Ga.: Historic Savannah Foundation, 1967. 12 pp., illus.

Historic Savannah Foundation, Inc. *Historic Savannah.* Savannah, Ga.: The Foundation, 1968. 247 pp., photos, prints, drawings, diagrams, maps, charts, bibliog. footnotes.

Savannah. *Historic Preservation Plan for the Central Area, General Neighborhood Renewal Area.* Savannah, Ga.: Savannah, 1968? 32 pp., illus.

HAWAII

Community Planning, Inc., Honolulu. *Proposal for the Historical Restoration and Preservation of Lahaina, Island of Maui, State of Hawaii.* Prepared for the Board of Supervisors and Lahaina Restoration Committee. Honolulu: 1961. 74 pp., illus., maps.

Hawaii. Division of State Parks, Outdoor Recreation and Historic Sites. *Historic Preservation: Annual Report.* Honolulu: 1967- .

Iolani Palace Restoration Project. *Iolani Palace Restoration.* Written, designed, and produced by the Iolani Palace Restoration project staff and special consultants. Project

director, George Moore. Honolulu: Friends of Iolani Palace, 1970. 203 pp., illus., plans, bibliog., paper.

Maui County Planning Commission. *A General Plan for the Lahaina District, County of Maui.* Maui: The Commission, 1968. 31 pp., folding map, graphs, tables, plans. ◆ Joint venture of Hiroshi Kasamoto, and Muroda and Tanaka, Inc. Report written by Anthony N. Hodges.

ILLINOIS

Bartholomew (Harland) and Associates. *A Report Upon the Comprehensive Plan, Nauvoo, Illinois.* Prepared for the Nauvoo Planning Commission. St. Louis: 1966. 59 pp., illus., maps. ◆ Historic area report, pp. 31-34.

Hodne Associates. *Planning Studies: A Basis for Comprehensive Planning for the City of Galena, Illinois.* Prepared for the Galena Planning Commission. Minneapolis: 1966. 108 pp., illus., maps.

Hodne Associates. *Proposed Comprehensive Plan for the Future Development of the City of Galena, Illinois.* Prepared for the Galena Planning Commission. Minneapolis: 1966. 90 pp., illus., maps, plans.

Kriviskey, Bruce M. "Galena's Feasibility Study," *Historic Preservation,* 20:1 (January-March 1968), pp. 32-36.

Pointner, Norbert J., II. "Pullman: A New Town Takes Shape on the Illinois Prairie," *Historic Preservation,* 22:2 (April-June 1970), pp. 26-35.

INDIANA

City Planning Associates, Inc. *Historic Richmond: Toward Architectural Preservation.* Richmond, Indiana: Community Renewal Program, 1970. Various pagings, photos, drawings.

KENTUCKY

Kentucky Heritage Commission. *Kentucky's Plan for Historic Preservation.* Frankfort, Ky.: The Commission, 1971. 86 pp., drawings, appendix, paper.

Kentucky. University. Kentucky Research Foundation, Institute for Environmental Studies. *Historical Survey and Plan for Lexington and Fayette County, Kentucky.* Report prepared primarily by the Institute for Environmental Studies, University of Kentucky,

Research Foundation in cooperation with the Lexington-Fayette County Planning Commission staff. Lexington: Lexington-Fayette County Planning Commission, 1969? 76 pp., illus., maps.

Louisville, Kentucky. Urban Renewal and Community Development Agency. *Rebirth and the Road to Vigor: The Renewal of Old Louisville; A Descriptive Report on the General Neighborhood Plans for the Restoration of Old Louisville.* Text by John Hazard Wildman, drawings by Robert York. Louisville, Ky.: 1966? 112 pp., illus., maps, plans.

LOUISIANA

Bureau of Governmental Research. New Orleans. *Plan and Program for the Preservation of the Vieux Carré: Historic District Demonstration Study, Conducted by the Bureau of Governmental Research for the City of New Orleans.* Prepared under the supervision of Marcou, O'Leary and Associates, Washington, D.C. New Orleans, La.: 1968. 170 pp., illus., maps, bibliog.

Bureau of Governmental Research. New Orleans. *Vieux Carré Historic District Demonstration Study.* Technical Supplements to *Plan and Program for the Preservation of the Vieux Carré.* New Orleans, La.: The Bureau, 1968. 7 vols., illus., maps. ◆ Supplements: *Technical Report on the Environmental Survey; Legal and Administrative Report; Economic and Social Study; The Vieux Carré, New Orleans, Its Plan, Its Growth, Its Architecture; New Orleans Central Business District Traffic Study; Summary Report–Evaluation of the Effects of the Proposed Riverfront Expressway; Technical Report on the Effects of the Proposed Riverfront Expressway.*

Heck, Robert W. *Historic Baton Rouge: An Urban Planning Perspective for the Preservation of Its Heritage.* Baton Rouge, La.: Community Renewal Program, 1970. 80 pp., photos, maps, reading list, paper.

Lemann, Bernard. *Historic Areas and Structures.* Report prepared as a part of the Community Renewal Program of New Orleans for the New Orleans City Planning Commission. New Orleans, La.: New Orleans City Planning Commission, 1967. 97 pp., illus.

Lemann, Bernard. *The Vieux Carré: A General Statement.* New Orleans, La.: Tulane University, School of Architecture, 1966. 91 pp., illus., paper.

MARYLAND

Baltimore. Department of Planning. *Baltimore: Preservation of the City's Character.* Baltimore, Md.: The Department, 1967. 32 pp., illus., map.

Committee for Annapolis, Inc. *Reconnaissance Report: Old City of Annapolis.* Annapolis, Md.: 1960. 26 pp., illus., maps, plans.

Historic Annapolis, Inc. *Three Ancient Blocks of Annapolis, Maryland's Capitol City: A Documented Account.* Annapolis, Md.: 1963. 16 pp.

Maryland. Maryland-National Capital Park and Planning Commission. *Gaithersburg Vicinity: Approved and Adopted Master Plan.* Silver Spring, Md.: The Commission, 1971. 63 pp., photos, charts, plans, appendices, set of pocket maps, paper.

Maryland. Maryland-National Capital Park and Planning Commission. *Historic Preservation Needs: An Aspect of Open Space Planning in the Bi-County Region.* Commission Working Paper no. 6. Silver Spring, Md.: The Commission, 1968. 30 pp.

Maryland Historical Trust. *The State of Maryland Historic Preservation Plan: 1970 Plan.* Prepared with the assistance of Maryland Department of State Planning and Raymond, Parish, Pine & Plavnick, Washington, D.C. Annapolis, Md.: 1970. 60 pp.

Montgomery County Planning Board. *Feasibility Study: National Park Seminary Site Preservation, Forest Glen, Maryland.* Silver Spring, Md.: Maryland–National Capital Park and Planning Commission, 1973. 82 pp., photos, maps. ◆ Keyes, Lethbridge & Condon, Consultants. Prepared for the Montgomery County Planning Board of the Maryland–National Capital Park and Planning Commission.

Plavnick, Robert L. *St. Mary's City: A Plan for the Preservation and Development of Maryland's First Capital.* St. Mary's City, Md.: St. Mary's City Commission, 1970. 58 pp., illus., maps.

Raymond, May, Parish & Plavnick. *The State of Maryland Historic Preservation Plan: Technical Report No. 1 – Goals and Criteria.* Prepared for the Maryland Historical Trust and the Maryland Department of Planning. Annapolis(?): Maryland Historical Trust, 1970. 68 pp., paper.

MASSACHUSETTS

Blair Associates, Inc. *Salem, Massachusetts: Historic Area Study.* Prepared by Blair Associates in cooperation with the Salem Planning Board and the Massachusetts Department of Commerce. Providence, R.I.: Blair Associates, Inc., 1963. 53 pp., illus., maps.

Boston. Architectural Center. *Highlands Study.* Report on a Pilot Project under a grant from the National Foundation for the Arts and Humanities, 1969-1971. Boston: The Center, 1971. Various pagings, maps, plans, appendix.

Corinthian Conservation Company. *Reconnaissance Report: Waterfront Historic Area, New Bedford, Massachusetts.* Phase I summary submitted to Waterfront Historic Area League. Annapolis, Md.: The Company, 1964. 36 pp., illus., plates.

Hale, Richard W., Jr. "The Shirley-Eustis House," *Historic Preservation,* 20:1 (January-March 1968), pp. 22-25.

Kerr, Robert J., II. "Preservation and Rehabilitation of Historic Urban Areas and Monuments: A Contemporary Challenge," *Curator,* 11:4 (1968), pp. 319-336. ◆ Waterfront Historic District, New Bedford, Massachusetts.

McGinley, Paul J. "Newburyport and a New Kind of Urban Renewal," *Old-Time New England,* LXI:4 (April-June 1971), pp. 111-115.

Massachusetts Legislative Research Bureau. *An Historic Preservation Program for Cities and Towns.* Prepared for the Legislative Research Council, January 10, 1966. Boston, Mass.: The Bureau, 1966. 72 pp.

New Bedford, Massachusetts, Redevelopment Authority. *Preservation and Rehabilitation of a Historic Commercial Area: A Demonstration Study of the Waterfront Historic District, New Bedford, Massachusetts.* New Bedford, Mass.: The Authority, 1973. 132 pp., appendices. ◆ Study done in cooperation with the City Planning Department and the Waterfront Historic Area League, funded by an Urban Renewal Demonstration Grant from HUD.

U.S. Boston National Historic Sites Commission. *Final Report of the Boston National Historic Sites Commission.* Letter from the Secretary of the Interior, transmitting the final report of the Boston National Historic Sites Commission pertaining in particular to major problems of historical preservation in the municipality of Boston, pursuant to the Act of August 4, 1959 (73 Stat. 297). Eighty-seventh Congress, first session, House document no. 107. Washington, D.C.: U.S. Government Printing Office, 1961. 261 pp., illus., maps.

MICHIGAN

Detroit. City Plan Commission. *Orchestra Place.* Detroit: The Commission, n.d. Unpaged, maps, plans, models.

Johnson, Johnson & Roy, Inc. *Marshall: A Plan for Preservation.* Marshall, Mich.: Marshall Historical Society, 1973. 85 pp., photos, drawings, maps, appendices. ◆ Appendices include preservation organizations, preservation values of Marshall properties, historic district ordinance.

Lansing Historic District Study Commission. *Yesterday, Today, Tomorrow: Memorandum '76: Historic Lansing.* Lansing, Mich.: The Commission, 1960. 48 pp., photos, maps, appendix.

Marshall City Planning Commission. *Central Business District Analysis, Marshall, Michigan.* Prepared by Vilican-Leman & Associates, Inc. Marshall, Mich.: The Commission (?), 1970. 21 pp., plans, maps.

Weisman, Leslie. *Flight from Suburbia: West Canfield Historic District.* Detroit: University of Detroit Press, 1973. Unpaged, illus., bibliog., paper.

Wilson, Richard Guy. "Old West Side," *Historic Preservation,* 25:3 (July-September 1973), pp. 16-21.

Wilson, Richard G., and Edward J. Vaughn. *Old West Side, Ann Arbor, Michigan.* Ann Arbor, Mich.: Old West Side Association, 1971. 85 pp., photos, drawings, maps, bibliog., appendix. ◆ Survey of total environment of a neighborhood including structures, landscape features, street furniture and other amenities to identify physical character, assets and problems.

MINNESOTA

Barton-Aschman Associates, Inc. *St. Anthony Falls-Nicollet Island: Landmarks at the Continent's Heart.* A prospective for their development, prepared for the Citizen's (sic) Committee for the Nicollet Island, under the sponsorship of the Downtown Council of Minneapolis. Minneapolis: 1961. 24 pp., illus., maps.

Coddington, Donn M. *Historic Preservation in Minnesota.* Report no. 1, 1969-1973. St. Paul, Minn.: Minnesota Historical Society, 1971. 166 pp., drawings, maps, paper.

Minnesota Legislature, Outdoor Recreation Resources Commission. *An Historic Sites Program for Minnesota.* Prepared by the Minnesota Outdoor Recreation Commission in cooperation with the Minnesota Historical Society, the Minnesota Highway Department, and the Division of State Parks, Conservation Department. St. Paul, Minn.: The Commission, 1964. 94 pp., maps, tables.

MISSOURI

Allied Engineers and Architects. *Investigation and Development of Master Plan for Restoration, Ste. Genevieve, Missouri.* St. Louis, 1966. 47 pp., illus., maps, plans.

Heritage/St. Louis. *Preliminary Research Report: Soulard Neighborhood Historic District.* St. Louis, Mo.: Heritage St. Louis, 1973. 8 pp., map, paper.

Landmarks Association of St. Louis, Inc. *Laclede's Landing Area, Third Street Highway to Wharf Eads Bridge to Veteran's Bridge.* St. Louis, Mo.: 1968. 26 pp., illus., maps.

McCue, George. "Private Renewal Without Federal Aid: Gaslight Square, St. Louis, Mo.," *Historic Preservation,* 16:1 (1964), pp. 24-29.

Missouri. State Park Board, State Historical Survey and Planning Office. *Foundations From the Past: Missouri's Historic Preservation Program.* 1st ed. Columbia, Mo.: Missouri State Park Board, 1971. 40 pp., photos, map, chart, appendices.

Raiche, Stephen J. "Soulard: An Ethnic Neighborhood, Past and Present," *Historic Preservation,* 35:3 (July-September 1973), pp. 37-41.

St. Louis. City Plan Commission. *Lafayette Square Restoration Plan.* St. Louis, Mo.: 1971. 48 pp., illus., maps. ◆ Prepared in cooperation with the Lafayette Square Restoration Committee and the Lafayette Park Neighborhood Association.

NEBRASKA

Nebraska Historical Society. *Historic Preservation in Nebraska.* Nebraska State Historical Society Preservation Series Report no. 1. Lincoln, Neb.: The Society, 1971. 158 pp., photos, appendices.

NEVADA

Nevada. Department of Conservation and Natural Resources. Nevada State Park System. *A Plan for Historical Preservation in Nevada: Vol. III–Annual Preservation Program.* 3rd ed. Carson City, Nev.: The Department, 1973. 28 pp., maps, charts, paper.

NEW JERSEY

Brown, James S., Jr. "Clinton's Headquarters: Its History and Restoration," *The Monmouth Historian,* 1 (1972), pp. 14-31.

NEW MEXICO

Conron, John P. "The Treaty of Santa Fe," *Historic Preservation,* 20:1 (January-March 1968), pp. 26-31. ◆ Las Trampas Foundation, New Mexico, and State Highway Department agreement to redesign highway through the historic community.

New Mexico, State Planning Office. *Historic Preservation: A Plan for New Mexico.* Santa Fe, N.M.: State Planning Office, 1971. 176 pp., photos, diagrams, forms, maps, property inventory, appendices. ◆ Appendix A, Existing Legislation; Appendix B, Organizations.

NEW YORK

Malo, Paul. *The Binghamton Commission on Architecture and Urban Design: The First Three Years, 1964-1967.* Binghamton, N.Y.: The Binghamton Commission on Architecture and Urban Design, 1968. 84 pp., bibliog. references.

New York (City). Department of Parks. *Richmondtown Restoration, Staten Island, City of New York.* Prepared by the Staten Island Historical Society and the Department of Parks of the City of New York. New York: 1956. 32 pp., photos, diagrams, map, paper.

New York State Historic Trust. *A Compilation of Historical and Architectural Data on the New York State Maritime Block in New York City.* By John G. Waite, Paul R. Huey, and Geoffrey Stein. Albany, N.Y.: The Trust, 1972. 94 pp., photos, drawings, charts, bibliog. ◆ Expands and updates *A Compilation of Data and Reports on the New York State Maritime Museum Block in New York City* (1969).

New York State Historic Trust. *Herkimer House: An Historic Structure Report.* Prepared by John G. Waite and Paul R. Huey. Albany, N.Y.: The Trust, 1972. Various pagings, photos, measured drawings, diagrams, maps, bibliog. footnotes, paper.

New York State Historical Trust. *John Jay House: An Historic Structure Report.* By John G. Waite, Paul R. Huey and Martha Truax. Albany, N.Y.: The Trust, 1972. 212 pp., photos, drawings, maps, bibliog.

New York State Historic Trust. *Northwest Stonehouse, Johnson Hall: An Historic Structure Report.* By John G. Waite and Paul R. Huey. Albany, N.Y.: The Trust, 1971. 65 pp., photos, drawings, maps.

New York State Historic Trust. *A Report on the L. M. Hoyt Estate, Staatsburgh, Dutchess County, New York.* Prepared by the New York State Historic Trust Staff. Albany, N.Y.: The Trust, 1969. Various pagings, illus., maps, plan.

New York State Historic Trust. *Senate House: An Historic Structure Report.* By John G. Waite and Paul R. Huey. Albany, N.Y.: The Trust, 1971. 75 pp., 16 pp. photos and prints, drawings, diagrams, maps, bibliog., paper.

New York State Historic Trust. *Washington's Headquarters, the Hasbrouck House: An Historic Structure Report.* By John G. Waite and Paul R. Huey. Albany, N.Y.: The Trust, 1971. 99 pp., 35 pp. photos and prints, drawings, diagrams, maps, bibliog., paper.

Rochester, New York. *Third Ward Urban Renewal Project, Rochester, New York: Urban Renewal Plan.* Rochester, N.Y.: 1966. 43 pp., ♦ Includes section on special provisions for buildings of significance or architectural merit.

Seligmann, Werner, and Roger Sherwood. *Binghamton City Hall Restoration.* Binghamton, N.Y.: Valley Development Foundation, 1972. 55 pp., photos, drawings, plans, maps, diagrams, tables, appendices, forms.

Society for the Preservation of Landmarks in Western New York. *The Landmark Society Views the Third Ward.* Rochester, N.Y.: The Society, 1965. 39 pp., map, appendices, paper.

Society for the Preservation of Landmarks in Western New York. Third Ward Committee. *This is Rochester: The Third Ward Today: A Report.* Rochester: 1965. 30 pp., illus., map.

South Street Seaport Museum. "Special Issue: Report on the South Street Plan," *South Street Reporter,* 2 (October 1973), special

issue. ♦ Includes introduction to the project, history of the organization, use of the waterfront, use of the buildings, statement of value and costs of the project to date.

U. S. National Park Service. *U.S. Military Academy, West Point, New York: Summary Report on the Academy Development Plan for the Advisory Council on Historic Preservation.* Washington, D.C.: National Park Service, Office of Archeology and Historic Preservation, 1970. 55 pp., photos, drawings, maps, paper.

Van Der Bogert, Giles Y. "The Stockade Story," *American Institute of Architects Journal,* 40:4 (October 1963), pp. 42-48.

Van Derpool, James Grote. "The Fraunces Tavern Block Project in Old New York," *Historic Presevation,* 16:4 (1964), pp. 156-158.

NORTH CAROLINA

Griffin, Frances. *Old Salem: An Adventure in Historic Preservation.* Winston-Salem, N.C.: Old Salem, Inc., 1970. 74 pp., photos, maps, appendix, paper. ♦ Includes experiences with historic zoning, community support, traffic control, property acquisition, financing, restoration methods, adaptive use, and complete texts of historic zoning ordinances.

Murfreesboro Historical Association. *Renaissance in Carolina: 1971-1976.* By E. Frank Stephenson, Jr. Murfreesboro, N.C.: The Association, 1971. 212 pp., photos, drawings. ♦ A community publication designed to raise funds for a restoration program.

North Carolina. Division of Community Planning. *Historic District Development Plan, Wilmington, North Carolina.* Prepared for the City of Wilmington. Raleigh, N.C.: Department of Conservation and Development, Division of Community Planning, 1968. 64 pp., illus., maps, o.p.

North Carolina. Division of Community Planning. *Wilmington, North Carolina, Historic Area: A Part of the Future Land-Use Plan.* Report prepared for the City of Wilmington. Raleigh, N.C.: 1962. 57 pp., illus., bibliog.

North Carolina. State Department of Archives and History. *An Interim North Carolina State Plan for Historic Preservation.* Prepared by the Department of Archives and History and the Institute of Government, University of North Carolina. Raleigh, N.C.: 1970. 1 vol.

North Carolina. State Department of Archives and History. *A Lonesome Place Against the*

Sky. Raleigh, N.C.: The Department, 1971. 35 pp., photos, maps.

Stephenson, E. Frank, Jr. *Renaissance in Carolina II: A Report to Potential Contributors of the Activities of the Murfreesboro Historical Association, Incorporated, and the Historic Murfreesboro Commission,* Murfreesboro, N.C.: Murfreesboro Historical Association, 1973. 168 pp., photos, maps, plans.

Wrenn, Tony P. *Beaufort, North Carolina.* Raleigh, N.C.: North Carolina Department of Archives and History, 1970. 72 pp., photos, tables, bibliog., appendix. ◆ Historical and architectural information for preservation planning. Includes forms and legislative information.

OHIO

Cincinnati. City Planning Commission. *Dayton Street Preservation Area Study.* Cincinnati, O.: The Commission, 1965. 26 pp., illus.

Ohio. Legislative Service Commission. *Preservation of Historic Sites.* Staff Research Report No. 77. Columbus, O.: The Commission, 1966. 26 pp. ◆ Report and recommendations of the Commission's Committee to Study Historic Site Preservation, based on replies to a questionnaire sent to the state's active historical societies.

Visnapuu and Gaede, Inc. *Fisher Hall, Miami University, Oxford, Ohio: Its Preservation Potential.* Consultant Service Grant Report no. 1. Washington, D.C.: National Trust for Historic Preservation, 1973. 25 pp., photos, tables, plans, maps, bibliog., appendices, paper.

Visnapuu and Gaede, Inc. *Water Street Study, Chillicothe, Ohio: Suggestions for Rehabilitation.* Consultant Service Grant Report no. 3. Washington, D.C.: National Trust for Historic Preservation, 1973. 10 pp., photos, map, drawings, paper.

OKLAHOMA

Oklahoma Historical Society. *Annual Preservation Program for 1972.* Vol. III, Oklahoma Preservation Plan (PL 89-665). Oklahoma City, Okla.: The Society, 1972. 112 pp., photos, charts, maps, index, paper.

Oklahoma Historical Society. *Historic Sites Preservation in Oklahoma: A Handbook.* Oklahoma City, Okla.: The Society, 1971. 17 pp., unnumbered. ◆ Includes National Historic Preservation Act of 1966 and Title 53,

Oklahoma statutes; duties of the Oklahoma Historical Society.

PENNSYLVANIA

Delaware Valley Regional Planning Commission. *A Report on Historic Preservation.* Philadelphia, Pa.: 1969. 70 pp., illus., map, plans, forms, bibliog. ◆ Includes setting and recommendations for historic preservation, action to aid preservation, funding, government and private roles.

Harbeson, Hough, Livingston, and Larson. *Plan for the Old City: A Report to the Philadelphia Planning Commission.* n.p.: 1960. 18 pp., illus., maps.

Kane, Thomas J. *Master Plan for Historic Bethlehem.* Bethlehem, Pa.: Historic Bethlehem, Inc., 1963. 24 pp., map, o.p.

Lee, Ronald F., et al. "Philadelphia 20th Century," *Historic Preservation,* 18:5 (September-October 1966), pp. 184-195.

Lehigh-Northampton Counties Joint Planning Commission. *Regional Recreation and Open Space Plan: Historic Structures and Sites.* Report no. 3. Allentown (?), Pa.: The Commission, 1970. 117 pp., photos, charts, bibliog., appendices.

Miller, Donald. "Pittsburgh's Old Post Office," *Antiques,* 102:3 (Septembr 1972), pp. 460-463.

Philadelphia. Architects Committee. *The Proposal for a Covered Below-Grade Expressway Through Philadelphia's Historic Waterfront.* Prepared in cooperation with the Committee to Preserve Philadelphia's Historic Gateway. Philadelphia: 1965. 28 pp.

Philadelphia. City Planning Commission. *Independence Mall: Center City Redevelopment Area.* Philadelphia: 1966. 27 pp., illus., plans, paper.

Philadelphia. Redevelopment Authority. *Society Hill: A Modern Community That Lives with History.* Philadelphia: 1969. 16 pp., illus., plans.

Pittsburgh History and Landmarks Foundation. *Five Year Report to Our Members and to the Community.* Pittsburgh, Pa.: The Foundation, 1969. 24 pp., photos, drawings, paper.

Pittsburgh History and Landmarks Foundation. *The Mexican War Streets Restoration Program of the Pittsburgh History and Land-*

marks Foundation. Pittsburgh: The Foundation, 1969. 8 pp., illus., pamphlet.

Van Trump, James D. *1300-1335 Liverpool Street, Manchester, Old Allegheny, Pittsburgh.* The Stones of Pittsburgh no. 2. Pittsburgh: Pittsburgh History and Landmarks Foundation, n.d. 34 pp., photos, diagrams, charts, bibliog., paper. ♦ History and evaluation of a Victorian residential block with architectural studies for rehabilitating together with cost estimates.

RHODE ISLAND

Newport, Rhode Island. Redevelopment Agency. *The Urban Design Plan, Historic Hill, Newport, Rhode Island, Project No. R.I. R-23.* Prepared by the Providence Partnership, Providence, Rhode Island, and Russell Wright, Reston, Virginia. Newport, R.I.: The Agency, 1971. 44 pp., photos, drawings, charts, maps, paper. ♦ A survey of physical and environmental features of the urban renewal area, including proposed land-use maps, illustrative site plans, proposals for public improvements, and design criteria for review of new construction.

Providence. City Plan Commission. *College Hill: A Demonstration Study of Historic Area Renewal.* 2nd ed. Providence, R.I.: The Commission, c1959, 1967. 231 pp., photos, maps, paper. ♦ Conducted in cooperation with Providence Preservation Society and Housing and Home Finance Agency.

Providence. City Plan Commission. *College Hill 1961: Progress After Planning.* Providence, R.I.: The Commission, April 1961. 16 pp., illus., paper.

Rhode Island. Statewide Comprehensive Transportation and Land Use Program. *Historic Preservation Plan.* Prepared by the Rhode Island Statewide Planning Program and the Rhode Island Historical Preservation Commission. Report No. 13. Providence, R.I.: The Planning Program, 1970. 150 pp., illus., maps.

SOUTH CAROLINA

Edmunds, Mrs. S. Henry; George C. Rogers, Jr.; and Joseph H. McGee, Jr. "The Charleston Story," *Historic Preservation,* 23:1 (January-March 1971), pp. 5-15. ♦ Reviews historic district and preservation program, city's cultural development, and zoning in Charleston.

McCahill, Peter J. "Saving a Neighborhood Through Historic Preservation," *Journal of Housing,* 24:3 (April 1967), pp. 168-172. ♦ Discussion of Ansonborough area rehabilitation program of Historic Charleston.

South Carolina Appalachian Council of Governments. *Historic Preservation Plan for Appalachian South Carolina: Greenville County Summary.* Prepared by South Carolina Appalachian Council of Governments for the Greenville County Historic Preservation Commission. Greenville, S.C. (?): The Council, 1973. 169 pp. ♦ Part of a statewide survey and preservation plan, with the survey to be compiled from ten districts.

TENNESSEE

Buchart-Horn. *Port Royal Covered Bridge Restoration Project.* Memphis, Tenn.: The Author, 1969. 32 pp., photos, measured drawings, diagrams, maps, bibliog.

Eberling, May Dean. "History in Towns: Jonesboro, Tennessee's Oldest Town," *Antiques,* 100:3 (September 1971), pp. 420-424.

Sternberg, Irma O. *Overton Park Is Your Park, Memphis!* Memphis, Tenn.: Tri-State Press, 1971. 72 pp., appendices, paper. ♦ Appendices include health effects of air pollution, legal citations and selected references, "Letter to the Editor."

Tennessee. State Historical Commission *Tennessee's Plan for Historic Preservation (An Interim Plan).* Rev. ed. Nashville, Tenn.: The Commission, c1970, 1971. 131 pp., photos, maps, forms, appendices, paper.

Tennessee. State Planning Commission. Upper East Tennessee Office. *Historic District Plan, Jonesboro, Tennessee.* Johnson City, Tenn.: 1972. 113 pp., maps, plans, drawings, appendix.

TEXAS

Brightman, Anna. "The Winedale Stagecoach Inn Near Round Top, Texas," *Antiques,* 94:1 (July 1968), pp. 96-100.

Graham, Roy Eugene, and Ben Calloway Jones. *Progressive Preservation: A Guide to the Understanding and Implementation of the Preservation of Historic Architecture in Texas.* Austin, Tex.: University of Texas, 1972. 122 pp., photos, drawings, bibliog. ♦ Includes definitions, policy decisions, public and private implementation.

San Antonio. Community Renewal Program. *San Antonio Historic Survey 1972.* Prepared by O'Neill, Perez, Lance, Larcade, architects. San Antonio, Tex.: City Planning Department, 1972. 32 pp., photos. ♦ Statement of program for historic preservation, objectives, special recommendations to be enacted by the city council, and survey description.

San Antonio. Community Renewal Program. *San Antonio Historic Survey 1972: Appendix.* Prepared by O'Neill, Perez, Lance, Larcade, architects. San Antonio, Tex.: City Planning Department, 1972. 60 pp., charts, bibliog. ♦ Includes survey methodology, map and resource index, text of laws, and data sources.

Skidmore, Owings & Merrill. *Urban Design Mechanisms for San Antonio.* San Antonio, Tex.: City Planning Department, Community Renewal Program, 1972. 108 pp., photos, drawings, diagrams, maps, plans, tables, bibliog., appendix.

Texas. Legislative Council. *Historic Forts and Missions in Texas; Restoration and Preservation: A Report to the 60th Legislature.* Council Report no. 59-7. Austin, Tex.: The Council, 1966. 110 pp.

VERMONT

Rovetti, Paul R.; Richard A. Haberlen; and Barbara Franco. *The Park-McCullogh House, North Bennington, Vermont: A Program of Use.* Consultant Service Grant Report no. 2. Washington, D.C.: National Trust for Historic Preservation, 1973. 14 pp., photos, drawings, plans, bibliog., paper.

Vermont. State Division of Historic Sites. *Historic Preservation in Vermont.* State Preservation Plan, Vol. III. Montpelier, Vt.: The Division, 1972. 39 pp., charts, tables, inserts, maps, forms, appendices.

VIRGINIA

The Architectural Record. *The Restoration of Colonial Williamsburg in Virginia.* New York: F.W. Dodge Corp., c1935. 355-458 pp. incl., illus. ♦ Reprinted from *Architectural Record,* December 1935. Contents include: "The Restoration of Colonial Williamsburg in Virginia," by Fiske Kimball; "The Historical Background," and "Notes on the Architecture," by W. G. Perry; "City Plan and Landscaping Problems," by A. A. Shurcliff; "Paints, Furniture and Furnishings," by Mrs. Susan Higgins Nash.

Fairfax County, Virginia. Planning Division. *Historic Preservation for Fairfax County, Virginia.* Rev. ed. Fairfax County, Va.: Division of Planning, 1967, 1969. 84 pp., photos, drawings, bibliog., appendix.

Fairfax County, Virginia. Planning Division. *A Proposal for the Pohick Church Historic District.* Fairfax County, Va.: Department of Planning and Financial Management, Division of Planning, 1969. 20 pp.

Green Springs Association. *Comments and Information on Environmental Impact of Proposed Reception and Diagnostic Center in Green Springs.* Green Springs, Va.: The Association, 1971. Unpaged, photos, maps, bibliog., paper. ♦ Statements by experts on the environmental impact on the historic community. Mentions alternate sites and alternate considerations. Compiled for inclusion in Law Enforcement Impact Report. See also: U.S. Department of Justice. *Green Springs Environmental Impact Statement.*

Rasmussen, Paul W. "Planning and Historic Preservation: The Old Town of Alexandria Experience," *Planners Notebook,* 3:1 (February 1973). ♦ Case study of preservation effort where preservation is an integral part of city planning process and is supported by both city hall and citizen groups.

U. S. Department of Justice. *Green Springs Environmental Impact Statement.* (Draft). Washington, D.C.: U.S. Government Printing Office, n.d. 90 pp., photos, drawings, diagrams, maps, tables. ♦ See also: "Environmental Impact Statement," three volumes of supporting material on alternatives, results of the proposal and exhibits in support and opposition, prepared for the U.S. Department of Justice, Law Enforcement Assistance Administration by the Environmental Impact Statement Section, National Clearinghouse for Criminal Justice, Planning and Architecture. Volume I also prepared by Impact Report Committee, Department of Welfare and Institutions, Virginia, for the Division of Corrections, Department of Welfare and Institutions, Virginia. Copies available at the library of the National Trust for Historic Preservation. See also: Green Springs Association, *Comments and Information. . . .*

Virginia. Division of State Planning and Community Affairs. *A Comprehensive Plan for Fredericksburg, Virginia.* Richmond, Va.: The Division, 1970. 120 pp., plans, folding maps, bibliog.

Waterford Foundation. *A Plan for the Conservation of Waterford.* Waterford, Va.: The Foundation, 1972? 12 pp., photos, maps.

Wrenn, Tony P. *Cherry Hill: Falls Church, Virginia.* Falls Church, Va.: Falls Church Historical Commission, 1971. 108 pp., photos, drawings, maps, plans, bibliog., appendix. ♦ Historical, architectural, and legal aspects of the estate.

Wrenn, Tony P. *The Dranesville Tavern: Proposals for Its Relocation, Restoration and Use as a Tourist and Information Center.* Fairfax County, Va.: Fairfax County Historical Landmarks Preservation Commission, 1967. 30 pp., illus.

Wrenn, Tony P. *Huntley: A Mason Family Country House.* Fairfax, Va.: Fairfax County Division of Planning, 1971. 56 pp., illus., bibliog.

WASHINGTON

Uhlman, Wes. "Preserving Pioneer Square in Seattle." Reprinted from *HUD Challenge,* June 1973. 4 pp., photos. ♦ Restoration of a historic town square when the city formed a public corporation to renovate and sell old buildings. Available as part of *Your Community Workbook* of the New York State Council on Architecture, Public Awareness Program.

WEST VIRGINIA

West Virginia. Community Affairs Division. *Comprehensive Plan: Phase One – Basic Research, Surveys and Analyses, Town of Moorefield, Hardy County, West Virginia.* Moorefield, W. Va.: The Division, 1969. 79 pp., maps, plans, charts, bibliog., appendix.

Wrenn, Tony P. *West Virginia Independence Hall, Wheeling, West Virginia: A Master Plan for Restoration and Use.* Consultant Service Grant Report no. 4. Washington, D.C.: National Trust for Historic Preservation, 1973. 14 pp., photos, prints, map, paper. ♦ Adaptive reuse study of old custom house.

WISCONSIN

University of Wisconsin. Department of Urban and Regional Planning, and Department of Landscape Architecture. *A Historic District Concept for Madison: A Background Study.* Madison, Wis.: The University , 1972? 61 pp., plans, charts, paper.

PUERTO RICO

Delgado, Mercado, Osiris. *Proyecto Para la Conservacion del San Juan Antiguo.* San Juan: Instituto de Cultura Puertorriquena, 1956. 77 pp., plans.

Puerto Rico. Urban Renewal and Housing Administration. *Old San Juan and Puerta de Tierra: A General Neighborhood Renewal Plan.* Report . . . prepared by the Puerto Rico Urban Renewal and Housing Administration, Long Range Planning Office. Rio Piedras: available from the Urban Renewal and Housing Corp., 1964. 81 pp., illus., maps.

VIRGIN ISLANDS

Royal Danish Academy of Fine Arts, Department of Town Planning. *Three Towns: Conservation and Renewal of Charlotte Amalie, Christiansted, and Frederiksted of the U.S. Virgin Islands.* Copenhagen: Tutein and Koch, 1964. 122 pp., drawings, maps. ♦ Analysis and historical development of three towns, conservation of buildings, and renewal proposals.

CANADA, GREAT BRITAIN, AND OTHER

Bland, John. "A Possible Programme for the Preservation and Restoration of Quebec," *Community Planning Review,* 13 (Autumn 1963), pp. 6-17.

Bland, John. "Preservation and Restoration of Quebec," *Historic Preservation,* 16:5 (September-October 1964), pp. 190-194.

Buchanan (Colin) and Partners. *Bath: A Study in Conservation.* Report to the Minister of Housing and Bath City Council. London: Her Majesty's Stationery Office, 1968. 141 pp., illus., maps.

Burrows, George Stokes. *Chichester: A Study in Conservation.* Report to the Minister of Housing and Local Government. London: Her Majesty's Stationery Office (distr. by British Information Services, New York), 1968. 203 pp., illus., maps, plans, bibliog.

Cambridge, England. Department of Architecture and Planning. *Cambridge Townscape: An Analysis.* Cambridge: City of Cambridge, Department of Architecture and Planning, 1971. 150 pp., 30 pp., illus., maps.

Donald W. Insall and Associates. *Blandford Forum: Conserve and Enhance.* Prepared for the County Planning Department of Dorset. London: 1970. 73 pp., illus., maps, plans.

Donald W. Insall and Associates. *Chester: A Study in Conservation.* Report to the Minister of Housing and Local Government and the City and County of Chester. London: Her Majesty's Stationery Office, 1968. 257 pp., folding plates, illus., maps, plans.

Esher, Lionel Gordon Baliol Brett, 4th Viscount. *York: A Study in Conservation.* Report to the Minister of Housing and Local Government and York City Council. London: Her Majesty's Stationery Office, 1968. 249 pp., illus., maps, plans. ◆ Four-page leaflet inserted, "Studies in Conservation: Classified Guide to Selected Topics."

"Halifax: Preservation of Nova Scotia's Architecture," *Urban Renewal and Public Housing in Canada,* 1 (July-September 1965), pp. 12-14.

Robbins, J. Stanton. *The Distinctive Architecture of Willemstad: Its Conservation and Enforcement.* A report prepared by J. Stanton Robbins (Stanton Robbins & Co.), and Lachlan F. Blair (Blair Associates). New York?: 1961. 50 pp., photos, maps, tables. ◆ Contents: Historic preservation in Curacao, Willemstad today, architectural inventory, historic area preservation, positive programs.

Robert Matthew, Johnson-Marshall & Partners. *New Life in Old Towns: Report by Robert Matthew, Johnson-Marshall & Partners on Two Studies on Urban Renewal in Nelson and Rawtenstall Municipal Boroughs for the Department of the Environment.* London: Her Majesty's Stationery Office, 1971. 212 pp., illus., bibliog. ◆ Study of two historic Lancashire towns and proposals to rehabilitate and revitalize them.

Seelig, Michael Y. *Time Present and Time Past: Proposals for Area Conservation in Vancouver.* Vancouver, B.C.: Department of Social Planning, 1973. 75 pp., drawings, bibliog.

5

Preservation Action

Equally as important as the fundamentals of law, research, and planning, there is preservation action, the necessary ingredient for raising funds, for restoring and re- habilitating structures, and for promoting preservation in the community.

Basically, action must be taken to finance a preservation project if there is to be any project at all. Although there are no magic formulas, if you have done your research and planning well, the chance of finding funds is certainly better— to say the least! To aid in the search, the first section of the chapter lists written material as well as places where further information about financial assistance may be procured.

The practical and special problems of restoration, the subject of the next several sections, are manifold and deserve particular attention. Fortunately, increasing concern for the analysis and conservation of buildings and building materials has led to more solutions and better restoration techniques. But the end is not in sight, for continued environmental pollution creates still more problems. Nonetheless, we know a great deal more today than we knew yesterday. As we will know more tomorrow, restorationists must keep up with developments through specialized organizations and periodicals.

Among the developments in the "new preservation" is greater attention to an old idea — rehabilitation and adaptive use. Since time immemorial man has been adapting structures that could be rehabilitated. Examples of today's uses are included in their own section. What is more important, perhaps, is that during the last twenty-five years there has been a rising consciousness that not all structures significant enough to be saved need to become museums of some variety. The lesson has been brought home especially in the movement to save historic districts, neighborhoods, and areas where a community of people can still live and work and enjoy their "renewed" scenic and historic environment.

Finally, the key to any successful project is the continuing effort by preservationists to relate and communicate — to financial supporters, public officials, restoration experts, and the community. The value of a good public relations program must not be under- estimated. Basically, preservation is for people, and it is heartwarming to note the burgeoning of interest in recent years on the part of a concerned citizenry. Throughout the process of their participation in the legal techniques, the research and surveys, the planning and the fund raising, the public must be continually inspired, educated, and rewarded. Many of these techniques are demonstrated in a selected number of books and articles in the last section of this chapter. The community is where today's action is, and where it ought to continue to be.

Funding and Fund Raising

Adler, Leopold, II. "Historic Savannah Foundation, Inc.," *Antiques,* 91:3 (March 1967), pp. 334-338.

Alderson, William T., Jr. "Securing Grant Support: Effective Planning and Preparation," *History News,* 27:12 (December 1972), Technical Leaflet no. 62 (new series). ◆ Suggests guidelines found successful by agencies that have received grants, and points out pitfalls.

Andrews, F. Emerson. "Applications for Foundation Grants." Reprinted from *Bulletin* of the American Association of Fund-Raising Counsel, n.d. 8 pp., bibliog., leaflet.

Berlin, Roisman & Kessler. *Law and Taxation: A Guide for Conservation and Other Nonprofit Organizations.* Washington, D.C.: The Conservation Foundation, 1970. 47 pp., paper.

Civic Trust. *Financing the Preservation of Old Buildings: A Civic Trust Report to the Department of the Environment.* London: The Trust, 1971. 47 pp.

Costonis, John J. "The Cost of Preservation: The Chicago Plan and the Economics of Keeping Landmarks in the Marketplace," *Architectural Forum,* 140 (January-February 1974), pp. 61-67. ◆ Detailed, technical analysis of the Chicago Plan as applied to four landmark buildings of the Chicago School of the late 1800's, which seeks to fund the municipal preservation program by transferring development rights as opposed to tax revenues.

Costonis, John J. *Space Adrift: Landmark Preservation and the Marketplace.* Urbana, Ill.: University of Illinois Press, 1974. 224 pp., illus., tables, drawings. ◆ Discusses the Chicago Plan which provides for the sale of unused development potential of landmark buildings for use on nonlandmark sites, transferring the cost of preservation from the owner or the city to the development process itself.

Costonis, John J. *Space Adrift: Saving Urban Landmarks Through the Chicago Plan.* Urbana, Ill.: Published for the National Trust for Historic Preservation by the University of Chicago Press, 1974. 207 pp., photos, tables, charts, graphs, bibliog., index, paper. ◆ Paperback edition of *Space Adrift: Landmark Preservation and the Marketplace* (cited above).

Dermer, Joseph. *How to Write Successful Foundation Presentations.* New York: Public Service Materials Center, 1970. 64 pp., paper.

Dermer, Joseph, ed. *Where America's Large Foundations Make Their Grants.* New York: Public Service Materials Center, 1971. 190 pp., paper. ◆ Includes list of foundations and grants by state.

The Foundation Directory. 4th ed. Edited by Marianna O. Lewis. New York: Columbia University Press, 1971. 642 pp., graphs, charts, indexes.

Foundation Grants Index. New York: distributed by Columbia University Press. 1 vol., annual. ◆ Compiled by the Foundation Center, Lee Noe, ed. 1972 edition.

Grantsmanship: Money and How to Get It. Orange, N.J.: Academic Media. 1973. 27 pp., bibliog., appendices, paper.

Grove, Richard. "Taken for Granted: Notes on the Pursuit of Money," *Museum News,* 49:10 (June 1971), pp. 18-19.

Lynn, James T. "Preservation and Revenue Sharing," *Preservation News,* 13:9 (September 1973), p. 8.

Maryland Historical Trust. *Sources of Funding for Historic Preservation.* MHT Guides to Historic Preservation Activity, no. 4. Annapolis, Md.: The Trust, n.d. 30 pp., bibliog., paper.

"Millions for the Arts"; Federal and State Cultural Programs, An Exhaustive Senate Report. By the editors of the Washington International Arts Letter. Arts Patronage Series. Washington, D.C.: Washington International Arts Letter, c1972. 58 pp., paper.

Morton, Terry Brust. "Town Hall Tonite," *Historic Preservation,* 18:1 (January-February 1966), pp. 8-19. ◆ Discusses National Endowment for the Arts/Humanities as potential sources of funding for remodeling opera houses and theaters.

Murtagh, William J. "Financing Landmark Preservation." Reprinted from "New Twists in Financing Historic Preservation," American Institute of Architects *Journal,* 45:3 (March 1966), pp. 70-74. 6 pp., photos. ◆ Reviews briefly examples of acquiring historic properties by purchase, gift, bequest, federal aid, adaptive use, foundation support, mortgage, and revolving funds.

The National Trust (England). *The National Trust and the Preservation of Historic Build-*

ings. London: The Trust, n.d. 8 pp. ◆ Describes the Country House Scheme for acquiring properties.

National Trust for Historic Preservation. *Consultant Service Grant Program: A Progress Report, July 1973.* Washington, D.C.: The Trust, 1973. 60 pp., photos, tables, paper. ◆ Contents include grant procedures, grant recipients, summary of grants, consultants, and grant application form.

National Trust for Historic Preservation. "Dollars and Sense: Preservation Economics." Reprinted from *Historic Preservation,* 23:2 (April-June 1971), pp. 15-33. ◆ Four articles on economic determinants, real estate values, economic incentives, and revolving funds.

National Trust for Historic Preservation. *A Guide to State Programs.* 1972 ed. Washington, D.C.: The Trust, 1972. 200 pp., paper. ◆ Information for each state is divided into two sections: preservation framework, giving the basis for the state program, the state's laws relating to preservation, and various state preservation programs and relationships with other state offices; and, preservation programs, outlining the programs undertaken by the state in response to preservation legislation. Rev. ed. in preparation.

National Trust for Historic Preservation. *National Historic Preservation Fund, Annual Report, Fiscal Year 1973.* Washington, D.C.: The Trust, 1973. 19, 5 pp., photos, paper. ◆ Contents include description of a revolving fund, administration of the NHPF, summaries of loans and grants, accounting of NHPF and its funding sources, and a NHPF application.

National Trust for Historic Preservation. *Sources of Project Implementation Funds.* Washington, D.C.: The Trust, September 1973. 6 pp., mimeo. ◆ Includes revolving funds, foundation support, federal financial assistance (National Register of Historic Places, revenue sharing), guides to financial support, other sources.

National Trust for Historic Preservation. *Technical Assistance Funds and Services.* Washington, D.C.: The Trust, August 1973. 5 pp., mimeo. ◆ Reprinted with *Sources of Project Implementation Funds* (cited above) in a four-page leaflet by the New York State Council on Architecture, Public Awareness Program, 1974.

New York (State). Commission on Cultural Resources. *State Financial Assistance to Cul-*

tural Resources: Report. New York: 1971. 163 pp., illus.

Pfeiffer, Norman. "Right Side of the Tracks: An Investigation into the Economics of Redeeming America's Old Train Depots," *Architectural Forum,* 139 (November 1973), pp. 66-73. ◆ Also available as part of *Your Community Workbook* of the New York State Council on Architecture, Public Awareness Program.

Private Foundations Active in the Arts. By the editors of the Washington International Arts Letter. Arts Patronage Series, vol. 1. Washington, D.C.: Washington International Arts Letter, c1970. 138 pp., paper. ◆ See also: *Private Foundations Active in the Arts Since Volume I: Lists 8-11* (Reprints of Newsletters).

Rowland, Howard S. *The New York Times Guide to Federal Aid for Cities and Towns.* New York: Quadrangle Books, 1972. 1243 pp.

Sheehan, Donald T. "Programming for Fund-Raising," *Historic Preservation,* 18:3 (May-June 1966), pp. 118-125. ◆ Also available as National Trust for Historic Preservation leaflet, 8 pp.

SPA/REDCO, Inc. *An Unsolicited Proposal to Provide a Basic Resource Tool for Historic Preservation.* Chicago, Ill.: The Company, n.d. 38 pp., tables, appendix. ◆ Suggestions for fund raising for preservation groups by consulting firm specializing in legislative analysis, market and economic feasibility analysis, and intergovernmental relations.

Turner, Bob. "Preservation at a Profit?" *Preservation News,* 14:3 (March 1974), p. 5. ◆ Columbus, Georgia, Historic Development Group organized as an investment partnership.

U.S. Advisory Council on Historic Preservation. *The Environmental Protection Tax Act of 1973: An Analysis for the Advisory Council on Historic Preservation, September 24, 1973.* Washington, D.C.: The Council, 1973. 13 pp., photocopy. ◆ Legislation is pending in U.S. House of Representatives Ways and Means Committee.

U.S. Advisory Council on Historic Preservation. *Issue Paper on Revenue Sharing, August 1, 1973.* 2nd paper. Washington, D.C.: The Council, 1973. 25 pp., photocopy.

U.S. Department of Commerce. Office of Area Development. *Your Community Can Profit from the Tourist Business.* Prepared by

Harry Clement. Washington, D.C.: U.S. Government Printing Office, 1957. 25 pp., illus. ◆ Economic value of tourist trade, tourism as dimension in community development, individual and community benefits, tourist attractions as a lure for industry, and how to sell and promote what you have.

U.S. Department of Housing and Urban Development. *Grants for Historic Preservation: Information for Applicants.* Washington, D.C.: The Department, 1970. Loose-leaf.

U.S. Office of Archeology and Historic Preservation. *Historic Preservation Grants-in-Aid (as of October 31, 1972).* Washington, D.C.: National Park Service, 1972. 42 pp. ◆ A complete list of all existing grants as of title date awarded since the passage of the Historic Preservation Act of 1966, giving a summary of the historical significance of a project site and the assistance work, by state, as well as site ownership and dollar amount of assistance.

U.S. Office of Archeology and Historic Preservation. *Historic Preservation Grants-in-Aid: Policies and Procedures.* Washington, D.C.: National Park Service, National Register of Historic Places, 1973. 101 pp., diagrams, charts, forms, index, paper. ◆ Outlines the format, scope, and content of the state historic preservation plan, the annual program grant, and administration of grants. The appendices include sample forms and charts.

U.S. Office of Management and Budget. Executive Office of the President. *Catalog of Federal Domestic Assistance.* Washington, D.C.: U.S. Government Printing Office, 1973. Various pagings, indexes, paper. ◆ Comprehensive listing and description of federal government domestic programs to assist in furthering social and economic progress. Includes 868 domestic assistance programs and activities administered by over forty-nine federal departments and agencies. See also: *Update to the 1973 Catalog of Federal Domestic Assistance.*

Washington and the Arts: *A Guide and Directory to Federal Programs and Dollars for the Arts.* Edited by Janet English Gracey and Sally Gardner. New York: Associated Councils of the Arts, 1971. 176 pp., appendices, paper.

Wilkes, Paul, and Joy Wilkes. *You Don't Have to Be Rich to Own a Brownstone.* New York: Quadrangle Books/The New York Times Book Co., 1973. 139 pp., illus., appendix, bibliog. ◆ How-to-do-it guide to restoring a brownstone including background on city houses, alternative to single-party ownership, evaluating neighborhoods and houses, buying your house, financing, estimating costs, legal information, insurance, tax information, building codes, and renovation problems.

Ziegler, Arthur P., Jr. *The Restoration Fund of Pittsburgh History and Landmarks Foundation: A Report.* Pittsburgh, Pa.: Pittsburgh History and Landmarks Foundation, 1970. 24 pp., appendix, paper. ◆ Describes use of funds to restore Liverpool Street and Mexican War Streets residential areas; background, work, summary, and future use of funds.

NOTES AND PERIODICALS

America the Beautiful Fund, 219 Shoreham Building, Washington, D.C. 20005. The Fund was established in 1965 as an environment-oriented, nonprofit organization, supported by private contributions, grants from the National Endowment for the Arts and the Lilly Endowment, Inc., to enrich the quality of the natural, historic, and man-made environment. Since 1965 the Fund has supported over 750 projects throughout the country in environmental planning, civic design, conservation, recreation, and cultural and historic preservation. In addition to providing technical assistance in planning and fund raising, the Fund offers small grants as "seed money" to initiate projects. The Fund also offers an Information Exchange as a clearinghouse for local history and preservation projects.

American Association of Fund-Raising Counsel. *Bulletin.* n.d., monthly, free. American Association of Fund-Raising Counsel, 500 Fifth Avenue, New York, New York 10036.

National Endowment for the Arts, Office of Museum Programs, 806 Fifteenth Street, N.W., Washington, D.C. 20506. The National Endowment for the Arts was created by Congress in 1965 as part of the National Foundation on the Arts and the Humanities. Its goals are to make the arts more widely available to preserve our cultural heritage; to strengthen cultural organizations; and to encourage creative development of talent. Grants are awarded as fellowships or matching grants in the fields of architecture and environmental arts, dance, education, expansion arts, crafts, literature, museums, music, public media, theater, and the visual arts. A City Options program focuses upon design and planning opportunities and concentrates on special settings, areas, and places within a city that provide its distinctive character and identity. Guidelines and an information leaflet are available from the Office of Museum Programs.

National Endowment for the Humanities, Office of Museum Programs, 806 Fifteenth Street, N.W., Washington, D.C. 20506. The National Endowment for the Humanities was created by Congress in 1965 as part of the National Foundation on the Arts and the Humanities. It supports a variety of activities in the humanities: education programs, public programs, research, fellowships and stipends, and projects designed and conducted by young people. Funds may be granted as outright grants or on a gifts and matching grant basis. A brochure and calendar of application dates are available from the Office of Museum Programs.

National Museum Act, Office of Museum Programs, Smithsonian Institution, Washington, D.C. 20560. Under the National Museum Act of 1970, the Smithsonian Institution provides technical aid and assistance to museums throughout the United States. An informal consultant service is available, as well as funding for formal proposals in a variety of program areas such as museum operations, exhibit techniques, conservation of artifacts, archival work, education programs, and management studies. Guidelines and a calendar of application dates are available from the Office of Museum Programs.

National Trust for Historic Preservation. "Guide to Federal Programs," in preparation. Description of federal programs supporting preservation-related activities.

National Trust for Historic Preservation. "Preservation in Your Town," in preparation. Proceedings of the 1973 Annual Preservation Conference, Cleveland, Ohio, October 10-14, to be published in 1974. Contents include: Preservationists Speak; Preservation Education Activities; Publications on a Budget; How to Raise Funds; Publicity and Public Relations; Observations from the Field; Preparation and Funding of Bicentennial Projects; Business Procedures of a Preservation Group; Marshall, Michigan, Preservation Project.

The Washington International Arts Letter. 1962, monthly, except July and December, subscription. Washington International Arts Letter, 115 Fifth Street, S.E., Washington, D.C.

20003. Information on current support programs for the arts including private foundations in the arts.

Restoration Techniques

General Principles and Practice

Baker, Roy W. "To Keep an Old House in Good Standing," *Old-Time New England,* 46:4, Serial no. 164 (Spring 1956), pp. 100-105.

Braun, Hugh. *The Restoration of Old Houses.* London: Faber and Faber, 1954. 192 pp., illus.

Builder's and Decorator's Reference Book: A Comprehensive Handbook Providing a Standard Day-to-Day Reference on the Construction, Repair, Redecoration and Renovation. 5th ed. Edited by E. Drury. London: George Newnes, 1962. 1 vol., various pagings, illus., diagrams, tables. ◆ Includes sections on building repair work, inspection of property, and shoring dangerous structures.

Building Research Institute. "Restoration and Preservation of Historic Buildings," *Building Research,* 1:5 (September-October 1964), entire issue. 64 pp., photos, drawings. ◆ Includes architecture and engineering; history research; archaeology; entomology; photogrammetry; photography; measured drawings and landscaping; pertinent data on details of restoring and preserving masonry, woodwork, paint, hardware, and lighting.

Bullock, Orin M., Jr. "The Friends Meeting House, 1699-1922; An Architectural Research Report," *Newport History,* 42:134, Part 2 (Spring 1969), pp. 25-57.

Bullock, Orin M., Jr. *The Restoration Manual: An Illustrated Guide to the Preservation and Restoration of Old Buildings.* Norwalk, Conn.: Silvermine Publishing Co., 1966. 181 pp., photos, prints, drawings, glossary, bibliog. ◆ Chapters include: architecture and engineering, historical research, archeological research, architectural research, restoration and specifications, building maintenance, building interpretation. The appendix, "Restoration and Preservation of Historic Buildings," is reprinted from *Building Research,* 1:5 (September-October 1964), entire issue.

Church of England. Council for the Care of Churches. *The Conservation of Churches and*

Their Treasures: A Bibliography. London: The Council, 1970. 73 pp., mimeo.

Church of England. Council of Diocesan Advisory Committees for the Care of Churches. *Redecorating Your Church.* Westminster: Church Information Service, 1971. 16 pp., photos. ◆ Discussion of approaches to various styles of churches and technical procedures on redecoration.

Civic Trust. *Pride of Place: A Manual for Those Wishing to Improve Your Surroundings.* London: The Trust, 1972. 126 pp., photos, diagrams, bibliog. ◆ Includes basic operation, problems and opportunities, checklist for restoration, landscaping, parks, playgrounds, etc.

Council of Europe. Council for Cultural Cooperation. *Principles and Practice of Active Preservation and Rehabilitation of Groups and Areas of Buildings of Historical or Artistic Interest; Preservation and Rehabilitation of Groups and Areas of Buildings of Historical or Artistic Interest.* Symposium C, Bath, 3-7 October, 1966; Report. Strasbourg: 1967. 126 pp.

Council of Europe. Council for Cultural Cooperation. *The Reviving of Monuments; Preservation and Development of Groups and Areas of Buildings of Historical or Artistic Interst.* Symposium B, Vienna, 4-8 October, 1965; Report. Strasbourg: 1965. 142 pp.

Fairfax, Geoffrey W. *Iolani Palace Restoration: Architectural Report.* Honolulu, Hawaii: Geoffrey W. Fairfax, Inc., 1972. 209 pp., illus., appendices. ◆ Copy on deposit in the National Trust for Historic Preservation library.

Hargreaves, June M. *Historic Buildings: Problems of Their Preservation.* Reprinted with additions, November 1965. York, Eng.: York Civic Trust, c1964, 1965. 34 pp., illus., bibliog.

Harvey, John. *Conservation of Buildings.* London: John Baker, 1972. 240 pp., photos, appendices, bibliog. notes, index. ◆ Includes "What to Save and How to Save It," "Craftsmen and Materials," "Continuing Conservation."

Harvey, John, comp. "Conservation of Old Buildings: A Select Bibliography," rev. ed. Reprinted from *Transactions* of the Ancient Monuments Society, new series, 16 (1969), pp. 115-144. 30 pp., paper. ◆ Annotated bibliography compiled for the use of architects and others directly concerned with the conservation and repair of individual buildings. Sections include general works, national

and international; acoustics; damage; chimneys; churches; fire protection; special problems; surveys; weathering.

"Historic Building Restoration," *Architectural and Engineering News,* 6:6 (June 1964), pp. 74-81.

Insall, Donald W. *The Care of Old Buildings Today: A Practical Guide.* London: The Architectural Press, 1972. 197 pp., photos, diagrams, bibliog. ◆ Published in conjunction with the Society for the Protection of Ancient Buildings, the book shows owners and architects how to dispel the threats of decay, neglect, and the developer's bulldozer. The first section deals with the administrative problems, legal background, and sources of financial help in Great Britain, and the second section covers specific restoration techniques.

Iolani Palace Restoration Project. *Iolani Palace Restoration.* Written, designed, and produced by the Iolani Palace Restoration Project staff and special consultants. Project director: George Moore. Honolulu: Friends of Iolani Palace, 1970. 203 pp., illus., plans, bibliog., paper. ◆ Includes concepts of environment and historical relationship; architectural philosophy; building research; restoration program; feasibility study; resources and fiscal matters.

Johnson, Sidney M. *Deterioration, Maintenance, and Repair of Structures.* New York: McGraw-Hill, 1965. 373 pp., photos, diagrams, tables, bibliog., index. ◆ Manual on repair and restoration, prevention of deterioration in steel, concrete, and timber structures.

Judd, Henry A. "Before Restoration Begins: Keeping Your Historic House Intact," *History News,* 28:10 (October 1973), Technical Leaflet no. 67 (new series).

Judd, Henry A. "Before Restoration Starts," *Bulletin of APT,* 3:1 (1971), pp. 30-37.

Judd, Henry A. "What to Do Before the Restorationist Comes," *Antiques,* 101:1 (January 1972), pp. 209-216.

Kelsall, Moultrie R., and Stuart Harris. *A Future for the Past.* London: Oliver and Boyd, 1961. 151 pp., photos, diagrams, index. ◆ Development of a policy of restoration in Scotland which includes practical notes on restoration techniques and case histories.

Lockwood, Alice G. B. "Problems and Responsibilities of Restoration," *Old-Time New England,* 28:2 (October 1937), pp. 49-59.

Melville, Ian A., and Ian A. Gordon. *The Repair and Maintenance of Houses.* 1st ed. London: The Estates Gazette, Ltd., 1973. 1050 pp., technical drawings. ◆ Diagnosis and remedies, for British conditions, regarding brick walls, stone walls, foundations, timber, shoring, roof coverings, dampness, internal and general matters, drainage, and contracts.

Nelson, Lee H. "Restoration in Independence Hall: A Continuum of Historic Preservation," *Antiques,* 90:1 (July 1966), pp. 64-68.

Nichols, Frederick D. "Primer for Preservation: Techniques and Problems," *History News,* 19:4 (February 1964), Technical Leaflet no. 17 (old series). ◆ See also: *Primer for Preservation: A Handbook for Historic-House Keeping* (Cooperstown: New York State Historical Association, 1956), pp. 13-15; *New York History,* 37:2 (1956), pp. 165-170.

Noblecourt, Andre. *Protection of Cultural Property in the Event of Armed Conflict.* Museums and Monuments series no. VIII. Paris: UNESCO, 1958. 346 pp., illus., bibliog.

Olszewski, George J. *Restoration of Ford's Theatre, Washington, D.C.* Washington, D.C.: U.S. Department of the Interior, National Park Service, National Capital Region (for sale by the U.S. Government Printing Office), 1963. 138 pp., photos, prints, diagrams, appendix, bibliog., index, paper. ◆ Detailed historical investigation of construction, design and furnishing of the building prior to restoration.

Peterson, Charles E., ed. "American Notes: Burning Buildings for Nails," *Journal of the Society of Architectural Historians,* 9:3 (October 1950), p. 23.

Phillips, Morgan W. "The Philosophy of Total Preservation," *Bulletin of APT,* 3:1 (1971), pp. 38-43. ◆ Society for the Preservation of New England Antiquities philosophy of building restoration.

Plenderleith, H.J. "Problems in the Preservation of Monuments." In *The Conservation of Cultural Property With Special Reference to Tropical Conditions* (Paris: UNESCO, 1968), pp. 124-134. ◆ Includes foundations and pavements; walls; damage from accumulated soluble salts; value of external screening; consolidation; anastylosis; mortars; cement; concrete; organic growths; salvage and transport; the museum and the antiquarium; major problems of tropical monuments; bibliography.

Powys, Albert Reginald. *Repair of Ancient Buildings.* 1929. Reprint. Ann Arbor, Mich.: The Finch Press, 1972. 208 pp., illus.

"Principles of Historic Restoration: A Symposium," *Antiques,* 58:1 (July 1950), pp. 29-32.

"Restoration and Preservation," *Architectural Review,* 148:885 (November 1970), special issue. ◆ Includes general comments on preservation and conservation, several accounts of European and British restoration projects, training, and listing sites.

Richards, J.M., and Abraham Rogatnick. "Venice: Problems and Possibilities," *Architectural Review,* 149:891 (May 1971), pp. 258-324, special issue.

Russell, Nadine Carter. "Restoring Architect Gallier's House in New Orleans," *Historic Preservation,* 23:4 (October-December 1971), pp. 27-29. ◆ Discusses restoration of special innovative architectural ideas and interior details.

Society for the Protection of Ancient Buildings. *The Protection of Ancient Buildings.* Prepared for the General Assembly of International Council of Monuments and Sites, Oxford, 1969. London: The Society, 1969. 46 pp., photos, drawings, paper. ◆ Examples of the Society's work, illustrations of repair methods, and before and after views of buildings saved.

United Nations Educational, Scientific and Cultural Organization. *Preserving and Restoring Monuments and Historic Buildings.* Museums and Monuments series no. XIV. Paris: UNESCO, 1972. 267 pp., photos, diagrams, charts, bibliog. references, paper and hardcover.

United Nations Educational, Scientific and Cultural Organization. *Venice Restored.* Paris: UNESCO, 1973. 95 pp., photos, bibliog. ◆ Illustrated report on the restoration of architecture in Venice, review of contributions by country, and future needs.

U.S. Commission on Renovation of the Executive Mansion. *Report.* Compiled under the direction of Edwin Bateman Morris. Washington, D.C.: U.S. Government Printing Office, 1952. 109, 4 pp., plans, photos, drawings, appendix.

U.S. Office of Archeology and Historic Preservation. *A Brief Bibliography for the Restoration of Historic Buildings.* Compiled by Paul Goeldner. Washington, D.C.: Historic American Buildings Survey, 1971. 6 pp., mimeo. ◆ Annotated bibliography.

Wilkes, Paul, and Joy Wilkes. *You Don't Have to Be Rich to Own a Brownstone.* New York: Quadrangle Books/The New York Times Book Co., 1973. 139 pp., illus., appendix, bibliog. ◆ How-to-do-it guide to restoring a brownstone, including evaluating neighborhoods and houses, financing, costs, legal information, building codes, renovation problems, and inconvenience.

Wofford, Theodore J., and W. Philip Cotton, Jr. *Recommendations for Restoring and Rejuvenating the Wainwright Building.* St. Louis, Mo.: St. Louis Chapter of the American Institute of Architects, Committee for the Preservation of Historic Buildings, 1966. 13 pp., plans, prints, paper.

NOTES AND PERIODICALS

Association for Preservation Technology, Meredith H. Sykes, Secretary-Treasurer, Box 2682, Ottawa 4, Ontario, Canada. Founded in 1968, the Association was organized for professional preservationists, restoration architects, furnishings consultants involved directly or indirectly in preservation activities. It publishes *Bulletin of APT* (cited below), and *Newsletter of APT* (cited below). A list of members with area of special interest is in *Bulletin of APT,* III:1 (1971), pp. 67-90.

Building Research: The Journal of the Building Research Institute. 1964, quarterly, membership. Building Research Institute, 2101 Constitution Avenue, N.W., Washington, D.C. 20418.

Building Research Establishment, Scottish Laboratory, Kelvin Road, East Kilbride, Glasgow, Scotland G75 ORZ. Formed in 1972, the Establishment is an amalgamation of the Building Research Station, Fire Research Station, and The Forest Products Research Laboratory. It integrates construction research efforts within the Department of the Environment, some of which is relevant to the profession in the private sector. It publishes *BRE News,* quarterly, covering recent publications, research reports, application of research and events; and *Information Directory,* annual, containing current publications, films, and services of the BRE. Topics covered in the Building Research Digest series include moulds and growths on building materials, cracking in buildings, waterproofing, stone preservatives, with current numbers listed in the Directory. The series is available through subscription or as single copies. The Building Research Advisory Service, begun in 1970, gives advice on a wide range of construction topics and publishes reports which are explained in an information brochure. The BRE also sponsors seminars and symposia based on its research programs.

Bulletin of APT. 1969, quarterly, membership. Association for Preservation Technology, Meredith H. Sykes, Secretary-Treasurer, Box 2682, Ottawa 4, Ontario, Canada. ◆ American Editor: Lee H. Nelson, 4708 Twinbrook Road, Fairfax, Virginia 22030.

Council for the Care of Churches. Publications in the Care of Churches series are written by experts on the maintenance of churches and cover such topics as repair of stone buildings, church timberwork, books and fabrics, moving churches, damage by bats and birds, and replacement of ancient lead roofs with cooper. A catalogue is available from the Church Information Office, Church House, Dean's Yard, London SW1 P 3NZ, England.

National Inventory of Building Crafts. Sponsored by the National Trust for Historic Preservation with the assistance of such organizations as the Department of Labor, AFL-CIO, and American Crafts Council, the Inventory will comprise a listing of traditional building craftsmen. The National Trust will research the historic nature of the crafts, develop a traditional criterion, and design a questionnaire for surveying the field. Once the Inventory is established it will be available as a labor pool of traditional craftsmen for public and private projects. The individual craftsmen would also be available for educational documentation and for training programs.

Newsletter of APT. 1972, bimonthly, membership. Martin Eli Weil, Editor, Association for Preservation Technology, 400 Stewart Street, Apartment 2211, Ottawa, Ontario K1N 6L2, Canada. ◆ Includes information about the organization; exchange of information on particular research and technical problems; listings of suppliers, services, and research resources; reports on new publications, courses, techniques, and works in progress.

North American International Regional Conference, Williamsburg and Philadelphia, 1972. The National Trust for Historic Preservation and the Rome Centre Committee of the Advisory Council on Historic Preservation cosponsored a conference, "Preservation and

Conservation: Principles and Practices, 1972," in Williamsburg and Philadelphia, September 10-16, 1972. The papers presented at the conference are being edited by the National Trust and are scheduled for publication by the Smithsonian Institution in early 1975.

The Old House Journal: Renovation and Maintenance Ideas for the Antique House. October 1973, monthly, subscription. The Old House Journal, 199 Berkeley Place, Brooklyn, New York 11217. ◆ Includes practical tips on general repairs, plumbing, and wiring, and readers' problems and solutions by the journal's technical staff.

Preservation and Building Codes, First National Conference, 1974. The National Trust for Historic Preservation sponsored the first national conference on preservation and building codes in Washington, D.C. on May 18-19, 1974. It was designed to analyze the problem of the divergence between modern building code requirements and historic preservation needs, and to explore some of the possibilities for modifying existing conditions. Experts from preservation organizations, national code organizations, National Fire Protection Association, and General Services Administration were among the participants.

Society for the Protection of Ancient Buildings, 55 Great Ormond Street, London, SC1N 3JA. Founded in 1877 to advise on the repair and treatment of old buildings. Complete description is given in Chapter 1, Preservation Organizations.

Technical Handbook for Historic Preservation. The National Park Service is collecting and organizing the knowledge and expertise developed over the past 40 years by the governmental and private sectors relating to historic preservation. The material will be edited and published as a technical handbook dealing with professional methods and techniques for preserving, improving, restoring, and maintaining historic properties. Lee H. Nelson, Project Director, Office of Archeology and Historic Preservation, National Park Service, 1100 L Street, N.W., Room 3413, Washington, D.C. 20005.

Buildings and Grounds Maintenance

Carroll, Orville. "Linoleum Used in Restoration Work," *Bulletin of APT*, 1:3 (December 1969), p. 8-11.

Emerick, Robert H. "Heating of Restorations." Reprinted from *Progressive Architecture,* August 1957. 12 pp., table, leaflet.

Fire Protection Association, England. *Fire Protection of Country Houses.* Rev. ed. Booklet no. 22. London: The Association, c1954. 24 pp., photos, drawings, paper. ◆ Prepared in consultation with a committee of the Royal Institute of British Architects and with the Society for the Protection of Ancient Buildings to illustrate causes of fires in country houses and recommended installations.

Fire Protection Association, England. *Prevention and Control of Fire in Cathedrals and Churches.* London: The Association, 1973. 14 pp., photos, drawings, paper. ◆ Includes examples of fires, ignition sources, dangers and precautions, fire fighting and fire protection equipment, and a fire prevention checklist.

Garston, Eng. Building Research Station. *Cleaning External Surfaces of Buildings.* Digest 113. London: Her Majesty's Stationery Office, 1970. 4 pp., leaflet. ◆ A descriptive outline of various techniques for cleaning different materials.

Moore, Alma (Chestnut). *How to Clean Everything: An Encyclopedia of What to Use and How to Use It.* Rev. ed. New York: Simon and Schuster, 1968. 224 pp., illus., bibliog. ◆ Describes use of every readily available cleaning agent and lists precise steps to take for cleaning all kinds of materials based on methods tested and checked by experts in many fields. Much is applicable to historic houses and buildings.

National Fire Protection Association, Committee on Libraries, Museums and Historic Buildings. *Protecting Our Heritage: A Discourse on Fire Prevention in Historic Buildings and Landmarks.* 2nd ed. Edited by Joseph F. Jenkins. Boston: National Fire Protection Association, with the assistance of the American Association for State and Local History, 1970. 29 pp., photos, appendices, glossary of fire protection equipment, paper.

Stewart, John J. "Historic Gardens in Canada and the United States," *Newsletter of APT,* 2:3 (June 1973), entire issue. ◆ Initial study includes location and description of gardens, historic garden experts, sources of plant materials and seeds. See also: Sykes, Meredith, and John Stewart, cited below, for bibliography on research on historic gardens.

Streatfield, David. "Standards for Historic Garden Preservation and Restoration." Reprinted from *Landscape Architecture,* 59:3 (April 1969), pp. 198-204. 8 pp., photos.

Sykes, Meredith, and John Stewart. "Historic Landscape Restoration in the United States and Canada; An Annotated Source Outline," *Bulletin of APT,* 4:3-4 (1972), pp. 114-158.

Symons, Vivian. *Church Maintenance.* London: Marshall, Morgan & Scott, 1968. 153 pp., photos, diagrams, tables, bibliog., index. ♦ A manual on maintaining the fabric of churches.

U.S. Department of Agriculture. *Making Basements Dry.* By Richard H. Rule. Home and Garden Bulletin no. 115. Rev. ed. Washington, D.C.: U.S. Government Printing Office, 1970. 10 pp., diagrams, paper.

Moving Buildings

Curtis, John O. "Moving Historic Buildings," American Institute of Architects *Journal,* 43 (March 1965), pp. 41-46.

Elder, William Voss, III. "The Dismantling and Restoration of an Historic Room," *Museum News,* 45:8 (April 1967), pp. 51-56, Technical Supplement no. 17.

Gold, Michael W. "Bogardus Cast Iron: Designed to be Dismantled and Rebuilt," *Historic Preservation,* 23:3 (July-September 1971), pp. 12-19. ♦ New York City Landmarks Preservation Commission plan to save cast iron buildings in an urban renewal project.

Kirk, Frode, and Bjarne Stoklund. "Moving Old Buildings." Offprint from *Dansk Folkemuseum & Frilandsmuseet: History and Activities,* 1966, pp. 245-263. ♦ Techniques used to move Danish farm houses to open-air museums.

Special Problems

Eeles, Francis Carolus. *Wall Surfaces: Ancient Usage and Modern Care.* Pamphlets on the Care of Churches no. 3. London: Church Information Board, 1958. 9 pp., photos, drawings. ♦ Historical and technical study.

MacGregor, John E. M. *Outward Leaning Walls.* Technical Pamphlet no. 1. London: Society for the Protection of Ancient Buildings, 1971. 8 pp., photos, diagrams. ♦ Seven sections covering cause of failure, resulting damage, restraining walls, pulling back walls, leaning west towers, eliminating basic cause, and summary.

New York State Historic Trust. *The Stabilization of an Eighteenth Century Ceiling at Philipse Manor: A Restoration Report.* By John G. Waite. Albany: The Trust, 1972. 37 pp., photos, drawings, diagrams, maps, bibliog., paper.

"The Problems with Preservation." Reprinted from *The Atom,* January-February 1973. 6 pp., photos. ♦ Subterrene program at National Park Service sites and other ruins stabilization proposals. Reprinted by Los Alamos Scientific Laboratory, University of California, Los Alamos, New Mexico 87544.

Society for the Protection of Ancient Buildings. *Rising Damp and Leaning Walls.* London: The Society, 1971. 3 pp., diagram, mimeo.

U.S. National Park Service. *Prehistoric Ruins Stabilization Handbook: Part 2–Field Methods.* Compiled by Roland Richert and Gordon Vivian. Release no. 1. Washington, D.C.: U.S. Department of the Interior, 1962. Various pagings, photos, diagrams, tables, forms. ♦ Cover title: *Handbook for Ruins Stabilization.*

Williams, R.E., and J.E. Griggs. *Use of the Rock-Melting Subterrene for Formation of Drainage Holes in Archaeological Sites.* Informal Report no. LA-5370-MS. Los Alamos, New Mexico: Los Alamos Scientific Laboratory of the University of California, 1973. 8 pp., photos, diagrams, ♦ Technique of boring holes in the earth to drain water from archeological ruins.

Care and Restoration of Building Materials

EXAMINATION AND ANALYSIS

Conference on the Problems of Moisture in Historic Monuments, Rome, 1967. *Conference on the Problems of Moisture in Historic Monuments, Rome, 11-14 X 1967.* Paris: ICOMOS, 1969. 332 pp., photos, diagrams, charts, bibliog. ♦ Sponsored by ICOMOS and the International Centre for the Study of the Preservation and the Restoration of Cultural Property. Includes list of experts and laboratories; text in French and English.

Gratwick, Reginald Thomas. *Dampness in Buildings.* Vol. 1: "Basement and Ground-Floor Conditions"; Vol. II: "Condensation and Penetration Above Ground." London: Crosby

Lockwood, 1966-67. 2 vols., illus., diagrams. ◆ Standard study with details of all treatments including electroosmosis.

Hart, David. "Exposing the Elements," *Museum News,* 51:7 (March 1973), pp. 50-53. ◆ Describes an x-ray process used to determine conditions hidden from view in historic structures.

Hart, David M. "X-ray Analysis of the Narbonne House," *Bulletin of APT,* 6:1 (1974), pp. 78-98.

Hart, David M. "X-ray Investigation of Buildings," *Bulletin of APT,* 5:1 (1973), pp. 9-21.

International Centre for the Study of the Preservation and the Restoration of Cultural Property. *Guide to the Methodical Study of Monuments and Causes of Their Deterioration.* By Guglielmo De Angelis D'Ossat. Rome, Italy: The International Centre, 1972. 47 pp., charts, paper. ◆ Study of monuments from the historical, artistic, and technical point of view, and causes of deterioration. English and Italian text.

International Centre for the Study of the Preservation and the Restoration of Cultural Property. *Humidity in Monuments.* By Giovanni Massari. Rome, Italy: The International Centre, 1971. 47 pp., diagrams, paper. ◆ Explanation of harmful results of exposure to damp, and instruments used for the study, illustrated by five examples.

International Centre for the Study of the Preservation and the Restoration of Cultural Property. *Pathology of Building Materials.* By Marc Mamillan. Rome, Italy: The International Centre, 1970. 53 pp., paper. ◆ Technical remarks on all kinds of stone, terracotta materials, mortars, and coatings.

Stambolov, T., and J. R. J. Van Asperen De Boer. *The Deterioration and Conservation of Porous Building Materials in Monuments: A Literature Review.* Rome: International Centre for the Study of the Preservation and the Restoration of Cultural Property, 1972. 70 pp., bibliog. ◆ A survey of deterioration phenomena and conservation methods in relation to ancient monuments. Includes weathering by moisture and salts (rocks, bricks, mortar, and plaster); moisture in porous building materials; fire damage; frost damage; wind erosion; dust pollution; fungi; microorganisms; animals; metal corrosion; remedial measures against moisture; cleaning; consolidation and protection.

Stumes, Paul. "The Application of Epoxy Resins for the Restoration of Historic Structures," *Bulletin of APT,* 3:1 (1971), pp. 59-63.

U.S. Department of Agriculture. *Controlling Household Pests.* Home and Garden Bulletin no. 96. Rev. ed. Washington, D.C.: U. S. Government Printing Office, 1971. 32 pp., photos, drawings, recipe table, paper.

Vos, B.H. "Moisture in Monuments." In *Application of Science in the Examination of Works of Art; Proceedings of the Seminar; June 15-19, 1970* (Boston: Museum of Fine Arts, 1973), pp. 147-153. ◆ Includes humidity of air; hygroscopic moisture; suction of water from the ground; rain penetration; condensation.

BRICK

Bonnell, D. G. R., and W. R. Pippard. *Some Common Defects in Brickwork.* 1950. Reprint. Department of Scientific and Industrial Research, National Building Studies Bulletin no. 9. London: Her Majesty's Stationery Office, 1965. 22 pp., photos, bibliog. ◆ Description of six kinds of defects arising in brickwork and means of prevention.

Claiborne, Herbert A. *Comments on Virginia Brickwork Before 1800.* Boston: Walpole Society, 1957. 47 pp., illus.

Historic Structures Training Conference, 3d, Philadelphia, 1963. *Early American Brick Masonry and Restoration of Exterior Brick Walls.* Edited by Lee H. Nelson. Philadelphia, Pa.: U. S. Department of the Interior, National Park Service, Eastern Office, Design and Construction, 1963. 40 pp., illus., bibliog.

Ritchie, T. *On Using Old Bricks in New Buildings.* Canadian Building Digest Leaflet 138. Ottawa: Division of Building Research, National Research Council of Canada, June 1971. 4 pp., photos.

MASONRY, MORTAR, PLASTER

Cliver, E. Blaine. "Tests for the Analysis of Mortar Samples," *Bulletin of APT,* 6:1 (1974), pp. 68-73.

Granquist, Charles. "Ornamental Plastering," *Historic Preservation,* 22:2 (April-June 1970), pp. 11-16.

McKee, Harley J. *Early American Masonry Materials in Walls, Floors and Ceilings: Notes on Prototypes, Sources, Preparation and Manner of Use.* Syracuse, N.Y.: The Author,

1971. 33 pp., drawings, maps, tables, bibliog. notes, mimeo.

McKee, Harley J. *Introduction to Early American Masonry: Stone, Brick, Mortar and Plaster.* National Trust — Columbia University Series on the Technology of Early American Buildings no. 1. Washington, D.C.: National Trust for Historic Preservation, 1973. 92 pp., photos, diagrams, drawings, tables, bibliog. footnotes, appendix (bibliog.), index, paper. ◆ History of the production, building use and techniques, deterioration and repair.

Phillips, Morgan W. "SPNEA-APT Conference on Mortar, Boston, March 15-16, 1973," *Bulletin of APT,* 6:1 (1974), pp. 9-39. ◆ Chaired and written summary by Morgan W. Phillips. Subject of the conference was performance of old and new mortars in old masonry walls. Includes list of conference participants and bibliography.

Santa Fe. Museum of New Mexico. *Adobe: Past and Present.* Reprinted from *El Palacio,* 77:4. Santa Fe, N.M.: 1972. 40 pp., photos, drawings, table, bibliog. notes, paper. ◆ See articles, "A Distinguished Architect Writes on Adobe," by William Lumpkins, dealing with adobe construction; and, "An Archaeologist's Summary of Adobe," by Charlie Steen, dealing with adobe's history, use, and preservation.

Schultz, Karl V. *Adobe Craft.* Castro Valley, Calif.: Adobe-Craft, 1972. 56 pp., drawings, photos, tables, bibliog., list of sources and suppliers, paper. ◆ Illustrated manual of technology of brickmaking, building and landscaping with adobe.

PAINT

Batcheler, Penelope Hartshorne. "Paint Color Research and Restoration," rev. ed., *History News,* 23:10 (October 1968), Technical Leaflet no. 15 (new series).

Candee, Richard M. "Housepaints in Colonial America: Their Materials, Manufacture and Application." Reprinted from *Color Engineering,* September-October 1966, November-December 1966, January-February 1967, March-April 1967. 26 pp., drawings, bibliog., o.p.

Candee, Richard M. "The Rediscovery of Milk-Based House Paint and the Myth of 'Brickdust and Buttermilk' Paints," *Old-Time New England,* LVIII:3 (January-March 1968), pp. 79-81.

"Paint Color Research and House Painting Practices," *Newsletter of APT,* 1:2 (August 1969), pp. 5-20.

Phillips, Morgan W. "Discoloration of Old House Paints: Restoration of Paint Colors at the Harrison Gray Otis House, Boston," *Bulletin of APT,* 3:4 (1971), pp. 40-47.

Phillips, Morgan, and Christopher Whitney. "The Restoration of Original Paints at Otis House," *Old-Time New England,* LXII:1 (Summer 1971), pp. 25-28. ◆ Explains how samples from original surfaces can be analyzed and duplicated. Revised and enlarged article in preparation.

U. S. Environmental Protection Agency. Office of Air Programs. *Paint Technology and Air Pollution: An Economic Assessment.* By J. W. Spence and G. H. Haynie. Washington, D.C.: U. S. Government Printing Office, 1972. 44 pp. ◆ Includes historical developments, industrial trends, effects of air pollution, bibliography on testing paints.

STONE

Cobblestone Society, Albion, New York. *Preservation and Restoration of Cobblestone Architecture.* Albion, N.Y.: The Society, 1963. Various pagings, paper. ◆ Contents: masonry, research, landscaping, repair of masonry, doorways and entrances, windows, roof restoration, guide for restoration.

Conferences on the Weathering of Stones, Brussels, 1966-1967. *Conferences on the Weathering of Stones, Brussels, 25-26 February 1966 and 20-21 December 1967.* Vol. I. Paris: ICOMOS, 1968. 176 pp., photos, drawings, charts, bibliog.

International Institute for Conservation of Historic and Artistic Works. *Conservation of Stone. Vol. I. Preprints of the Contributors to the New York Conference on Conservation of Stone and Wooden Objects, June 7-13, 1970.* 2nd ed., rev. London: The Institute, 1971. 134 pp., illus., charts, diagrams, references. ◆ Decay of stone, impregnation, removal of soluble salts, mud-brick preservation, stabilizing adobe and stone, preservation with silicates, degeneration of sculptural stone.

Lewin, S. Z. "The Preservation of Natural Stone, 1839-1965: An Annotated Bibliography," *Art and Archaeology Technical Abstracts,* 6:1 (1966), pp. 183-272.

Martin, D. G. *Maintenance and Repair of Stone Buildings.* London: Church Information

Office for the Council for the Care of Churches, 1970. 15 pp., drawings, bibliog., paper. ◆ Nature of stone, causes of decay, repair techniques, structural problems, mortars. Also available from the Society for the Protection of Ancient Buildings.

Purcell, Donovan. "Stone Preservation in Europe and the British Isles," *Bulletin of APT,* 3:4 (1971), pp. 65-67.

Rawlins, F. I. G. "The Cleaning of Stonework," *Studies in Conservation,* 3:1 (April 1957), pp. 1-23. ◆ Illustrated summary of methods of cleaning old masonry used at cathedrals and other buildings. Also reprinted by University Press, Aberdeen, Scotland, 1957.

Schaffer, Robert John. . . . *The Weathering of Natural Building Stones.* Department of Scientific and Industrial Research Special Report no. 18. London: Her Majesty's Stationery Office, 1932. 149 pp., illus., tables, diagrams, plates, bibliog. references. ◆ Comprehensive scientific study of forms of decay in stone, methods of prevention, and testing of materials.

Stambolov, T. "Notes on the Removal of Iron Stains from Calcareous Stone," *Studies in Conservation,* 13:1 (1968), pp. 45-47.

Warnes, Arthur Robert. *Building Stones: Their Properties, Decay and Preservation.* London: Ernest Benn, Ltd., 1926. 269 pp., photos, tables, formulae, bibliog., index.

Winkler, Erhard M. "Salt Action on Stone in Urban Buildings." In *Application of Science in the Examination of Works of Art; Proceedings of the Seminar: June 15-19, 1970* (Boston: Museum of Fine Arts, 1973), pp. 139-146. ◆ Includes ionic diffusion, osmotic pressures, efflorescence, hydration pressure.

NOTES

Center of Research in the Conservation of Stone, Graduate School of the University of Louisville, Louisville, Kentucky. Professor K. Lal Gauri has developed a process for the treatment of exposed stone, permitting deep pentration of resin in weathered stone and application in the open. It reconsolidates worn strata, and renders the treated stone impervious to further chemical decay, while altering the appearance of the treated stone minimally.

WOOD

Bryan, J. *Non-Pressure Methods of Applying Wood Preservatives.* By J. Bryan and D. F.

Purslow. Forest Products Research Records no. 31. London: 1961. 14 pp.

Findlay, Walter Philip Kennedy. *Dry Rot and Other Timber Troubles.* London; New York: Hutchinson's Scientific and Technical Publications, 1953. 267 pp., photos, tables, diagrams, bibliog., index. ◆ Contents include nature of wood, causes of deterioration in timber, fungal decay, destruction of wood by insects, wood preservatives and their use, and decay of timber in buildings.

Findlay, Walter Philip Kennedy. *The Preservation of Timber.* London: A. & C. Black, 1962. 162 pp., illus., bibliog.

Findlay, Walter Philip Kennedy. *Timber Pests and Diseases.* 1st ed. Pergamon Monographs on Furniture and Timber no. 5. Oxford; New York: Pergamon Press, 1967. 280 pp., illus., bibliog. ◆ A comprehensive study of all forms of decay and infestation of timber and their treatments.

Fitzsimmons, K. R. "Termite Control in Historic Landmarks," *Historic Preservation,* 22:4 (October-December 1970), pp. 40-44.

Great Britain. Ministry of Public Buildings and Works. *Notes on the Repair and Preservation of Historic Buildings: Timberwork.* London: Her Majesty's Stationery Office, 1965. 20 pp., drawings, diagrams, paper.

Hickin, Norman E. *The Conservation of Building Timbers: A Study of the Incidence of Wood-boring Insects and Wood-rotting Fungi in Buildings and Other Contributions Towards the Conservation of Building Timbers.* London: Hutchinson and Co., Ltd., 1967. 144 pp., illus., maps, tables, diagrams, bibliog.

Hickin, Norman E. *The Dry Rot Problem.* 2nd ed. London: Hutchinson & Co., Ltd., 1972. 115 pp., photos, drawings, bibliog., index.

Hickin, Norman E. *The Insect Factor in Wood Decay: An Account of Wood-boring Insects with Particular Reference to Timber Indoors.* 2nd ed. London: Hutchinson and Co., Ltd., 1968. 344 pp., illus., maps, bibliog.

Hickin, Norman E. *Termites: A World Problem.* London: Hutchinson and Co., Ltd., 1971. 232 pp., illus., bibliog.

Hickin, Norman E. *Wood Preservation: A Guide to the Meaning of Terms.* London: Hutchinson and Co., Ltd., 1971. 109 pp., bibliog., glossary of terms.

International Institute for Conservation of Historic and Artistic Works. *Conservation of*

Wooden Objects. Vol. II. Preprints of the Contributions to the New York Conference on Conservation of Stone and Wooden Objects, June 7-13, 1970. 2nd ed. London: The Institute, 1971. 140 pp., illus., diagrams, graphs, charts, bibliogs. ◆ Deterioration and prevention, consolidation, dimensional stabilization of timber, freeze-drying, insects.

Nicholas, Darrel D., ed. Wood Deterioration, and Its Prevention by Preservation Treatments. 1st ed. Syracuse, N.Y.: Syracuse University Press, 1973. Vol I, 380 pp.; Vol. II, 402 pp.; photos, tables, bibliog., graphs, index. ◆ A collection of articles by various authors on preventive treatments for preservation.

Princes Risborough, England. Forest Products Research Laboratory. Decay of Timber and Its Prevention. By K. St. George Cartwright and W. P. K. Findlay. 2nd ed. London: Her Majesty's Stationery Office, 1958. 332 pp., illus. ◆ A comprehensive scientific study of fungal decay of timber and methods of restoration.

Society for the Protection of Ancient Buildings. The Surface Treatment of Timber-framed Houses. London: The Society, 1971. 2 pp., mimeo.

Symposium on the Weathering of Wood, Ludwigsburg, Germany, 8-11 VI 1969. Vol. IV. Paris: ICOMOS, 1972. 259 pp., photos, diagrams, tables. ◆ Includes an extensive bibliography covering publications in French, English, German, and Polish, and a list of experts and specialized institutions. Text in French and English.

U. S. Department of Agriculture. Controlling Wood-Destroying Beetles in Buildings and Furniture. By Lonnie H. Williams and Harmon R. Johnston. Leaflet no. 558. Washington, D.C.: U. S. Government Printing Office, 1972. 8 pp., photos, drawings, bibliog., paper.

U. S. Department of Agriculture. The Old House Borer. By T. McIntyre and R. A. St. George. Leaflet no. 501, rev. Washington, D.C.: U.S. Goverment Printing Office, 1970. 8 pp.

U. S. Department of Agriculture. Protecting Log Cabins, Rustic Work, and Unseasoned Wood from Injurious Insects in the Eastern United States. Farmer's Bulletin no. 2104, rev. Washington, D.C.: U. S. Government Printing Office, 1970. 18 pp.

U.S. Department of Agriculture. Subterranean Termites: Their Prevention and Control in Buildings. By H. R. Johnston, Virgil K. Smith, and Raymond H. Beal. Home and Garden Bulletin no. 64, rev. ed. Washington, D.C.: U.S. Government Printing Office, 1972. 30 pp., photos, drawings, diagrams, map, paper.

U.S. Department of Agriculture. Wood Decay in Houses: How to Prevent and Control It. Home and Garden Bulletin no. 73, rev. ed. Washington, D.C.: U. S. Government Printing Office, 1973. 17 pp., photos, diagrams, paper. ◆ Contents: cause of damage, general safeguards, safeguarding woodwork close to ground, safeguarding parts of house exposed to rain, using new types of building material, care of houses.

U.S. Office of History and Historic Architecture, Eastern Service Center. "Simplified Methods for Reproducing Wood Mouldings," Bulletin of APT, 3:4 (1971), pp. 48-53.

NOTES

American Heritage Program, Shell Chemical Company, 235 Peachtree Street, N.E., Atlanta, Georgia 30303. Termite Treatment Program. Shell donates enough insecticide to treat any building of significant national or local historic value. To obtain approval of a specific building, send a brief description and historical background to the Company which will also assist in contacting a pest control firm if there is difficulty in finding a local firm.

Technical assistance, wood. Mimeographed listing of trade associations in the U. S. dealing with technical assistance with wood in historic preservation has been compiled by Lou Sloat, Alabama Historical Commission, 305 South Lawrence Street, Montgomery, Alabama 36104.

Rehabilitation and Adaptive Use

American Society of Planning Officials. Row Houses. Planning Advisory Service Information Report no. 164. Chicago: The Society, 1962. 20 pp., illus.

Amery, Colin; Mark Girouard; and Dan Cruickshank. "Save the Garden," Architectural Review, 152:905 (July 1972), pp. 16-32. ◆ Factors involved in saving Covent Garden including history, roads and transportation, housing, alternative uses and plans, architectural and human scale, economics, environmental space, warehouse storage, rights of local merchants, habitants, and developers.

Boston Redevelopment Authority. *Back Bay Residential District: Guidelines for Exterior Rehabilitation and Restoration.* Sponsored by the Boston Redevelopment Authority, Back Bay Federation for Community Development, and Neighborhood Association of the Back Bay. Boston: The Authority, n.d. 36 pp., photos, maps, short bibliog., paper. ◆ Includes topographical history; description of district and commission; and guidelines for masonry, entrances, windows, ironwork, roofs, signs/utility equipment, landscaping.

Boston Redevelopment Authority. *Revitalizing Older Houses in Charlestown.* Boston: The Authority, 1973. 28 pp., photos, drawings, maps.

Boyd, John W. "The Trains Don't Stop Here Anymore," *Museum News,* 52:3 (November 1973), pp. 16-20. ◆ Omaha's Art Deco Union Pacific Railroad Station adapted for use as a major museum.

Brown, Charles Bernard. *The Conversion of Old Buildings into New Homes for Occupation and Investment.* London: Batsford, 1955. 218 pp., drawings, photos. ◆ Detailed aspects of conversion including financial, legal, and architectural matters.

"Business as Usual — In a Period Setting," *Historic Preservation,* 16:1 (1964), pp. 17-23. ◆ Photos and captions illustrating adaptive use or rehabilitation for the same use.

Cantacuzino, Sherban, ed. "New Uses for Old Buildings," *Architectural Review,* 151:903 (May 1972), pp. 262-328, special issue. 67 pp., photos, drawings, plans. ◆ Contents include rehabilitation discussions for European exemplars, churches, breweries and maltings, warehouses, mills, barns, schools, and pumping stations.

Clifford, Henry Dalton, and R. E. Enthove. *New Homes From Old Buildings.* London: Country Life, Ltd., 1954. 119 pp., illus. ◆ Detailed treatment for the conversion of buildings, largely from a technical point of view.

Council of Europe. Council for Cultural Cooperation. *Principles and Practice of Active Preservation and Rehabilitation of Groups and Areas of Buildings of Historical or Artistic Interest; Preservation and Rehabilitation of Groups and Areas of Buildings of Historical or*

Artistic Interest. Symposium C, Bath, 3-7 October 1966; Report. Strasbourg: 1967. 126 pp.

Crawford, Dana. "Economics of Rehabilitated Downtown Areas," *Historic Preservation,* 21:1 (January-March 1969), pp. 29-31.

Edgerton, William H. et al. *How to Renovate a Brownstone.* New York: Halsey Publishing Company, 1970. 373 pp., charts, forms, appendices, paper. ◆ Appendix III—Additional Source Material.

Edmunds, Frances R. "The Adaptive Use of Charleston Buildings in Historic Preservation," *Antiques,* 97:4 (April 1970), pp. 590-595.

Great Britain. Department of the Environment. *New Life for Historic Areas: Aspects of Conservation: 2.* Issued by the Department of the Environment, Scottish Development Department and Welsh Office. London: Her Majesty's Stationery Office, 1972. 28 pp., photos, plans. ◆ Environmental improvement projects (buildings and spaces) in England and Scotland, including costs, briefly outlined.

Great Britain. Department of the Environment. *New Life for Old Buildings: Aspects of Conservation: 1.* Issued by the Department of the Environment, Scottish Development Department and Welsh Office. London: Her Majesty's Stationery Office, 1971. 52 pp., photos, diagrams, maps, paper. ◆ Sections include how differing official, voluntary, and private agencies can restore and use historic buildings; rehabilitation in business districts; and adaptive usage, in England and Scotland.

Great Britain. Ministry of Housing and Local Government. *Old Houses into New Homes.* London: Her Majesty's Stationery Office, 1968. 29 pp.

Haas, Walter A., Jr. "Levi's Old/New Pants Factory," *Historic Preservation,* 23:4 (October-December 1971), pp. 14-17. ◆ Description of Levi Strauss & Company renovation and restoration of its oldest factory in San Francisco.

Harrison, Myra F. *Adaptive Use of Historic Structures: A Series of Case Studies.* Report on a study done through a grant from the National Endowment for the Humanities. Washington, D.C.: National Trust for Historic Preservation, 1971. Unpublished. ◆ Copy available through interlibrary loan from the National Trust for Historic Preservation library.

Hawkins, Reginald R., and C. H. Abbe. *New Houses from Old: A Guide to the Planning and*

Practice of House Remodeling. New York: McGraw-Hill, 1948. 558 pp., illus.

Hieronymus, Bill. "Firms Renovate Buildings: Eye on History, Energy Crisis," *Preservation News,* 14:2 (February 1974), p. 12. ◆ Article reprinted from *Wall Street Journal,* January 2, 1974.

Historic Preservation, 18:3 (May-June 1966), pp. 95-129. ◆ Special issue on adaptive uses of historic buildings including specific examples.

Kidney, Walter. "New Life for a Dead Letter Office," *Progressive Architecture,* 53 (November 1972), pp. 100-105. ◆ Pittsburgh's old North Side Post Office restored to new use as the Pittsburgh History and Landmarks Museum.

McKenna, H. Dickson. *A House in the City: A Guide to Buying and Renovating Old Row Houses.* New York: Van Nostrand Reinhold Co., 1971. 159 pp., photos, drawings, diagrams, prints, maps, appendices, bibliog., index.

McLeod, Ferrara and Ensign. *Franklin School Building.* Washington, D.C.: The Authors, c1969, 1973. 58 pp., photos, drawings, map. ◆ A proposal including architectural history, to restore a public building with adaptive use.

Nash, William W. *Residential Rehabilitations: Private Profits and Public Purposes.* Series in Housing and Community Development. New York: McGraw-Hill, 1959. 272 pp., table, maps, bibliog., appendices, index.

New Bedford, Massachusetts. Redevelopment Authority. *Preservation and Rehabilitation of a Historic Commercial Area: A Demonstration of the Waterfront Historic District, New Bedford, Massachusetts.* New Bedford, Mass: The Authority, 1973. 132 pp., appendices. ◆ Study done in cooperation with the City Planning Department and the Waterfront Historic Area League, funded by an Urban Renewal Demonstration Grant, HUD. Includes study and evaluation, project plan, methods of implementation, relative costs and benefits, historic development standards, minimum property standards for rehabilitation, proposed format and content for civic design ordinance, reference sources and supporting documentation.

"New Life for Old Buildings," *Preservation News,* 13:4 (April 1973), Supplement, 4 pp. ◆ Pictorial report on adaptive uses.

"New Life for Old Buildings: The Architect's Renewed Commitment to Preservation." Building Types Study 429. *Architectural Record,* 150:6 (December 1971), special issue. 212 pp., photos, diagrams, maps.

Orofino, John J. *An Architect's Odyssey: Case Study in Rehabilitating Housing.* Washington, D.C.: American Institute of Architects, n.d. 10 pp., photos, paper.

"Portfolio: The Facets of Renovation," *Progressive Architecture,* 53 (November 1972), pp. 92-99. ◆ Report of rehabilitation of historic and architectural sites in Detroit; New York City; Winona, Minn.; Rochester, N.Y.; Dallas, Tex.; Cincinnati, Ohio; St. Charles, Mo.; Lincoln, Neb.

"Recycling," *Architecture Plus,* 2:2 (March/April 1974), pp. 36-87. ◆ A series of articles on adaptive use of buildings in Italy, India, Spain, West Germany, Massachusetts, New Jersey, and California.

"Rehabilitation," *Journal of Housing,* 24:4 (May 1967), pp. 199-225, special issue. ◆ Includes projects in St. Louis, Pittsburgh, Boston, and Philadelphia.

Shopsin, William C. *Adapting Old Buildings to New Uses.* New York: New York State Council on Architecture, April 1974. 12 pp., photos. ◆ Includes a new preservation vocabulary, and selected bibliography. Available as part of *Your Community Workbook* of the Council's Public Awareness Program.

Snow, Barbara. "Preservation for Use," *Antiques,* 77:4 (April 1960), 370-377.

Stanforth, Deirdre, and Martha Stamm. *Buying and Renovating a House in the City: A Practical Guide.* New York: Alfred A. Knopf, 1972. 414 pp., photos, diagrams, appendix, list of organizations, index, paper and hardcover.

Stephen, George. *Remodeling Old Houses Without Destroying Their Character.* New York: Alfred A. Knopf, 1972. 235 pp., drawings, diagrams, tables, glossary, appendices, index, paper and hard-cover.

Tunnard, Christopher. "Urban Rehabilitation and Adaptive Use in the United States." In *Historic Preservation Today: . . . (Charlottesville, Va.: University Press of Virginia, 1966),* pp. 225-237.

U.S. Department of Housing and Urban Development. Library. *Neighborhood Conservation and Property: A Bibliography.*

Washington, D.C.: U. S. Government Printing Office, 1969. 78 pp. ◆ Lists publications dealing with various phases of housing and property rehabilitation including appraisals, code enforcement, financing, land use, nonresidential rehabilitation, relocation, and a list of films, training aids, and courses.

Wilson, Richard G., and Edward J. Vaughn. *Old West Side, Ann Arbor, Michigan.* Ann Arbor, Mich.: Old West Side Association, 1971. 85 pp., photos, drawings, maps, bibliog., appendix. ◆ A survey of the total environment of a neighborhood including structures, landscape features, street furniture, and other amenities to identify its physical character, assets, and problems and to suggest guidelines for preservation.

Ziegler, Arthur P., Jr. *Historic Preservation in Inner City Areas: A Manual of Practice.* Pittsburgh, Pa.: Allegeny Press, 1971. 77 pp., photos, drawings, paper. ◆ A practical manual of principles, directions, and experience of the Pittsburgh History and Landmarks Foundation, focusing on restoration in historic districts without dislocating the residents. The manual also emphasizes the importance of community participation.

Ziegler, Arthur P., Jr. "New Lives from Old Buildings." Reprinted from the *Journal of Property Management,* September-October 1969. 6 pp., photos.

Ziegler, Arthur P., Jr. "Renovate, Don't Relocate," *Museum News,* 51:4 (December 1972), pp. 21-24. ◆ Pittsburgh History and Landmarks Foundation programs to revitalize inner-city neighborhoods without relocating their residents, in the districts of Birmingham, South Side, Mexican War Streets, Manchester, and the Post Office museum.

Preservation and the Community

Booker, Christopher, and Candida L. Green. *Goodbye London: An Illustrated Guide to Threatened Buildings.* London: Fontana, 1973. 160 pp., photos, maps, paper. ◆ Contents include a list of developers, planners, buildings, and conservation areas and the role of the public.

Civic Trust. *Pride of Place: A Manual for Those Wishing to Improve Your Surroundings.* London: The Trust, 1972. 126 pp., photos, diagrams, bibliog. ◆ Contents include basic

operation; problems and opportunities; checklist on restoration, landscaping, parks, playgrounds, etc.; addresses, model letters, and questionnaires.

Feiss, Carl. "Historic Town Keeping," *Journal of the Society of Architectural Historians,* 15:4 (December 1956), pp. 2-6.

Frisbee, John L., III. *Historic Preservation and the Tourist Industry: A Cooperative Project of the National Trust for Historic Preservation and the Pittsburgh History and Landmarks Foundation.* Washington, D.C.: National Trust for Historic Preservation (Preservation Leaflet Series), 1970. 16 pp., photos, charts, bibliog.

Hillman, Ernest, Jr. "Marshaling Public Opinion and Public Support," *Historic Preservation,* 15:1 (1963), pp. 22-25.

Huenefeld, John. *The Community Activist's Handbook: A Guide to Organizing, Financing, and Publicizing Community Campaigns.* Boston: Beacon Press, 1970. 160 pp., ◆ Practical techniques of planning, recruiting, publicity, fund-raising, conducting meetings, and campaign management.

Hutton, Ann Hawkes. "Politicians Are People," *Historic Preservation,* 15:1 (1963), pp. 6-11. ◆ Importance of learning to work with politicians.

Huxtable, Ada Louise. "Preservation Features: Only You Can Help Yourselves." Reprinted from *Historic Preservation,* 23:2 (April-June 1971), pp. 2-3. 2 pp., photos. ◆ First published in the New York *Times,* April 25, 1971.

"Keep Your Town's Historic Landmarks." Reprinted from *Changing Times,* September 1965. 4 pp.

Landmarks Association of St. Louis, Inc. *Laclede's Landing Area, Third Street Highway to Wharf Eads Bridge to Veteran's Bridge.* St. Louis, Mo.: 1968 26 pp., illus., maps. ◆ Promotional pamphlet to focus on historic area slated for demolition and renewal and includes Landmarks Association resolution on the proposal which preserves and incorporates the area's historic sites.

Leibert, Edwin R., and Bernice E. Sheldon. *Handbook of Special Events for Non-Profit Organizations: Tested Ideas for Fund Raising and Public Relations.* New York: Association Press, 1972. 224 pp., illus., bibliog.

"Let's Be Realistic," *Historic Preservation,* 16:1 (1964), p. 38. ◆ Favors a more realistic, conservative appraisal of history as a crowd-getter.

McCaskey, Thomas G. "Promotion and Development of Landmarks," *Historic Preservation,* 21:1 (January-March 1969), pp. 25-28.

Miller, Amelia F. "Preserving a New England Burying Ground: A Community Improvement Project," *Old-Time New England,* IV:4 (April-June 1965), pp. 85-95.

Milo Smith and Associates. *The Beach, the Bay, and the City: Tourism at the Crossroads.* Prepared for the Escambia-Santa Rosa Regional Planning Council and Pensacola-Escambia County Development Commission. Pensacola, Fla: Escambia-Santa Rosa Regional Planning Council, 1971. 69 pp., illus. ♦ Contents: tourist market, existing tourist facilities, tourist behavior and attitudes, future of tourism, proposal for quayside Pensacola, undeveloped potential of historic sites in the area.

Mobile, Alabama. Historic Development Commission. *Preservation with a Purpose: An Outline of How Preservation of Mobile's Traditional Architecture and Development of Mobile's Historic Districts Can Create a Multi-Million Dollar Industry.* Mobile, Ala.: The Commission, 1963. 12 pp., drawings, folding map insert.

Morton, Terry Brust. *A Guide to Preparing Better Press Releases.* Washington, D.C.: National Trust for Historic Preservation (Preservation Leaflet Series), n.d. 7 pp., bibliog.

Murphy, Paul A. "The Kanawha Canal: Linking the Atlantic Ocean with the Ohio River," *Historic Preservation,* 23:3 (July-September 1971), pp. 4-11. ♦ Reynolds Metals Company, Richmond, Va., incorporated canal lock preservation in new construction for community benefit.

National Trust for Historic Preservation. *Films: Historic Preservation and Related Subjects.* Washington, D.C.: The Trust, 1973. 17 pp., list of films. ♦ Included in Preservation for the Bicentennial kit.

National Trust for Historic Preservation. *Preservation for the Bicentennial.* Washington, D.C.: The Trust, 1971. ♦ Kit containing pamphlets relevant to Bicentennial celebration.

National Trust for Historic Preservation. *Seven Basic Steps Toward an Effective Program for Preserving an Historic Site or Building.* Washington, D.C.: The Trust, n.d. 2 pp.

"The New Preservation and Yorkers," *The Yorker,* 31:2 (December 1972), pp. 7-8, 13-14. ♦ Junior historians of the New York State Historical Association contribute to federal and state preservation agencies through surveys in their own communities and regions.

New York State Bar Association, Committee for the Preservation of Historic Courthouses. "How to Save a Courthouse," *Historic Preservation,* 14:2 (1962), p. 49. ♦ Also available as a leaflet from New York State Bar Association, 1 Elk Street, Albany, N.Y. 12210.

Pittsburgh History and Landmarks Foundation. *Birmingham, Pittsburgh, South Side, An Area With a Past That Has A Future.* The Stones of Pittsburgh no. 7. Pittsburgh: Foundation, 1968. 15 pp., photos, paper. ♦ Birmingham self-help, community renewal program brochure with dos and do nots of restoration.

Reed, Henry Hope, Jr., and Jill Sullivan Spelman. *Historic Preservation . . . Through Walking Tours.* Washington, D. C.: National Trust for Historic Preservation (Preservation Leaflet Series), n.d. 4 pp., photo.

Stephenson, E. Frank, Jr. *Renaissance in Carolina II: A Report to Potential Contributors of the Activities of the Murfreesboro Historical Association Incorporated, and Historic Murfreesboro Commission.* Murfreesboro, N.C.: Murfreesboro Historical Association, Inc., and the Historic Murfreesboro Commission, 1973. 168 pp., photos, maps, plans. ♦ Table of Contents: Who We Are; What We Do; Where We're Going; Contributors; The Public Speaks; The Press; Acquisitions; Private Restorations; Potpourri; Riverside Park; Epilogue; Guidelines for Giving.

Sternberg, Irma O. *Overton Park Is Your Park, Memphis!* Memphis, Tenn.: Tri-State Press, 1971. 72 pp., paper. ♦ Booklet explaining effects of highway plan through the park.

"Traditions of Christmas Project Attracts Interest and Funds to Save Historic House," *History News,* 26:12 (December 1971), pp. 260-261. ♦ Grinter Place, near Kansas City, Kansas.

U.S. Department of Commerce. Office of Area Development. *Your Community Can Profit from the Tourist Business.* Prepared by Harry Clement. Washington, D.C.: U.S. Government Printing Office, 1957. 25 pp., illus. ♦ Economic value of tourist trade, tourism as dimension in community development, individual and community benefits, tourist attractions as a lure for industry, how to sell and promote what you have.

Van Trump, James D. *Pittsburgh's Neglected Gateway: The Rotunda of the Pennsylvania Railroad Station.* The Stones of Pittsburgh no. 6. Pittsburgh: Pittsburgh History and Landmarks Foundation, 1967. 8 pp., illus., plan.

Wall, Ned L. *The Press, the Public, and Planning.* Planning Advisory Service Information Report no. 134. Chicago: American Society of Planning Officials, 1960. 20 pp.

Willensky, Elliot. *Guide to Developing a Neighborhood Marker System.* New York: Museum of the City of New York, 1972. 63 pp., illus.

Willensky, Elliot. *An Urban Information System for New York City.* New York: Museum of the City of New York, 1972. 203 pp., illus., appendices, bibliog. ◆ Appendices: Out-of-Town Marker and Tour Programs; Existing Marker and Tour Programs in New York City; Tape Cassettes for Sightseeing; Bibliography; *Guide to Developing a Neighborhood Marker System,* separately bound and paginated, see above.

Wolfe, Andrew D. "Promoting the Preservation Cause," *Historic Preservation,* 21:1 (January-March 1969), pp. 32-35.

Wrenn, Tony P. "The Tourist Industry and Promotional Publications," *Historic Preservation,* 16:3 (1964), pp. 111-118. ◆ Study of historical architecture in promotion of tourist trade, its economic value, and value of well-designed, factual promotional literature.

APPENDIX
Periodicals Cited

ACLS Newsletter. 1949, quarterly, free. American Council of Learned Societies, 345 East 46th Street, New York, New York 10017.

AIA Journal (formerly American Institute of Architects *Journal*). 1944, monthly, subscription. American Institute of Architects, Octagon, 1735 New York Avenue, N.W., Washington, D.C. 20006.

American Antiquity. 1935, quarterly, membership. Society for American Archaeology, 1703 New Hampshire Avenue, N.W., Washington, D.C. 20009.

American Association of Fund-Raising Counsel. *Bulletin.* n.d., monthly, free. American Association of Fund-Raising Counsel, 500 Fifth Avenue, New York 10036.

American City. 1909, monthly, subscription. Buttenheim Publishing Corporation, Berkshire Common, Pittsfield, Massachusetts 01201.

American-German Review. 1934-1970, bimonthly. National Carl Schurz Association, Inc., 339 Walnut Street, Philadelphia, Pennsylvania 19106. ◆ Superseded by *Rundschau, An American-German Review.*

American Institute of Planners Journal. 1925, bimonthly, membership. American Institute of Planners, 1776 Massachusetts Avenue, N.W., Washington, D.C. 20036.

American Journal of Archaeology. 1885, quarterly, subscription. Archaeological Institute of America, 260 W. Broadway, New York, New York 10013.

American Quarterly. 1949, 5 issues/year, membership. American Studies Association, Box 1, Logan Hall, University of Pennsylvania, Philadelphia, Pennsylvania 19174.

Antiques. 1922, monthly, subscription. Straight Enterprises, 551 Fifth Avenue, New York, New York 10017.

Appraisal Journal. 1932, quarterly. American Institute of Real Estate Appraisers, National Association of Real Estate Boards, 155 East Superior Street, Chicago, Illinois 60611.

Archaeology. 1948, quarterly, subscription. Archaeological Institute of America, 260 W. Broadway, New York, New York 10013.

Architects' Journal. 1895, weekly, subscription. Architectural Press, Ltd., 9 Queen Anne's Gate, London, S.W.1, England.

Architectural and Engineering News. 1958, monthly, controlled circulation. Chilton Company, 56th and Chestnut Streets, Philadelphia, Pennsylvania 19139.

Architectural Forum. 1892-1974, 10 issues/year, subscription. Whitney Publications, Inc., 130 East 59th Street, New York, New York 10022. ◆ Ceased publication with March 1974 issue, absorbed by *Architecture Plus.*

Architectural Record. 1891, monthly, subscription. Architectural Record, 1221 Avenue of the Americas, New York, New York 10020.

Architectural Review. 1897, monthly, subscription. Architectural Press, Ltd., 13 Queen Anne's Gate, Westminster, London, S.W.1, England.

Architecture Canada. (formerly Royal Architectural Institute of Canada *Journal*). 1924, monthly, subscription. Royal Architectural Institute of Canada, 160 Eglinton Avenue E, Toronto 315, Canada.

Architecture Plus: The International Magazine of Architecture. 1973, bimonthly, subscription. Informat Publishing Corporation, 1345 Sixth Avenue, New York, New York 10019.

Art and Archaeology Technical Abstracts. 1955, irregular. Circulation Department,

114

AATA, c/o New York University, Conservation Center, Institute of Fine Arts, 1 East 78th Street, New York, New York 10021.

The Atom. 1964, monthly. Los Alamos Scientific Laboratory, University of California, Box 1663, Los Alamos, New Mexico 87544.

Building Research: The Journal of the Building Research Institute. 1964, quarterly, membership. Building Research Institute, 2101 Constitution Avenue, N.W., Washington, D.C. 20418.

Bulletin of APT. 1969, quarterly, membership. Association for Preservation Technology, Box 2682, Ottawa 4, Ontario, Canada.

C F Letter. n.d., monthly, subscription. The Conservation Foundation, 1717 Massachusetts Avenue, N.W., Washington, D.C. 20036.

Changing Times; The Kiplinger Magazine. 1947, monthly, subscription. Kiplinger Washington Editors, Inc., 1729 H Street, N.W., Washington, D.C. 20006.

Color Engineering. 1963, bimonthly, free to qualified personnel. Chromatic Communications, Inc., 799 Roosevelt Road, Building 4, Suite 300, Glen Ellyn, Illinois 60137.

Columbia Law Review. 1901, monthly (November-June). Columbia Law Students, 435 West 116th Street, New York, New York 10027.

Community Planning Review/Revue Canadienne D'Urbanisme. 1951, quarterly, membership. Community Planning Association of Canada, 425 Gloucester Street, Ottawa 4, Canada.

The Concrete Opposition. 1971, irregular newsletter. Highway Action Coalition, Room 731, 1346 Connecticut Avenue, N.W., Washington, D.C. 20036.

Congressional Action. 1956, weekly while Congress is in session, membership. Chamber of Commerce of the United States, 1615 H Street, N.W., Washington, D.C. 20006.

Curator. 1958, quarterly, subscription. American Museum of Natural History, 79th Street at Central Park West, New York, New York 10024.

Ekistics: The Journal of Human Settlement. 1955, monthly, subscription. Athens Center of Ekistics of the Athens Technological Organization, Box 471, Athens, 136, Greece.

El Palacio. 1913, quarterly, subscription.

Museum of New Mexico, P. O. Box 2087, Santa Fe, New Mexico 87501.

Field Studies; Journal of the Field Studies Council. 1967, once annually (5 annual parts constitute one volume). E. W. Classey, Ltd., 353, Hanworth Road, Hampton, Middlesex, England.

Habitat. 1958, bimonthly, free. Central Mortgage and Housing Corporation, Montreal Road, Ottawa, Canada.

Harvard Law Review. 1887, monthly (November-June). Harvard Law Review Association, Gannett House, Cambridge, Massachusetts 02138.

Historic Preservation. 1949, quarterly, membership. National Trust for Historic Preservation, 740-748 Jackson Place, N.W., Washington, D. C. 20006.

Historical Archaeology. 1967, annual, membership. Society for Historical Archaeology, Roderick Sprague, Sec.-Treas., Department of Sociology/Anthropology, University of Idaho, Moscow, Idaho 83843.

Historical New Hampshire. 1946, quarterly, membership. New Hampshire Historical Society, 30 Park Street, Concord, New Hampshire 03301.

History News. 1941, monthly, membership. American Association for State and Local History, 1400 Eighth Avenue South, Nashville, Tennessee 37203.

Housing and Planning References. 1948, bimonthly. U. S. Department of Housing and Urban Development, U. S. Government Printing Office, Washington, D.C. 20402.

HUD Challenge. 1969, monthly, subscription. U. S. Department of Housing and Urban Development, Washington, D.C. 20410.

Industrial Archaeology: The Journal of the History of Industry and Technology. 1964, quarterly, subscription. Dr. John Butt, ed., University of Strathclyde, Department of History, McCarie Building, Richmond Street, Glasgow C.1, Scotland.

International Federation for Housing and Planning. *Bulletin.* 1961, monthly (September-June), membership. International Federation for Housing and Planning, Wassenaarseweg 43, The Hague, Netherlands, 24 45 57.

Journal of Architectural Education. 1947, quarterly, membership. Association of Collegiate Schools of Architecture, 521 18th Street, N.W., Washington, D. C. 20006.

Journal of Housing. 1944, 11 issues/year, membership. National Association of Housing and Redevelopment Officials, 2600 Virginia Avenue, N.W., Washington, D. C. 20037.

Journal of Property Management. 1934, bimonthly. Institute of Real Estate Management, National Association of Real Estate Boards, 115 East Superior Street, Chicago, Illinois 60611.

Journal of the Society of Architectural Historians. 1941, quarterly, membership. Society of Architectural Historians, Room 716, 1700 Walnut Street, Philadelphia, Pennsylvania 19103.

Kiva. 1935, quarterly. The Arizona Archaeological and Historical Society, Arizona State Museum, Tucson, Arizona 85721.

Land-Use Controls Annual. Winter 1971-72, annual, included in subscription to *Zoning Digest.* Land-Use Controls Publications Service, American Society of Planning Officials, 1313 East 60th Street, Chicago, Illinois 60637.

Landscape Architecture. 1910, quarterly. American Society of Landscape Architects, Schuster Building, 1500 Bardstown Road, Louisville, Kentucky 40205.

Law and Contemporary Problems. 1933, quarterly. Duke University, School of Law, Durham, North Carolina 27706.

Man in the Northeast. 1971, semiannual, subscription. Man in the Northeast, Inc., Box 589, Center Harbor, New Hampshire 03226.

Massachusetts Historical Society. *Proceedings.* 1859, annual. Massachusetts Historical Society, 1154 Boylston Street, Boston, Massachusetts 02215.

Monmouth Historian. 1972, annual, subscription. Monmouth County Historical Association, 70 Court Street, Freehold, New Jersey 07728.

Museum News. 1924, 9 issues/year, membership. American Association of Museums, 2233 Wisconsin Avenue, N.W., Washington, D.C. 20007.

National Civic Review. 1911, monthly (September-June). National Municipal League, 47 E. 68th Street, New York, New York 10021.

New York History. 1919, quarterly, membership. New York State Historical Association, Cooperstown, New York 13326.

New York Times Magazine. 1896, weekly. New York Times Company, 229 West 43rd Street, New York, New York 10036. ♦ Section of *New York Times* Sunday edition.

Newport History. 1912, quarterly, membership. Newport Historical Society, 82 Touro Street, Newport, Rhode Island 02840.

Newsletter of APT. 1972, bimonthly, membership. Martin Eli Weil, ed., Association for Preservation Technology, 400 Stewart Street, Apt. 2211, Ottawa, Ontario K1N 6L2.

Notre Dame Lawyer. 1925, quarterly. Notre Dame Law School, Box 486, Notre Dame, Indiana 46556.

The Old House Journal: Renovation and Maintenance Ideas for the Antique House. 1973, monthly, subscription. The Old House Journal, 199 Berkeley Place, Brooklyn, New York 11217.

Old-Time New England. 1910, quarterly, membership. Society for the Preservation of New England Antiquities, Harrison Gray Otis House, 141 Cambridge Street, Boston, Massachusetts 02114.

Planners Notebook. 1970, bimonthly, subscription. American Institute of Planners, 1776 Massachusetts Avenue, N.W., Washington, D.C. 20036.

Planning (also called *Planning Yearbook*). 1909, annual, subscription. American Society of Planning Officials, 1313 East 60th Street, Chicago, Illinois 60637.

Planning (formerly *ASPO Newsletter).* 1935, monthly, membership. American Society of Planning Officials, 1313 East 60th Street, Chicago, Illinois 60637.

Popular Government. 1931, 9 issues/year, subscription. University of North Carolina, Institute of Government, Box 990, Chapel Hill, North Carolina 27515.

Preservation News. 1961, monthly newspaper, membership. National Trust for Historic Preservation, 740-748 Jackson Place, N.W., Washington, D.C. 20006.

Proceedings of the American Bar Association, Section of Real Property, Probate and Trust Law. 1938-1965, annual. American Bar Association, Section of Real Property, Probate and Trust Law, 1155 East 60th Street, Chicago, Illinois 60637. ♦ Proceedings now published in *Real Property, Probate and Trust Journal.*

Progressive Architecture. 1920, monthly, subscription. Circulation Department, Progressive Architecture, 25 Sullivan Street, Westwood, New Jersey 07675.

Reader's Digest. 1922, monthly, subscription. Reader's Digest Association, Inc., Pleasantville, New York 10570.

Royal Institute of British Architects Journal. 1893, monthly, membership. Royal Institute of British Architects, 66 Portland Place, London, W1N 4AD, England.

San Bernardino County Museum Association. *Quarterly.* 1953, quarterly, membership. San Bernardino County Museum Association, 18860 Orange Street, Bloomington, California 92316.

Saturday Review. 1924, weekly, subscription. Saturday Review, Inc., 380 Madison Avenue, New York, New York 10017.

Schenectady County Historical Society. *Bulletin* (later called *Quarterly*). 1957-1969, quarterly, membership. Schenectady County Historical Society, 32 Washington Avenue, Schenectady, New York 12305.

Society for Industrial Archeology. *Newsletter.* 1972, bimonthly, membership. Robert M. Vogel, ed., Room 5020, National Museum of History and Technology, Smithsonian Institution, Washington, D.C. 20560.

South Street Reporter. 1967, quarterly newsletter, membership. South Street Seaport Museum, 16 Fulton Street, New York, New York 10038.

Studies in Conservation/Etudes de Conservation. 1952, quarterly, membership or subscription. International Institute for Conservation of Historic and Artistic Works, 608 Grand Buildings, Trafalgar Square, London WC 2N 5HN, England.

Syracuse Law Review. 1949, quarterly. Syracuse University, College of Law, Syracuse, New York 13210.

Town Planning Institute. *Journal.* 1914, 10 issues/year. Town Planning Institute, 26 Portland Place, London W.1, England.

Traffic Quarterly. 1947, quarterly. Eno Foundation for Transportation, Inc., Saugatuck, Connecticut 06880.

Transactions of The Ancient Monuments Society. 1953, annual, membership. The Ancient Monuments Society, 33 Ladbroke Square, London W11 3NB, England.

UNESCO Courier. 1948, monthly, subscription. UNESCO Publications Center, Box 433, New York, New York 10016.

U.S. Federal Register. 1951, weekly. U. S. Government Printing Office, Washington, D.C. 20402.

U.S. Library of Congress. *Quarterly Journal.* 1943, quarterly, subscription. U.S. Government Printing Office, Washington, D.C. 20402.

Urban Renewal and Public Housing in Canada. 1965, quarterly, free. Central Mortgage and Housing Corporation, Information Division, Ottawa K1A OP7, Canada. ♦ Title changed to *Living Places* with vol. 9, no. 3 (1973).

Virginia Law Review. 1913, 8 issues/year. Virginia Law Review Association, University of Virginia, Clark Hall, Charlottesville, Virginia 22901.

Wake Forest Law Review (formerly *Wake Forest Intramural Law Review*). Vol. 7 (1970-71), quarterly. Wake Forest University, School of Law, Winston-Salem, North Carolina 27109.

The Wall Street Journal. 1889, daily, subscription. Subscriptions to The Wall Street Journal, 200 Burnett Road, Chicopee, Massachusetts 01021.

The Washington International Arts Letter. 1962, monthly except July and December, subscription. Washington International Arts Letter, 115 5th Street, S.E., Washington, D.C. 20003.

Yankee. 1935, monthly, subscription. Yankee, Inc., Dublin, New Hampshire 03444.

The Yorker. 1942, quarterly, membership. New York State Historical Association, Cooperstown, New York 13326.

Zoning Digest. 1948, 10-12 issues/year, subscription. Land-Use Controls Publications Service, American Society of Planning Officials, 1313 East 60th Street, Chicago, Illinois 60637.

Index